Diversity and Entrepreneurship

Whilst there has been an increased interest in minorities and their contribution to society, the literature on minorities and under-represented communities is still weak. This edited volume discusses entrepreneurship in the context of minorities and the role they play in society.

The book looks at under-represented communities, such as LGBTQ+, disadvantaged, ethnic minority, religious entrepreneurs, medically limited, indigenous, refugees, young/old and other socio-economic segments. It provides a holistic, comprehensive overview of how diversity in entrepreneurship facilitates increased levels of innovation. The book will be amongst the first to take a broad perspective of minority entrepreneurs.

Vanessa Ratten is an associate professor of Entrepreneurship and Innovation at La Trobe University, Australia.

Leo-Paul Dana is a professor of Entrepreneurship at the Montpellier Business School, Montpellier, France.

Routledge Advances in Management and Business Studies

Happiness, Wellbeing and Society
What Matters for Singaporeans
Siok Kuan Tambyah and Soo Jiuan Tan

Women in Business Families
From Past to Present
Jarna Heinonen and Kirsi Vainio-Korhonen

Transformative Management Education
The Role of the Humanities and Social Sciences
Ulrike Landfester and Jörg Metelmann

Operating Under High-Risk Conditions in Temporary Organizations
A Sociotechnical Systems Perspective
Matthijs Moorkamp

Decision-making for New Product Development in Small Businesses
Mary Haropoulou and Clive Smallman

Frugal Innovation and the New Product Development Process
Insights from Indonesia
Stephanie B.M. Cadeddu, Jerome D. Donovan, Cheree Topple,
Gerrit A. de Waal and Eryadi K. Masli

Ethical Branding and Marketing
Cases and Lessons
Edited by Hagai Gringarten and Raúl Fernández-Calienes

Diversity and Entrepreneurship
Edited by Vanessa Ratten and Leo-Paul Dana

For more information about this series, please visit www.routledge.com/
Routledge-Advances-in-Management-and-Business-Studies/book-series/SE0305

Diversity and Entrepreneurship

Edited by
Vanessa Ratten and
Leo-Paul Dana

LONDON AND NEW YORK

First published 2020
by Routledge
2 Park Square, Milton Park, Abingdon, Oxon OX14 4RN

and by Routledge
52 Vanderbilt Avenue, New York, NY 10017

Routledge is an imprint of the Taylor & Francis Group, an informa business

First issued in paperback 2021

© 2020 selection and editorial matter, Vanessa Ratten and Leo-Paul Dana; individual chapters, the contributors

The right of Vanessa Ratten and Leo-Paul Dana to be identified as the authors of the editorial material, and of the authors for their individual chapters, has been asserted in accordance with sections 77 and 78 of the Copyright, Designs and Patents Act 1988.

All rights reserved. No part of this book may be reprinted or reproduced or utilised in any form or by any electronic, mechanical, or other means, now known or hereafter invented, including photocopying and recording, or in any information storage or retrieval system, without permission in writing from the publishers.

Trademark notice: Product or corporate names may be trademarks or registered trademarks, and are used only for identification and explanation without intent to infringe.

British Library Cataloguing-in-Publication Data
A catalogue record for this book is available from the British Library

Library of Congress Cataloging-in-Publication Data
A catalog record for this book has been requested

ISBN: 978-0-367-26394-2 (hbk)
ISBN: 978-1-03-209002-3 (pbk)
ISBN: 978-0-429-29308-5 (ebk)

Typeset in Galliard
by codeMantra

To MB — LKJ with kindest thanks

Dedicated to my family: Kaye, David, Hamish, Stuart and Sakura Ratten

Contents

List of figures	ix
List of tables	xi
List of contributors	xiii

1 **Diversity in entrepreneurship**   1
VANESSA RATTEN

2 **Minority and under-represented communities in entrepreneurship**   9
VANESSA RATTEN

3 **Taking stock and moving forward in research on refugee entrepreneurship: a systematic review of the current field and future research directions**   23
SOLOMON AKELE ABEBE

4 **International research on social entrepreneurship: looking for an operational definition of the concept**   63
GIORGI JAMBURIA AND JEAN-MARIE COURRENT

5 **Eco-entrepreneurship as a promising drive for financial performance: a literature review**   108
CHANDRIKA HEMANTHI WIJAYASINGHE, DILRUKSHI
KRISHANTHI YAPA ABEYWARDHANA, AND
CHANDRALAL THILAKERATHNE

6 **Female empowerment through social entrepreneurship in Indonesia: a conceptual framework**   129
PRAMESHWARA ANGGAHEGARI, GATOT YUDOKO, BAMBANG
RUDITO AND MELIA FAMIOLA

viii *Contents*

7 Competences in social business: an analysis of the narratives about the experiences of a group of social entrepreneurs in the State of Alagoas 142
IBSEN MATEUS BITTENCOURT

8 Communities, diversity and entrepreneurship: future trends 163
VANESSA RATTEN

Index 171

Figures

3.1	Articles per year and citations	27
3.2	Publication channels for refugee entrepreneurship research	28
3.3	Characteristics of refugees versus immigrants	50
5.1	Graphical presentation of total citations	118
6.1	The process of data collection and dimensions of female social entrepreneur in Indonesia	134
6.2	Conceptual framework on female empowerment through social entrepreneurship	138
7.1	Flow of the central elements of analysis: MeuTutor and Hand Talk	147
7.2	Essential skills versus final MeuTutor products	151
7.3	Essential skills versus end products – Hand Talk	152
7.4	Flow of the central elements of analysis: Osório Cardoso and AAPPE	153

Tables

3.1	Review of refugee entrepreneurship literature (articles in descending order of year)	30
3.2	Differences between refugee entrepreneurs and other categories of migrant entrepreneurs	51
4.1	Different categorisations/typologies of social enterprises	76
4.2	Definitions of social entrepreneurship, social enterprise and social entrepreneur	80
5.1	Definitions of 'Ecopreneurs'	109
5.2	Distribution of papers by subcategory	113
5.3	Distribution of research papers by year (2000–2018)	114
5.4	Classification of top ranked, most cited research papers (2000–2018)	116
5.5	The link between green variables and GRI standards	118
A1	Summary of methodologies	120
A2	Reporting Principles and GRI Standards	122

Contributors

Solomon Akele Abebe is a PhD candidate at Sten K. Johnson Centre for Entrepreneurship, School of Economics & Management, Lund University, Sweden.

Dilrukshi Krishanthi Yapa Abeywardhana is a senior lecturer at the University of Kelaniya in Sri Lanka.

Prameshwara Anggahegari is a lecturer at the Bandung Institute of Technology, Bandung, Indonesia.

Ibsen Mateus Bittencourt is a professor at the Federal University of Alagoas, Alagoas, Brazil.

Janette Brunstein is a professor at the Federal University of Alagoas, Alagoas, Brazil.

Jean-Marie Courrent is a professor at the University of Montpellier, Montpellier, France.

Leo-Paul Dana is a professor of Entrepreneurship at the Montpellier Business School, Montpellier, France.

Melia Famiola is a lecturer at the Bandung Institute of Technology, Bandung, Indonesia.

Giorgi Jamburia is a PhD student at the University of Montpellier, Montpellier, France.

Vanessa Ratten is an associate professor of Entrepreneurship and Innovation at La Trobe University, Australia.

Bambang Rudito is a lecturer at the Bandung Institute of Technology, Bandung, Indonesia.

Chandralal Thilakerathne is a professor at University of Kelaniya, Sri Lanka.

Chandrika Hemanthi Wijayasinghe is an economist at the Ministry of Mahaweli Industry and Environment, Sri Lanka.

Gatot Yudoko is a lecturer at the Bandung Institute of Technology, Bandung, Indonesia.

1 Diversity in entrepreneurship

Vanessa Ratten

Introduction

Diversity in an entrepreneurial setting can take many different forms from those less represented in society to individuals neglected in the current research. During the past decade, the meaning of diversity has changed based on societal attitudes. This has led to fertile research areas that have been understudied from an entrepreneurship perspective. Whilst many studies in sociology have examined the meaning of diversity, it is less studied in an entrepreneurship setting. In addition, diversity tends to be viewed based on specific characteristics such as gender or age without considering other factors. This has meant that diversity is often seen as a benefit to entrepreneurs due to different lifestyle factors leading to new opportunities. However, currently the entrepreneurship literature considers diversity more in terms of gender, sexuality or location.

Entrepreneurs are increasingly investing in diversity management due to the need to focus on innovation and creativity within workplace practices (Ferreira, Fernandes and Ratten, 2017). They come from diverse backgrounds and need to consider different viewpoints when entering global marketplaces. In some industries, especially high technology, there is a high number of ethnic minorities. This has led to diversity being a competitive advantage in terms of providing a creative environment for new ideas to emerge (Ferreira, Ratten and Dana, 2017). There are different functions apparent in diversity management that utilise human resource management practices, which include increasing the level of human capital (Olsen and Martins, 2012). Madera (2018:100) defines diversity management as 'formal organizational policies and programs that develop and maintain a diverse workforce through selecting, developing and advancing employees from diverse backgrounds'. Thus, diversity management in entrepreneurship involves taking a proactive approach to solving problems.

A social perspective taking is useful in understanding diversity in entrepreneurship. Social perspective taking refers to 'the process of having individuals take the perspective of an out-group member by thinking and feeling the experience of an out-group member' (Madera, 2018:101). In-group members are those within society that are considered stereotypes and have common physical traits. Diversity includes out-group members by referring to the differences amongst

2 Vanessa Ratten

people (Manoharan and Singal, 2017). The concept of diversity in entrepreneurship originated from studies on ethnic minorities. Diversity management has come to be widely practised by entrepreneurs, but in some industries it is less common than others. Diversity involves differences amongst people and can include age, sexual preference and lifestyle choices (Dobbs, 1996). Thus, diversity can be classified using a broad or narrow category (Mor Barak, 2005). Taking a broad category approach means including many ways people are considered different, and a narrow category approach is more objective and normally includes traits that are easier to measure.

Diversity can be further evaluated in terms of primary-/surface-level or secondary-/deep-level differences (Manoharan and Singal, 2017). At the primary/surface level, it involves aspects that contribute to identity such as visible characteristics like height, weight and ethnicity. It is easier to study primary-/surface-level diversity due to the already existing research about this topic. Less difficult is secondary-/deep-level diversity that can be hidden in society due to perceived prejudices. Examples of surface-/deep-level diversity include personality traits, learning styles and religion (Lambert and Bell, 2012). In entrepreneurial settings, it may be more useful to focus on secondary-/deep-level diversity as this is an area less understood (Jonsen, Maznevski and Schneider, 2011). In addition, diversity can be examined in terms of shifting societal trends that fundamentally change business practice (White, 2018).

There has been more interest in how to measure and assess diversity in entrepreneurship. The management of diversity is defined as 'the policies and practices that are designed to not only allow and acknowledge and recognise diversity, but also to leverage these differences to support an organizational goal' (Manoharan and Singal, 2017:78). In this book, we attempt to take stock of research that relates to diversity in entrepreneurship as a way of identifying future research trends. This is due to changing definitions existing in research and practice about diversity. Entrepreneurs are a diverse group of individuals, with each person having a unique identity. Although entrepreneurs are sometimes classified as being all the same and interested in risk-taking activities, they each have different attributes, which impacts their success in the market. As Fuller-Love, Lim and Akehurst (2006:429) state, 'entrepreneurs are a diverse group whether they are men or women, those from different ethnic backgrounds, social groups, types of businesses or geographical areas'. Thus, it is necessary to further our understanding of diversity in entrepreneurship by examining their different cultural attributes. This involves focusing on how entrepreneurs utilise their networks to access information that can be located in distinct groups. This will enable more diversity in entrepreneurship to evolve that brings about better management skills.

The rationale for this book came from an examination of the literature on minority entrepreneurship, which found that most studies tend to focus on biology or ethnic traits without considering other diverse segments of society. The initial research found that whilst ethnic minority and female entrepreneurship are well studied in the literature, other diverse individuals are less researched.

Diversity in entrepreneurship 3

This has led to a concentration of studies on specific characteristics without considering what it means to be a minority in today's society. The chapters in this book address various issues concerning diversity in entrepreneurship, including (1) the changing notion of diversity in society, (2) how diverse communities help or hinder entrepreneurship and (3) the potential for entrepreneurship in underrepresented parts of society.

Based on the new societal meanings of diversity, this book was inspired to take a broad view as to how diversity is interpreted in an entrepreneurial setting. This enables an exploration about how diversity is important and the impact it has on research. As society begins to accept more diverse individuals, it is important to understand how these individuals contribute to entrepreneurship research (Dobbs, 1996). More importantly, how can we learn from diverse groups of people in society in terms of their attitudes and expectations regarding entrepreneurship? The purpose of this book is to open up the discussion on diversity and entrepreneurship in order to improve the literature. More concretely, the goal is to develop better theoretical and empirical studies about diversity. This can contribute to creating a better economic and social landscape for entrepreneurship. To achieve this goal, the book includes a number of chapters that have different theoretical and methodological approaches.

The remainder of this chapter is organised as follows. The meaning of diversity in entrepreneurship is discussed with an overview of how this has changed in recent years. Next, the rationale for specifically focusing on diversity from a holistic perspective is stated. This leads to a summary of the chapters included in this book and an agenda for future research. Finally, managerial and policy implications are stated.

Role of entrepreneurship in society

An entrepreneur is defined as 'someone who perceives an opportunity and creates an organization to pursue it' (Bygrave and Hofer, 1991:14). Culture involves learned behaviour that is communicated in a societal setting. Most forms of culture involve a language or way of acting that is common to all members (Anggadwita et al., 2017). Culture is normally passed down generations, but can be also learnt. There are different ways of looking at culture both from an entrepreneurship perspective and from a societal stance. Depending on the context, culture can be learnt via example or involve a set of behaviours to adhere to. Individuals behave in a certain way based on the values endemic in their culture. Some cultures have specific ideas that shape society. One of the most famous scholars on culture is Hofstede, who refers to culture as 'the collective programming of the mind which distinguishes the members of one human group from another' (Hofstede, 1980:25). The culture in a society influences how individuals define and react to diversity in entrepreneurship.

Entrepreneurs are often considered to be young, and this stereotype has restricted entrepreneurship research. Entrepreneurship education is often focused on young people and neglects other sectors of society. White (2018:2) states,

4   *Vanessa Ratten*

'minority entrepreneurship scholars have long studied the relationship between age and entrepreneurship practice'. However, a large proportion of society is now considered mature age or seniors. This is evident in some developed countries, such as Japan having a large proportion of people over sixty years of age. Whilst the average life span of individuals has increased, there has been a reluctance in entrepreneurship studies to understand these entrepreneurs who have been referred to as mature age, older, seniors, grey and baby boomers. There is also a debate in the entrepreneurship field about whether age matters in the proclivity to start a business. This issue about whether entrepreneurs are born or made keeps popping up in the entrepreneurship scholarship with no appropriate answer being found.

Entrepreneurs are not considered as members of mainstream society, as they have had to overcome obstacles in their personal life that help them deal with adverse conditions. Thus, in order to search for better economic opportunities or have greater independence, individuals become entrepreneurs. Altinay and Altinay (2008:24) state, 'society today is a mosaic of people from different backgrounds in terms of their histories, cultures, origins, religions and languages'. The diversity in terms of personality or behaviour helps contribute to entrepreneurial endeavours as gaps in the market are filled.

Minority entrepreneurship can be understood from a cultural or structural perspective. The cultural approach suggests that certain types of businesses are favoured by minorities. This may be related to food or lifestyle preferences that are different to what is currently in the marketplace. The structural approach focuses on the disadvantages minorities face due to different resources. This may include language or geographic differences that limit business opportunities. Another theory used to understand minority entrepreneurship is the mixed embeddedness approach, which focuses on regulations, sectoral and spatial differences in the environment (Kloosterman, Van der Leun and Rath, 1999). The food sector is a good example of an industry that has been impacted by minority entrepreneurs. For example, Patak's curry products when first introduced in the United Kingdom market were considered exotic, but now are common food items in many customers' cupboards. Greek yoghurt is another example of a specific ethnic product gaining mainstream market appeal. The spatial environment focuses more on geography in terms of how close individuals are to business locations. For agricultural products such as dairy and meat, the spatial environment can be used as a branding tool. This applies to milk and fruit where location is used as a way to distinguish the reputation of a product. The regulatory environment involves aspects such as taxes and tariffs that are influenced by the government.

In the entrepreneurship literature, diversity is seen as an asset because it brings in a new mindset. Although most of the literature on entrepreneurship has tended to use the same sample demographic that is easy to access and acquire, it has limited the number of studies that have diverse samples and takes into account modern living styles that are not typical of past research. Diversity is a complex subject and each person has their own entrepreneurial style. This book

Diversity in entrepreneurship 5

takes a holistic approach to diversity by confirming its important role in entrepreneurship research. Diversity, whilst considered a positive factor in entrepreneurship, can also have negative factors depending on the context. In the early stage of entrepreneurial development, diversity may make it hard for others to understand the business idea. In addition, it can act as a constraint in later entrepreneurial development when the entrepreneur wants to sell or divest the business. To counteract these positive and negative factors, a bridging approach that focuses more on the profitability and future income of the business is needed.

Theories about diversity

Social network theory is a commonly referred to theory in entrepreneurship research in order to understand diversity management. By engaging in a social forum, networks enable both formal and informal interaction. This helps to create a knowledge community and enable collaborative learning. Within these networks, there is a sense of trust, with members expected to behave in a reciprocal manner. Social networks enable entrepreneurs to access information and resources to make business decisions.

The block mobility theory suggests that certain individuals are stopped from entering certain professions due to their characteristics such as ethnicity, age or gender. Piperopoulos (2010:142) states that some ethnic groups 'are disadvantaged in the labour market due to racial discrimination, negative events, low education and qualifications, redundancy, under-paid salaried work, or language difficulty'. Thus, to understand minority entrepreneurship in the global economy, it can be examined through migration, settlement, identity and business. Migration is a topic often addressed in the media due to its impact on economic policy. There are regions migrants tend to settle in due to the cultural community that exists (Ratten, 2006). Moreover, some regions have a historical association with certain ethnic groups and have existing infrastructure. Other regions such as the Silicon Valley have migrants wanting to work in the technology industry. Thus, the personal connection a migrant has to a location can be based on occupation, language, religious or some other kind of connection. Government policy also contributes to migration, as some regions encourage it as a way to build their pool of human capital (Ratten, 2014). This is evident in more favoured locations based on migration traditions. Settlement involves looking into where diverse communities are located and the type of business in these areas. For older people, they might move to locations that have more health services. Other groups of people such as working professionals might prefer locations closer to cities. Identity means how individuals associate with their cultural and social background. Some minority groups might consider themselves part of communities because of their business skills, whilst others might prefer to be identified based on behaviour or culture. Business means the kind of economic activity an individual engages in.

Expectancy or valence, instrumentality, expectancy theory has been used to understand minority entrepreneurship (Edelman et al., 2010). This theory

6 Vanessa Ratten

suggests that when individuals believe their effort will result in an outcome, they are likely to behave in a certain way. The theory has been used to explain the reasons why individuals are motivated to become entrepreneurs.

The extant research explaining the impact of minorities on entrepreneurship has expanded over the past years. Culture has a strong influence on entrepreneurial ambitions, and research on this topic is informing our understanding about general entrepreneurship behaviour. Indeed, it is noted that there is a shifting research agenda to exploring what a minority is and how it is defined by society. The increased social acceptance and tolerance of different individuals has changed the research discourse on minority entrepreneurship. However, at the same time there is still a tendency to characterise individuals as a minority based on traditional ways such as gender without considering new conceptualisations. This presents a research gap and chance to build a better understanding of minority entrepreneurship. Politics plays a part in this debate as does funding that might specify research on a certain minority group. In addition, individual research preferences influence decisions about what kind of minority group to study. The aim of this book is to provide a theoretical and empirical foundation to understand diversity in entrepreneurship. It is difficult to group all minorities under one umbrella, so some care and effort is needed.

Support for future research

Each chapter in the book provides suggestions about where research on diversity in entrepreneurship is heading. Further on, I summarise the main issues yet to be addressed in this exciting and vibrant research field. All studies of entrepreneurship need to consider the context as it helps or hinders business activity. Increasingly, entrepreneurship is viewed as a by-product of its context, which impacts its success and knowledge spillover effect. It is beneficial to analyse entrepreneurship from a contextual perspective to understand what is supporting or constraining behaviour. This is also true for diversity in entrepreneurship, as culture and location have an effect on business performance. In addition, some contexts will lead to more diversity in entrepreneurship due to the flow of information generated. This means more research is required on what kind of contexts in terms of people and resources lead to diverse forms of entrepreneurship. To do this, a multiplicity of contexts may be needed to see if there are stages or processes followed that lead to entrepreneurship. In addition, there may be a number of different contexts at certain stages of an entrepreneur's lifecycle. Thus, at an early stage the context required may involve training and education, whilst at the later stages it may be internationalisation support. It would help if more scholars focused on longitudinal analysis of diversity to understand the journey taken by entrepreneurs. Moreover, the role of collaboration and public/private partnerships to help disadvantaged members of society is needed. This includes focusing on the approaches used by minority entrepreneurs as they enter the market and manage their business. Given that the way society views minorities is changing, it would be useful to focus on historical changes that have

Diversity in entrepreneurship 7

led to societal attitudes shifting. This can include focusing on cultural attitudes towards diverse groups of society and how they utilise social capital.

More theoretical frameworks are needed to understand diversity in entrepreneurship. There are a number of ways to understand diversity, so new theories need to be continually developed to take into account emerging societal trends. Theories that focus on one specific area of diversity such as a minority group might be useful, as in the past there tended to be general stereotypes existing in the research. For example, whilst the middleman, opportunity seeking and social network theories have been useful, it is time to develop new theories specific to diversity in entrepreneurship. This should consider the antecedents as well as the outcomes of diversity. For example, new theories or conceptual models that create new knowledge are needed. This would not only enhance our understanding of diversity, but can also extend existing theories. For example, signalling, institutional and transactional cost theory are well-established general entrepreneurship literature but could be adapted to suit diverse segments of society.

References

Altinay, L. and Altinay, E. (2008) 'Factors influencing business growth: The rise of Turkish entrepreneurship in the UK', *International Journal of Entrepreneurial Behaviour & Research*, 14(1): 24–46.

Anggadwita, G., Luturlean, B. S., Ramadani, V. and Ratten, V. (2017) 'Socio-cultural environments and emerging economy entrepreneurship: Women entrepreneurs in Indonesia', *Journal of Entrepreneurship in Emerging Economies*, 9(1): 85–96.

Bygrave, W. and Hofer, C. (1991) 'Theorizing about entrepreneurship', *Entrepreneurship Theory and Practice*, 16(2): 13–21.

Dobbs, M. (1996) 'Managing diversity: Lessons from the private sector', *Personnel Management*, 25(3): 351–367.

Edelman, L., Brush, C., Manolova, T. and Greene, P. (2010) 'Start-up motivations and growth intentions of minority nascent entrepreneurs', *Journal of Small Business Management*, 48(2): 174–196.

Ferreira, J. J., Fernandes, C. I. and Ratten, V. (2017) 'Entrepreneurship, innovation and competitiveness: What is the connection?', *International Journal of Business and Globalisation*, 18(1): 73–95.

Ferreira, J. J., Ratten, V. and Dana, L. P. (2017) 'Knowledge spillover-based strategic entrepreneurship', *International Entrepreneurship and Management Journal*, 13(1): 161–167.

Fuller-Love, N., Lim, L. and Akehurst, G. (2006) 'Guest editorial: Female and ethnic minority entrepreneurship', *Entrepreneurship Management*, 2: 429–439.

Hofstede, G. (1980) *Cultures consequences: International differences in work-related values*, Beverly Hills, Sage Publications.

Jonsen, K., Maznevski, M. and Schneider, S. (2011) 'Diversity and its not so diverse literature: An international perspective', *International Journal of Cross Cultural Management*, 11(1): 35–62.

Kloosterman, R., Van der Leun, J. and Rath, J. (1999) 'Mixed embeddedness: (In)formal economic activities and immigrant businesses in the Netherlands', *International Journal of Urban and Regional Research*, 23(2): 252–266.

8 Vanessa Ratten

Lambert, J. and Bell, M. (2012) 'Diverse forms of differences', In Robertson, Q. (Ed) *The Oxford Handbook of Diversity and Work*, Oxford, UK, Oxford University Press, pp. 13–31.

Madera, J. (2018) 'What's in it for me? Perspective taking as an intervention for improving attitudes toward diversity management', *Cornell Hospitality Quarterly*, 59(2): 100–111.

Manoharan, A. and Singal, M. (2017) 'A systematic literature review of research on diversity and diversity management in the hospitality literature', *International Journal of Hospitality Management*, 66: 77–91.

Mor Barak, M. (2005) *Managing diversity: Toward a globally inclusive workplace*, Thousand Oaks, Sage Publications.

Olsen, J. and Martins, J. (2012) 'Understanding organizational diversity management programs: A theoretical framework and directions for future research', *Journal of Organizational Behaviour*, 33(8): 1168–1187.

Piperopoulos, P. (2010) 'Ethnic minority businesses and immigrant entrepreneurship in Greece', *Journal of Small Business and Enterprise Development*, 17(1): 139–158.

Ratten, V. (2006) 'Policy drivers of international entrepreneurship in Europe', *Euromed Journal of Business*, 1(2): 15–28.

Ratten, V. (2014) 'Future research directions for collective entrepreneurship in developing countries: A small and medium-sized enterprise perspective', *International Journal of Entrepreneurship and Small Business*, 22(2): 266–274.

White, J. C. (2018) 'Toward a theory of minority entrepreneurship in the non-profit arts sector', *The Journal of Arts Management, Law and Society*, 48(4): 287–300.

2 Minority and under-represented communities in entrepreneurship

Vanessa Ratten

Introduction

This chapter reveals minority entrepreneurship as a vibrant field of research that will gain in ascendency in future years as it focuses more on under-represented communities. White (2018:1) defines minority entrepreneurship as 'self-employment or business ownership by any individual who is not of the majority population'. This chapter calls attention to a topic that has public policy importance due to the social inclusion often felt by minority groups and under-represented community groups. Minority groups are less likely to establish and sustain new businesses as they typically face higher levels of risk in starting their own business due to a myriad of factors – from lack of education to inadequate business experience. Minority entrepreneurs are a popular topic, as they provide a greater understanding about the diversity evident in entrepreneurship. By encouraging minority entrepreneurs, there are likely to be both social and economic benefits.

The social benefit derives from entrepreneurship providing a way for minorities to climb the ladder and increase their status in society and the economic benefits of entrepreneurship to minorities include more self-confidence and independence. Both these types of benefits help minority entrepreneurs play a unique role in the development of communities. This is due to the overall outcome of minority entrepreneurship to create value through sustained business practices and community engagement. This can occur through creative destruction that enables cultural capital to be used for business purposes whilst involving action through business practices. Minority entrepreneurs typically have had discriminatory barriers that limit their ability to grow their businesses. This has been through finance being harder to obtain and lacking the knowledge on how to circumvent barriers. Whilst there are famous large-scale minority entrepreneurs such as Patak's curry products or Chobani with Greek yoghurt, most are small sized. This has meant a great number of minority entrepreneurs who due to their small size are understudied but offer interesting research avenues.

Minority entrepreneurship enhances our understanding about the diversity of entrepreneurship and prospect for business ownership amongst the disadvantaged members of society. The emerging research on minority entrepreneurship is pioneering, as it pushes the boundaries of traditional entrepreneurship scholarship; but there is still much to do in developing this research field. As a

10   *Vanessa Ratten*

consequence, there is expected to be a surge of interest in minority entrepreneurship that further increases our understanding of this interesting research field due to its diversity.

Diversity can be understood at the micro or macro levels. The micro level usually refers to individual characteristics such as age, gender, ethnicity, linguistic ability and education. Normally, most studies on minority entrepreneurs tend to focus on individual characteristics, but increasingly, macro level features such as geographic location are being utilised in the literature. Diversity is often utilised in the creation of new businesses that focus on special skills or products for their competitive advantage. This is often seen through new food products from one minority group being mass marketed to the general population. Increasingly, this form of entrepreneurship is becoming more frequent due to the diaspora-based networks transferring information and knowledge at quicker rates.

Most research on minority entrepreneurship has tended to focus on immigrants or females whilst neglecting other under-represented groups such as gay, lesbian and transsexual. This is surprising as the entrepreneurship field prides itself on being innovative, but there needs to be more forward thinking in terms of some community groups. This has led to studies of minority entrepreneurs tending to be published more in the sociology literature, with the mainstream entrepreneurship journals tending to focus on other areas. Thus, it is important for entrepreneurship scholars to explore in more detail the topic of minority entrepreneurship and under-represented communities.

There has been a significant body of literature devoted to ethnic minority entrepreneurship, which implies there is a distinction based on ethnic origins in terms of entrepreneurship. This has led to the term 'ethnic minority entrepreneurship' gaining popularity in the literature as a way of understanding minority entrepreneurs. In this chapter, I remove the ethnic distinction to focus more broadly on minority entrepreneurs in the general sense and under-represented communities. This means ethnicity is not the defining characteristic, but rather that the number or status of the entrepreneur in society is the differentiating factor. Thus, minority entrepreneurship refers to disadvantaged or challenged members of society that engage in entrepreneurship.

The main objective of this chapter is to develop a conceptual overview of minority entrepreneurship and under-represented communities. The chapter begins by discussing the reasons for increased interest in minority entrepreneurship that is not defined only by ethnicity, but also by personal or other socio-demographic characteristics. The different types of minority entrepreneurs are then stated and the evolution of the field discussed. This leads to a discussion on the different theoretical frameworks that can be used to understand minority entrepreneurship. This chapter concludes by stating suggestions for future research on minority entrepreneurship.

Theories to describe minority entrepreneurship

There are a variety of theories that can be utilised to describe minority entrepreneurship and are often used as the theoretical foundation of research theories.

Minority and under-represented communities 11

Amongst the most popular is the disadvantage theory, which suggests that people who are excluded from the mainstream economy turn to business ownership because of necessity (Smith-Hunter and Boyd, 2004). This means that self-employment is needed by those who are not able to enter the labour market. Previous research by Horton and DeJong (1991) found that there are high levels of business ownership amongst minorities due to their need of entrepreneurship as a survival mechanism. Individuals with a disadvantage in the labour market have been found to be more likely to be entrepreneurs. This meant a culture of survivalist entrepreneurship emerging from minorities (Smith-Hunter and Boyd, 2004).

Expectancy theory is used in entrepreneurship research to explain human behaviour (Edelman et al., 2010). As entrepreneurship focuses on new venture creation, expectancy theory is used to understand the reasons why an individual will behave when their actions have a positive effect. Cultural theory suggests that some individuals have a higher propensity for entrepreneurship due to cultural norms and values (Smith-Hunter and Boyd, 2004). The explanation given for some minorities not participating in entrepreneurship is referred to as cultural deficiency because they lack the perceived skills (Smith-Hunter and Boyd, 2004). This is reflected in stereotypes such as the Protestant work ethic referring to individuals coming from certain religions being better workers (Weber, 1930). Cultural theory suggests that certain cultures have a predilection and aspiration to be entrepreneurs. This is due to the attitudes and personal motivations that come from belonging to a certain cultural group.

Individuals who expect certain outcomes from their actions will likely perform in a certain way (Olson et al., 1996). This is helpful in understanding the consequences of action that are a result of human behaviour (Miller and Brush, 1988). The main elements of expectancy theory involve the probability that an action will result in a desired outcome, which is anticipated as being beneficial to the individual (Van Eerde and Theirry, 1996). This involves some subjectivity in terms of the importance of the action and the results that follow. Individuals who exert more effort can, therefore, be expected to perform at a certain level. Thus, entrepreneurs who believe they have the appropriate skills and ability will normally exert more effort (Shaver et al., 2001). This is helpful in predicting entrepreneurial behavioural and the personal variables that will have an effect.

The opportunity structure theory suggests that minorities have knowledge about specific needs of their community that opens up business opportunities (Piperopoulos, 2010). Bates (2011) suggests that the main barriers to minorities in an economy involve (1) lack of financial resources, (2) inability to enter markets, (3) global competition and (4) inadequate training. By focusing on market opportunities overlooked by other businesses, there is often lower competition. This enables them to see market needs that serve a certain niche or segment of the market. The ethnic enclave theory was developed to explain the reason why some minority groups locate in the same geographic area (Portes and Bach, 1985). By having a spatial concentration of people from the same ethnic group can enable a more focused type of business activity (Wilson and Martin, 1982).

12 *Vanessa Ratten*

Middleman theory suggests that minorities employ themselves for the purpose of making money and sending it back to their original country (Butler, 2005). According to this theory, minorities face discrimination in a new country, so the need to make their own business opportunities (White, 2018). This means that by acting as a middleman, minorities can negotiate between different strata of society. The protected market theory focuses on 'the importance of the special skills or knowledge that business owners must have' (Smith-Hunter and Boyd, 2004:21). Minorities have special skills due to their experience and membership of a distinct group of society. This means that they have certain knowledge about needs due to the experience in society. At the core of the protected market theory is that current businesses will focus on specific racial groups, thereby prejudicing minority groups (Aldrich et al., 1985). This is seen in the mass production of goods without taking into account the needs of people with disabilities or special health needs. This has resulted in some niche businesses being established based on cultural or social needs such as gluten-free grains or vegetarianism to serve these market segments. In addition, the protected market theory has resulted in some ethnic minority groups being served by other members of their community because of their cultural understanding (Light, 1972).

The mixed embeddedness model focuses on how regions are affected by legal and institutional structures (Jones et al., 2002). Thus, it recognises that opportunities are often viewed by entrepreneurs who create businesses in a region based on availability and access to resources (Peters, 2002). Embeddedness recognises that people do not act outside a social context but are part of an ongoing system of social relations. Thus, as Wang and Altinay (2010:7) state, 'the embeddedness approach argues that the nature, depth and extent of an individual's ties into the environment are configuring elements of business'. This means that the entrepreneurial process for minorities is reflected in the socio-economic factors evident in a region. The embeddedness approach is useful in understanding the social networks' individuals have that relate to their socio-economic environment (Ram and Jones, 1998). Therefore, individuals are nested in a structure of institutional layers that influences their entrepreneurial behaviour. The next section will discuss these theories in terms of the current literature on minority entrepreneurship.

Current literature on minority entrepreneurship

The identification of belonging to a minority group involves thinking about an individual's place in society (Monterrubio, 2018). The concept of identify is hard to define as it encompasses a sense of belonging based on one's position in society. A basic definition involves knowing who we are that is based on a multifaceted understanding of the world (Lawler, 2008). Individuals have multiple identities that change over time (Robinson-Wood, 2016). The dynamic nature of an individual's identity is shaped by their situation or ideology. Identities can be based on attitudes, behaviours and feelings (Eliason, 1996). Individuals are defined by their identity and place within a social group. Increasingly, the

Minority and under-represented communities 13

social relations an individual has is based on their interaction with members of their community. Social groups involve a collection of individuals that have a consensus about their shared values (Tajfel and Turner, 2004). This includes the emotional involvement of individuals in a group because of their perceived similarities.

Gatewood and colleagues (2002) view this process as effort-performance-outcome model, as it explains expectations from entrepreneurship. In some minorities, there may be a higher propensity for entrepreneurship. Dillard and Campbell (1981) found that parents in African American households place more emphasis on entrepreneurship. This finding is supported by Kollinger and Minniti (2006), who found that African Americans start new businesses at a higher rate than other ethnic groups. Wilson and colleagues (2004) also found that African American youths have higher rates of interest in entrepreneurship than other groups. In addition, African Americans utilise social relationships from church and political leaders to help them with entrepreneurial endeavours (Hill et al., 1990). These social relationships are part of the learning process for minority entrepreneurs, who benefit from networks outside of their family (Butler and Herring, 1991).

There is history in entrepreneurship research of changing definitions based on new trends. This is evident with research viewing entrepreneurs in a negative light as social misfits or naughty individuals rebelling against perceived normal business structures (Evans and Leighton, 1989). This led to entrepreneurs being considered as risk takers who were willing to challenge existing business structures (Kao, 1989). By acknowledging entrepreneurs as different to managers, the personality characteristics such as commitment, perseverance and reliability have been used more in the literature (Nafukho and Muyia, 2010). However, there has been a debate about whether entrepreneurs have the same personalities, as there are some exceptions. This is reflected in Kets de Vries (1997) finding that some individuals become entrepreneurs due to a rejection from society and need to prove themselves.

Minority entrepreneurship reflects the changing socio-demographic structures in society and fulfils an important social role for minority communities. Waldinger and colleagues (1990) proposed the interactive model to explain the multiple factors that work together to influence ethnic entrepreneurship. In the model, opportunity structures influence resources available to ethnic minority groups, which influence to their strategy to act on opportunities. The opportunity structure includes market conditions, access to ownership and legal frameworks. Market conditions shape whether there is a gap in the business environments for niche products that are tied to ethnicity. This enables ethnic minorities to open up potential market opportunities by focusing on ethnic products that are not available in the mainstream market. Access to ownership refers to whether ethnic minorities have the resources to start their own business. This will depend on financial conditions and the type of capital needed for their businesses. Job market condition involves how easy or hard it is for an ethnic minority to find employment. This might be restricted to religious

14 *Vanessa Ratten*

beliefs, dress codes or role of gender in society. Some ethnic minorities become entrepreneurs due to necessity, as they might not have the language capabilities or social skills to fit into the mainstream marketplace. Legal frameworks refer to the status of ethnic minorities in society with some being illegal immigrants. This means that they might not have the proper legal status to work in certain jobs that restrict their financial situation. For this reason, the grey or informal economy might be the only option.

The different factors that comprise the opportunity structure influence both the ethnic strategies and resources available to ethnic minority entrepreneurs. The resources include cultural traditions and ethnic social networks. Increasingly, cultural traditions such as food and clothes have become a way for ethnic minorities to distinguish themselves in the marketplace. Due to the internationalisation of the global economy, consumers are more interested in how cultural traditions manifest in certain products and services. This is linked to tourism and the related service economy that is a part of cultural activities.

Entrepreneurs are social animals as they are dependent on other actors to accomplish various tasks (Dodd and Anderson, 2007). In order to function properly in society, entrepreneurs need to have social interaction that is the result of collective action (Lindgren and Packendorff, 2002). This involves a multilayered sociological approach that recognises there are different elements of society needed for entrepreneurship. The social approach to entrepreneurship recognises that entrepreneurs are practical and embedded in their social environment. Thus, the myth of entrepreneurs acting alone is not true as they need others in order to conduct their business activities. This means that entrepreneurs act based on trust and cooperation they receive from others (Johannisson and Petersonm, 1984). In the past, economics was considered as the main factor influencing entrepreneurship, but this has changed with the acknowledgement of entrepreneurship as a complex process (Dodd and Anderson, 2007).

Often, minority groups are highly motivated to become entrepreneurs to not only showcase their diversity, but also for financial reasons. The current assumptions of minority entrepreneurs being necessity-based and underprivileged need to be reassessed to take into account more current trends towards entrepreneurship. Minority entrepreneurs are individuals who are under-represented in the community because of cultural or social factors. A majority of studies on minority entrepreneurs has focused on ethnicity, immigrant or women whilst neglecting other forms such as those with health issues or physical limitations. This has led to a tendency of the minority entrepreneurship literature to stereotype individuals without focusing on individual entrepreneurs on a case-by-case basis. The discrimination of some minorities has encouraged them to find their own identity in entrepreneurship. The decision to be an entrepreneur is not necessarily attached to being a minority, but is rather a personality choice. Some minority entrepreneurs suppress their culture in order to fit into society. Minority entrepreneurs are fundamentally no different to other types of entrepreneurs, but their minority status has more significance for the type of entrepreneurship they are engaged in.

Minority and under-represented communities 15

There has been a tendency to have a hierarchical binary division with minority entrepreneurs such as women/men and ethnic/indigenous that restrict our understanding of entrepreneurship. There are other cultural ways to define minorities that need to be adopted in the literature. From a minority perspective, the long-standing demarcation of minority/non-minority is no longer relevant in today's society. As some minority groups are no longer minorities, there needs to be a new focus on research on under-represented groups. This would help build a better classification of minority entrepreneurship that is of more practical usage. By encompassing previously unidentified minority groups, there can be growth in research that facilitates a more holistic understanding of the field. This can lead to a reconceptualisation of what type of entrepreneur fits into the definition of being a minority entrepreneur. Entrepreneurship can play an important role in the formation of minority identity. By engaging in entrepreneurship, society attitudes towards minorities can change. This can enable minorities to be open about their differences in a way that encourages inclusiveness.

The definition of minority entrepreneurs is dynamic and fluid, based on the subjective norm of the society. Cultural conditions need to be considered in terms of conceptualising minorities but taking a broader view. The identification with being a part of a minority group is dependent on culture, place, situation and time. The notion of being a minority is a mixture of cultural and social identity. An individual's awareness of being a minority can take place at any time during their life. There are psychological and social factors associated with being identified as a minority. These can contribute to an understanding of what extent minority entrepreneurship is a socio-cultural phenomenon.

Types of under-represented communities in entrepreneurship research

Entrepreneurship has tended to be romanticised and considered a positive uplifting experience (Verduijn and Essers, 2013). Governments have increasingly used entrepreneurship as a way to increase the wealth in communities. The dominant entrepreneurship discourse is biased by ethnocentricity and gender (Verduijn and Essers, 2013). There is a myth of an entrepreneur being male and white, but this has changed with more internationalisation of entrepreneurship research. Entrepreneurs normally have certain behavioural traits such as being creative, innovative and risk taking. These traits are associated with assumptions about behaviours needed to be an entrepreneur. This view has changed with the realisation entrepreneurs can be both introverts and extroverts. Entrepreneurship is a subjective phenomenon as it differs based on culture and individual personality. The following section will discuss different types of minority entrepreneurs and under-represented communities.

Refugees are a minority in many countries due to their relatively disadvantaged status compared to other citizens. Often due to hardship in their own countries, refugees face difficulties finding employment because of social prejudices or language (Fuller-Love et al., 2006). This makes it hard for refugees to

16 *Vanessa Ratten*

set up their own business (Kloosterman and Van Der Lein, 1999). Compared to immigrants, refugees come to other countries more often because of necessity and not choice. This means that refugees have less social networks and are less integrated into communities (Gold, 1992). In addition, refugees might have other problems, including psychological or physical issues, limiting their ability to be a part of the workforce (Hauff and Vaglum, 1993). Refugees, despite their perceived negative characteristics, have the propensity and ability to be entrepreneurs (Wauters and Lambrecht, 2006).

Women entrepreneurs are a minority, but this may change in the future with more gender equality becoming evident in the workforce. Past research has focused on understanding the way women differ from men in entrepreneurship (Fuller-Love et al., 2006). Entrepreneurship normally has a masculine label attached to it due to the association with confidence and risk taking (Achtenhagen and Welter, 2011). There are historical reasons why some minorities are more entrepreneurial than others. In addition, sociological perspectives can explain how cultural factors explain entrepreneurship. Women entrepreneurs are considered to have less worthy traits such as being subordinate and supportive compared to males who are perceived as being more rational (Bruni et al., 2004).

Minorities can include those from certain religious groups such as Muslims, Amish and Mennonites. There has been a tendency in Western society to polarise some religious groups in a way that stereotypes certain minority groups. Some religious groups have specific values and habits that differ to the mainstream population. This occurs with Muslim's praying at certain times of the day and requiring halal food. This diversity means new forms of businesses can develop that relate to the cultural values. In addition, ethnic minorities have often close ties and family relations that can be both an advantage and a disadvantage in business (Verduijn and Essers, 2013).

There is a stereotype that minorities are less capable of being entrepreneurs than the majority of the population. This is not always the case, but rather depends on the individual characteristics of the entrepreneur. There are multiple meanings associated with minority entrepreneurship that depend on the cultural contexts. Normally, minorities refer to ethnicity such as Asian, black or African American, Hispanic or Latino, Indigenous, rural or Applachian (White, 2018). Sexuality is another way minority entrepreneurs are classified, but with gender neutral words becoming more used in society there has been a tendency to focus on sexuality. Minorities can be classified by culturally specific meanings such as European or Asian that are associated with ethnicity. Minorities have tended to be marginalised in society and overlooked in entrepreneurship research.

Diversity can include the number of people speaking difference languages. The linguistic diversity in a region can increase competitiveness by bringing in foreign customers and businesses. Minorities are an economic asset as they contribute to the competitiveness of a region. Resources are needed to exploit the diversity of minority entrepreneurs. Further systematic research is needed to understand the connections between minority entrepreneurship and competitiveness.

Minority and under-represented communities 17

Sexual identity is a way to distinguish minorities, and this can include gay, lesbian, bisexual, transgender, and gender-nonconforming people. Traditionally, those individuals considered not heterosexual have been a minority group, but this has changed with greater acceptance in society about sexual orientation. Monterrubio (2018:4) states that in queer theory 'sexual identity is quite a fluid and contentious social category'. Studies of gay and lesbian entrepreneurs remain a largely neglected area of research (Monterrubio, 2018). This has resulted in stereotypes of gay and lesbian people engaging in certain types of businesses typically associated with gender traits, especially evident in the tourism and hospitality sector with gay entrepreneurs. These stereotypes have limited the research on how sexuality influences entrepreneurship. The significance of sexual identity on entrepreneurship is a reciprocal relationship, as both are viewed as being different in society. Entrepreneurs by definition are considered innovative and holding progressive views, which is similar to individuals being dentified as minorities. In addition, the lifestyle patterns and social interactions of gay and lesbian people can shape their entrepreneurial behaviour.

At the moment retirees or senior people are minorities due to them being a small segment of the marketplace. Due to the ageing population and people living longer, this minority status may change in the future. Older people have tended to be entrepreneurs to supplement their incomes, but have a more flexible working arrangement. Compared to their younger counterparts, older entrepreneurs have human, financial and social capital that helps them establish businesses (Kautonen et al., 2008). In addition, older entrepreneurs have more industry experience that can be useful in building network capabilities (Singh and De Noble, 2003).

Future practitioner and research avenues

This chapter leaves many potential research questions unexplored that need to be answered. The issues discussed in this chapter are intended to be a starting point for further research. One of the most important conclusions of this chapter is presenting an overview of the different types of minority entrepreneurs. This chapter has major implications for different types of practitioners. For entrepreneurs and potential entrepreneurs, this chapter has discussed ways to utilise their minority status to turn ideas into inspirational businesses. This will enable more minorities to be successful entrepreneurs by embracing their diversity. Policymakers can help minorities improve their entrepreneurial activities by providing them with more guidance and support. This includes focusing on entrepreneurship training and education initiatives that take into account the needs of minorities. This will help nurture potential minority entrepreneurs by providing them with necessary resources for their development. Educators can also partner with nascent minority entrepreneurs with experienced entrepreneurs to help them build their social networks.

More interdisciplinary models need to be developed for minority entrepreneurship that draws on accounts of minority identity. This includes personal

18 *Vanessa Ratten*

experiences that can place more attention on the identity formation process. This can further enrich our understanding of minority entrepreneurship that reveals more about the socio-cultural dimensions. Minority perspectives offer a strong lens to examine the fluid nature of entrepreneurship. This helps to understand how the role of entrepreneurship in society is subjective and influenced by socio-spatial relations. The literature on minority entrepreneurship is still limited by being mostly conducted by researchers from the Western contexts. This limits in a way the empathy from research coming from minorities when they write about their experiences. There is a need for more studies to be undertaken by minorities to incorporate a more ethnographic view of their experiences with entrepreneurship. This includes research on different types of minorities overlooked in the mainstream entrepreneurship literature and often not recognised as a minority. For example, individuals with epilepsy or other health issues have not been studied in detail despite them being a part of society. The tendency to focus on gender or ethnicity has limited the personal experiences of other minorities and by researchers on new types of minorities that would further increase the depth of the field.

This chapter has explored the different types of minorities and their motivations to be entrepreneurs. Additional studies are needed to compare new types of minorities previously unexplored in the literature to see if there are significant differences between the more researched form of minorities such as women and immigrant entrepreneurs. This can enable new research to take into account changing societal perceptions about who is a minority entrepreneur. By focusing on more health-related minority entrepreneurs, it would also open up new research linkages with the health science and entrepreneurship literature. This can be fruitfully augmented by future work field, exploring from a personal narrative the industry barriers affecting health-related minority entrepreneurs. This can untangle some misconceptions about health issues that have been considered a weakness in some business settings but may be an asset in entrepreneurial ventures. This includes the use of creativity by physically challenged individuals.

It is hoped that this chapter will be used as a springboard for further research and policy implementation. More research is needed on understanding the motives and experiences of minority entrepreneurs. This will be useful in analysing the aspirations of minorities in terms of their impact on economic development. New research approaches are needed as some methodologies might be biased towards minority groups. This is reflected in the mostly positivist nature of data collected in entrepreneurship research that limits applicability to other settings (Brush et al., 2009). Much of the previous research on entrepreneurship has used firm level studies or samples without consideration of individual differences. Whilst often positivist approaches can result in good data, there is a tendency to utilise statistical packages to make assumptions without considering the complex nature of responses. In addition, the halo effect and acquiescence bias can mean that minorities may be afraid to reveal their true feelings. This means that a mixed method approach recognises the

Minority and under-represented communities 19

benefit of statistical analysis, but more interpretivist approaches are needed in minority entrepreneurship research. As entrepreneurship is by nature creative, there also needs to be more imaginative approaches to data collection of minority entrepreneurs.

There needs to be a change in the methodological approach of minority entrepreneurship research to encourage more diversity. As most entrepreneurship research has tended to use a positivist approach with surveys or databases being the norm, due to the sensitive nature of being a minority these methodologies need to change. A way to do this is by taking a humanistic approach that takes a more empathetic view and personal approach to minority entrepreneurship. This will enable a more insightful way to understand minority entrepreneurship that incorporates the psychological experiences.

Minority entrepreneurship is vitally important for the social cohesion of the global economy as it is behind the increased cosmopolitism of regions. Despite the increased interest in diversity and culture in business, there continues to be a need to increase the number of successful minority entrepreneurs. Thus, more research is required to understand the nature of minority entrepreneurs in order to stimulate action. Much of the literature on minority entrepreneurship is segregated into specific socio-economic classes based on ethnicity, gender, religion, disability, age or other distinguishing features. Thus, this has meant there is no underlying theoretical framework to understand minority entrepreneurs in the general sense. This chapter will contribute to developing a theory of minority entrepreneurship based on the valuable insights and diversity in under-represented groups of society.

Minority entrepreneurship should be researched by taking a broad perspective in terms of focusing not just on business ventures, but also the position of minorities in society and their contribution to the formation of industry. There have been more global conversations about the role of minorities in economies, which has inspired policy initiatives around diversity. Building the research field of minority entrepreneurship is essential in order to understand more deeply the nature of entrepreneurship. More research projects that look into both small- and large-scale minority entrepreneurs are needed. This can include the use of policy think tanks to harness a community of researchers to study minority entrepreneurship. This research can inspire more dialogue about minority entrepreneurship and advance policy considerations.

References

Achtenhagen, L. and Welter, F. (2011). "Surfing on the ironing board' – the representation of women's entrepreneurship in German newspapers', *Entrepreneurship & Regional Development*, 23(9–10): 763–786.

Aldrich, H., Cater, J., Jones, T., McEvoy, D. and Velleman, P. (1985) 'Ethnic residential concentration and the protected market hypothesis', *Social Forces*, 63(4): 996–1009.

Bates, T. (2011) 'Minority entrepreneurship', *Foundation and Trends in Entrepreneurship*, 7(3–4): 151–311.

20 *Vanessa Ratten*

Bruni, A., Gherardi, S. and Poggio, B. (2004) 'Entrepreneur-mentality, gender and the study of women entrepreneurs', *Journal of Organizational Change Management*, 17(3): 256–268.

Brush, C.G., De Bruin, A. and Welter, F. (2009) 'A gender-aware framework for women's entrepreneurship', *International Journal of Gender and Entrepreneurship*, 1(1): 8–24.

Butler, J.S. (2005) *Entrepreneurship and self-help among black Americans*, State University of New York Press, Albany.

Butler, J.S. and Herring, C. (1991) 'Ethnicity and entrepreneurship in America: Towards an explanation of racial and ethnic group variations in self-employment', *Sociological Perspectives*, 34(1): 79–94.

Dillard, J.M. and Campbell, N.J. (1981) 'Influences of Puerto Rico, black, and Anglo parents' career behavior on their adolescent children's career development', *Vocational Guidance Quarterly*, 30: 139–148.

Dodd, D.S. and Anderson, A.R. (2007) 'Mumpsimus and the mything of the individualistic entrepreneur', *International Small Business Journal*, 25(4): 341–359.

Edelman, L.F., Brush, C.G., Manolova, T.J. and Greene, P.G. (2010) 'Start-up motivators and growth intentions of minority nascent entrepreneurs', *Journal of Small Business Management*, 48(2): 174–196.

Eliason, M.J. (1996) 'Identity formation for lesbian, bisexual and gay persons: Beyond a "minoritizing" view', *Journal of Homosexuality*, 30(3): 31–58.

Evans, D. and Leighton, L. (1989) 'Some empirical aspects of entrepreneurship', *The American Economic Review*, 79(3): 519–535.

Fuller-Love, N., Lim, L. and Akehurst, G. (2006) 'Guest editorial: Female and ethnic minority entrepreneurship', *Entrepreneurship Management*, 2: 429–439.

Gatewood, E.J., Shaver, K.J., Powers, J.B. and Gartner, W.B. (2002) 'Entrepreneurial expectancy, task effort and performance', *Entrepreneurship Theory and Practice*, 27(2): 187–206.

Gold, S.J. (1992) 'The employment potentials of refugee entrepreneurship: Soviet Jews and Vietnamese in California', *Policy Studies Review*, 11: 176–186.

Hauff, E. and Vaglum, P. (1993) 'Integration of Vietnamese refugees into the Norwegian labor market: The impact of war trauma', *International Migration Review*, 27: 388–405.

Hill, O.W., Petrus, W.C. and Hedin, B.A. (1990) 'Studies of factors affecting the attitudes of blacks and females toward the pursuit of science and science-related careers', *Journal of Research in Science Teaching*, 27: 289–314.

Horton, H. and De Jong, G. (1991). 'Black entrepreneurs: A socio-demographic analysis', *Research in Race and Ethnic Relations*, 6: 105–120.

Johannisson, B. and Peterson, R. (1984). The personal networks of entrepreneurs. In *Conference Proceedings*, ICSB, Ryerson Polytechnical Institute, Toronto.

Jones, T., McEvoy, D. and McGoldrick, C. (2002) 'The economic embeddedness of immigrant enterprises in Britain', *International Journal of Entrepreneurial Behavior & Research*, 8(1/2): 11–31.

Kao, J. (1989) *Entrepreneurship, creativity and organization*, Prentice-Hall, Englewood Cliffs, NJ.

Kautonen, T., Down, S. and South, L. (2008) 'Enterprise support for older entrepreneurs: The case of PRIME in the UK', *International Journal of Entrepreneurial Behavior & Research*, 14(2): 65–101.

Kets de Vries, M. (1997) 'Creative rebels with a cause', In Birley, S. and Muzyka, D. (Eds) *Mastering Enteprise*, Financial Times/Pitman, London, pp. 5–8.

Minority and under-represented communities 21

Kloosterman, R. and Van der Leun, J. (1999) 'Just for starters: Commercial gentrification by immigrant entrepreneurs in Amsterdam and Rotterdam neighbourhoods', *Housing Studies*, 14: 659–677.

Kolligner, P. and Minniti, M. (2006) 'Not for lack of trying: American entrepreneurship in black and white', *Small Business Economics*, 27(1): 50–79.

Lawler, S. (2008) *Identity: Sociological perspectives*, Polity Press, Cambridge, MA.

Light, I.H. (1972) *Ethnic enterprise in America: Business and welfare among Chinese, Japanese and Blacks*, University of California Press, Berkeley, CA.

Lindgren, M. and Packendorff, J. (2002, May). Interactive entrepreneurship: On the study of innovative social processes. In *2nd Annual Conference of the European Academy of Management*, Stockholm, Sweden, 9–11 May.

Miller, L.E. and Grush, J.E. (1988) 'Improving predictions in expectancy theory research: Effects of personality, expectancies and norms', *Academy of Management Journal*, 31(1): 107–122.

Monterrubio, C. (2018) 'Tourism and male homosexual identities: Directions for sociocultural research', *Tourism Review*. doi:10.1108/TR-08-2017-0125.

Nafukho, F.M. and Helen Muyia, M.A. (2010). 'Entrepreneurship and socioeconomic development in Africa: A reality or myth?', *Journal of European Industrial Training*, 34(2): 96–109.

Olson, J.M., Roese, N.J. and Zanna, M.P. (1996) 'Expectancies', In Higgins, E.T. and Kuglanski, A.W. (Eds) *Social Psychology Handbook of Basic Principles*, Guilford Press, New York, pp. 211–258.

Peters, N. (2002) 'Mixed embeddedness: Does it really explain immigrant enterprises in Western Australia?', *International Journal of Entrepreneurial Behavior & Research*, 8(1/2): 32–53.

Piperopoulos, P. (2010) 'Ethnic minority businesses and immigrant entrepreneurship in Greece', *Journal of Small Business and Enterprise Development*, 17(1): 139–158.

Portes, A. and Bach, R.L. (1985) *Latin Journey*, Berkeley, LA, University of California Press.

Ram, M. and Jones, T. (1998). Ethnic minorities in business. *University of Illinois at Urbana-Champaign's Academy for Entrepreneurial Leadership Historical Research Reference in Entrepreneurship.*

Robinson-Wood, T. (2016) *The convergence of race, ethnicity and gender: Multiple identities in counseling*, Sage Publications, Thousand Oaks, CA.

Shaver, K., Gatewood, E. and Gartner, W.B. (2001) 'Differing expectations: Comparing nascent entrepreneurs to non-entrepreneurs', Paper presented at the Academy of Management Research conference, Washington DC.

Singh, G. and De Noble, A. (2003) 'Early retirees as the next generation of entrepreneurs', *Entrepreneurship Theory and Practice*, 27(3): 2–7–226.

Smith-Hunter, A.E. and Boyd, R.L. (2004) 'Applying theories of entrepreneurship to a comparative analysis of white, and minority women business owners', *Women in Management Review*, 19(1): 18–28.

Tajfel, M. and Turner, J.C. (2004) 'The social identity theory of intergroup behavior', In Jost, J.T. and Sidanius, J. (Eds) *Political Psychology: Key Readings*, Psychology Press, New York, pp. 276–293.

Van Eerde, W. and Theirry, H. (1996) 'Vroom's expectancy model and work-related criteria: A meta-analysis', *Journal of Applied Psychology*, 81(5): 575–586.

Verduijn, K. and Essers, C. (2013) 'Questioning dominant entrepreneurship assumptions: The case of female ethnic minority entrepreneurs', *Entrepreneurship & Regional Development*, 25(7–8): 612–630.

22 *Vanessa Ratten*

Waldinger, R., Aldrich, H. and Ward, R. (1990) 'Opportunities, group characteristics and strategies', In Waldinger, R., Aldrich, H. and Ward, R. (Eds) *Ethnic Entrepreneurs: Immigrant Business in Industrial Societies*, Sage, London, 13–48.

Wang, C.L. and Altinay, L. (2008). 'International franchise partner selection and chain performance through the lens of organisational learning', *The Service Industries Journal*, 28(2): 225–238.

Wauters, B. and Lambrecht, J. (2006) 'Refugee entrepreneurship in Belgium: Potential and practice', *International Entrepreneurship and Management Journal*, 2: 509–525.

Weber, M. (1930) *The Protestant ethic and the spirit of capitalism*, Routledge, London.

White, J.C. (2018) 'Toward a theory of minority entrepreneurship in the non-profit arts sector', *The Journal of Arts, Management, Law and Society*, 48(4): 287–300.

Wilson, F., Marlino, D. and Kickul, J. (2004) 'Our entrepreneurial future: Examining the diverse attitudes and motivations of teens across gender and ethnic identity', *Journal of Developmental Entrepreneurship*, 9(3): 177–197.

Wilson, K.L. and Martin, W.A. (1982) 'Ethnic enclaves: A comparison of the Cuban and black economies in Miami', *Journal of Sociology*, 88(1): 135–160.

3 Taking stock and moving forward in research on refugee entrepreneurship

A systematic review of the current field and future research directions

Solomon Akele Abebe

Introduction

In recent years, entrepreneurship undertaken by refugees in their new host country –here, understood as refugee entrepreneurship – has garnered an increasing political and academic consideration (Bizri, 2017; Mawson & Kasem, 2019; Sandberg et al., 2019). A resurgence of interest around this phenomenon has specifically risen since the so-called 'refugee crisis' in 2015, when over 19.5 million people were displaced across the globe (Holmes & Castañeda, 2016). Refugee entrepreneurship has captured the attention of policymakers in their efforts to respond to the high pressures of integrating large numbers of refugees with diverse cultural backgrounds into their society (Obschonka & Hahn, 2018). For academics, the issue presents an opportunity to respond to the emergent demand for a theoretical and empirical understanding of entrepreneurial activities *for* and *by* refugees, along with the potential benefits and challenges that entrepreneurship as a career choice entails for them.

Notwithstanding the growing academic and political curiosity, scientific knowledge on the topic is underdeveloped. To begin with, research on refugees' entrepreneurial and self-employed activities has been rather marginal (Hauff & Vaglum, 1993; Samuel, 1984; Valtonen, 1999), given the wealth of scholarship dealing with their economic adaptation since the mid-1980s. Even though Gold (1988; 1992) earlier marked the distinct nature of refugee entrepreneurship research, the topic did not grow into the mobilisation of a large number of scholars, and previous research was multidisciplinary in nature. Researchers have explained refugee entrepreneurship by using an array of perspectives derived from sociology and anthropology (Campbell, 2007; Gold, 1988; 1992), psychology (Fass, 1986), political science and history (Halter, 1995; Moore, 1990), human and economic geography (Kaplan, 1997; Miyares, 1998) and economics (Basok, 1989; Gonzales et al., 2013), to name a few. As a result, the literature is broadly scattered across these different but often disconnected research areas that have been studied through a wide variety of theoretical orientations, sample

24 *Solomon Akele Abebe*

characteristics and methodologies. Consequently, there seems to be a lack of common theoretical vernacular, an agreed upon focus and research problems and questions, which bind researchers together in a common and distinguishing intellectual project.

However, there appears to be a rising consensus that refugee entrepreneurship is distinct from immigrant and ethnic minority entrepreneurship. The literature suggests that refugees are characterised by an uncontrolled nature in their movement (Gold, 1992), a lack of access to their home country (Wauters & Lambrecht, 2006), lengthy legal processes in their receiving countries (Cortes, 2004), traumatic experiences (Hutchinson & Dorsett, 2012) and an inability to prepare for and adapt to living in a new context (Takeda, 2000). Few scholars maintain that the combined effects of these factors position refugees in disadvantageous position compared to immigrants (Heilbrunn & Iannone, 2019), which ultimately result in a distinguishable entrepreneurial behaviour, experiences and outcomes they call 'refugee entrepreneurship' (Wauters & Lambrecht, 2006; 2008). Their argument is that refugee entrepreneurship, irrespective of sharing a few commonalities with immigrant entrepreneurship, has its own specificities and deserves a separate analysis and its own academic attention.

While the calls for a separate analysis refugee entrepreneurship seem to be pervasive in recent years (Bizri, 2017; Freiling & Harima, 2019; Heilbrunn & Iannone, 2019), the main challenge confronting researchers has been 'where to go from here'? The field needs clear definitions, distinct boundaries and an agreed upon research domain. The current fragmented state of research unfortunately makes it ambivalent for invested scholars, policymakers and practitioners. The complexity shows a considerable need for ordering and systemisation of the literature as well as a viable disciplinary brand and a distinct position to contribute towards its further advancement. This aligns with assumptions from a decidedly modernist construction of science that a research field advances and achieves academic legitimacy through developing a unified system of knowledge around a common domain of interest (Arnould & Thompson, 2005).

In line with these arguments, this chapter provides the following theoretical and practical contributions. First, from a theoretical perspective, it comprehensively covers and organises the literature. The analytical framework offers an overview of the dominant academic fields, motivating interests, scholarly focus, conceptual orientations and theoretical agendas that characterise this particular research stream. Second, this analysis lays a conceptual foundation for future research with explicatory efforts to define the field, demarcate its domain and propose suggestions for future research. The combined outcome provides (1) a better understanding of how the research has progressed since its formative years and (2) the base for creating a collective research ground that will serve to build a coherent theory and form the ontological and epistemological base for the field. From a policy perspective, this analysis is pertinent and timely, given the rapid surge in the influx of refugees across the globe. Furthermore, policymakers interested in the topic can achieve a better understanding of the relevant issues that need to be considered for encouraging refugee entrepreneurship.

Taking stock and moving forward 25

This chapter is organised as follows. The first section provides an overview of the systematic review methodology and the analysis process implemented in the study. The second section proceeds with key findings from the analysis followed by a discussion regarding the main challenges of refugee entrepreneurship research. The last section provides directions for future research followed by a conclusion.

The systematic review methodology

This chapter implements a systematic review methodology, as recommended in the management research field (Tranfield et al., 2003), to identify, evaluate and analyse the existing literature on refugee entrepreneurship in a replicable and transparent process. Entrepreneurship scholars have recently used this methodology for its ability to enhance the validity and rigour of a review process with a clear set of protocols and systematically generated evidence that allows generalisability of results (Cacciotti & Hayton, 2015; Hägg & Gabrielsson, 2017). Application of the review methodology in this research has resulted in 90 academic works[1] that focus exclusively on entrepreneurial self-employment and small business activities of refugees. These articles form the cornerstone for the analysis.

Planning the review

The systematic review began with identification and collection of the literature to build a database of articles aligned with the research objectives and conceptual frames of the study. Search boundaries were set to electronic databases with a focus on a peer-reviewed body of knowledge published as a final output in full text (Costa et al., 2016). Only databases with articles in English were included to extract knowledge for the international scholarly community. There was no particular limit on the selection of journals based on their rankings, publication house and time frame. The bibliographical databases that matched the demands for full coverage, and comprehensive article access included EB-SCO, SCOPUS, Web of Science and Google Scholar (Gusenbauer, 2019). Following directly from the definition of 'refugees' and 'refugee entrepreneurship' in the study, a series of keywords that constituted 'refugees' (refugee*), 'forced migrants' (forced migrant*), 'entrepreneur' (entrepreneur*), 'self-employment' (self-employ*), 'enterprise' (enterprise*), and 'small business' (small business*) were developed. These keywords were combined in all possible Boolean search terms, and were directly applied into each database to identify all relevant academic works under the conceptual boundary. The search process yielded 176 articles in Web of Science, 333 articles in Scopus and 152 articles in EBSCO that contained the keywords.

Systematically reviewing an undeveloped academic field requires looking beyond electronic databases. To this end, manually searching the bibliographies of identified studies through the so-called snowballing technique (Webster &

26 *Solomon Akele Abebe*

Watson, 2002) and reviewing the proceedings (Rauch & Frese, 2007) of entrepreneurship and migration conferences[2] further resulted in seven additional articles. A final independent literature search was conducted via Google Scholar to triangulate results of the search and eventually mitigate the potential loss of articles due to the rigidity of the systematic review methodology. The comparison of the top 20 items obtained from Google Scholar containing the exact phrase 'refugee entrepreneurship', along with 20 articles included in the review, showed a 60% match.

Conducting the review

Each set of results was imported into the reference manager software Mendeley (including full text.pdf file where available) for further screening procedure after removing duplicates. Titles, abstracts, keywords and conclusions of the identified publications were carefully scrutinised with respect to the review objectives to decide on whether to keep or discard each of them in the final data set. Only studies focusing on the entrepreneurial and self-employed activities of refugees and that contributed significantly to refugee entrepreneurship research were included. Publications that contained either of the search terms and keywords in their abstract and titles but that lacked any relevance for the field were excluded. Exclusions in this category included articles on the 'refugee effect' that refers to the positive effect of unemployment on self-employment (Aubry et al., 2015; Carree et al., 2015; Thurik et al., 2008). Publications broadly focusing on refugees' livelihood (Omata, 2012), economic potential, situation and adaptation (Mamgain & Collins, 2003; Pulla & Kharel, 2014; Roth et al., 2012) and refugee camp economies (Beehner, 2015) with limited allusions to refugee entrepreneurship were also debarred from the review. Besides, great precaution was also undertaken on academic works dealing with immigrant, ethnic minority and diaspora entrepreneurship.

The screening process was accompanied by a full text review and systematic documentation of the final set of articles using a coding structure. The coding structure was designed as organising framework to facilitate the standardisation of information about the authors, types of journals, focus of research, theoretical frameworks, classification of research methods, key findings and so on. The standardised information initially served as a basis for conducting a descriptive analysis of the full sample of articles. A configurative methodology (Gough et al., 2012) was followed, as existing research is heterogeneous in terms of theory, methods and samples. This approach involved inductive organisation and arrangement of patterns emerging from the data. The application of configurative analysis in this study helped to inductively extract theoretical debates and empirical evidences and group them into different themes and clusters in a manner that provides an evidence-based overview of the research on refugee entrepreneurship. Observations and patterns emerging from the data analysis were then transformed into graphs and tables.

Taking stock and moving forward 27

Results from the systematic review

Current status of research

The systematic analysis shows that refugee entrepreneurship is an underdeveloped field of research. Even though the phenomenon whetted academic curiosity since the mid-1980s (Fass, 1986), only a limited number of studies investigated the topic at great length prior to the so-called 'global refugee crisis' in 2015. Figure 3.1 shows that the number of academic articles investigating entrepreneurial activities *for* and *by* refugees has drastically increased during the last few years. The existing body of literature primarily constitutes published articles (42%), book chapters (27.8%), conference papers (10%), PhD dissertations (2.2%), articles in press (5.6%) and research-based policy report (7.8%). The sheer surge in the rate of scientific production is due to the scholarly urgency to respond to emerging interests from academic journals following the recent academic and political interest on the topic. However, the citation analysis indicates that the intellectual contribution and influence of refugee entrepreneurship research remains insignificant (Figure 3.1).

Disciplinary approach

Analysis of the disciplinary approach in refugee entrepreneurship research shows the fragmented nature of the field with contributions made from different academic areas. The widespread research shows that issues related to the phenomenon have garnered academic curiosity across a broad range of audiences.

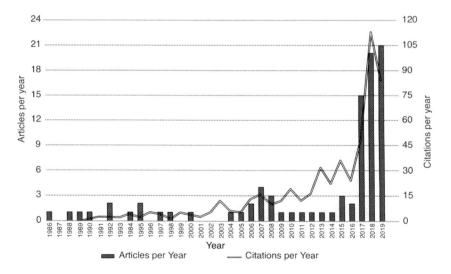

Figure 3.1 Articles per year and citations.
Source: Author's own figure.

28 *Solomon Akele Abebe*

The data specifically show that social and behavioural sciences (46%) provide the predominant disciplinary perspectives through which the topic has been studied. The literature predominantly comes from anthropologists, human and economic geographers, sociologists, psychologists and political scientists. Other disciplinary approaches to the topic include management science and economics (13.3%), arts and humanities (4.4%), strategy and organisation (2.2%) and business administration (34.4%). The overall conclusion is that social science scholars have dominated the research scene in refugee entrepreneurship since its formative years. However, the topic has begun to attract significant attention from management and entrepreneurship scholars in recent years.

Refugee entrepreneurship research also lacks few consistent publication channels to disseminate results. The published body of knowledge (n = 47) is scattered over a wide range of research outlets across multiple disciplines. Figure 3.2 indicates that academic journals in social sciences including those specifically focusing on ethnic, migration and refugee studies have disseminated most of the scholarship on the topic. The general pattern indicates that the role of entrepreneurship and management journals in the dissemination of research outputs has originally been limited, even though this trend appears to be changing in the last couple of years.

Empirical highlights

The empirical overview on refugee entrepreneurship research shows that the share of empirical studies (90%) by far surpasses conceptual contributions (10%). The implication is that empirical evidence on the phenomenon is not proportionally supported by a sufficient level of theorisation and conceptual foundation. Much of the empirical literature (n = 81) is generated through qualitative

Publication outlet for refugee entreprenurship research

- Earth and planetary sciences
- Entreprenurship
- Arts and humanites
- Economics, econometrics and finance
- Business, managment and accounting
- Ethnic, migration and refugee studies
- Other social sciences

Figure 3.2 Publication channels for refugee entrepreneurship research.
Source: Author's own figure.

Taking stock and moving forward 29

approach (79%) that include ethnographic interviews and focus groups, with refugee entrepreneurs involving smaller sample sizes. Qualitative methods are often complemented by a review of policy documents, organisational reports and previous research. Articles with quantitative and mixed-methods research strategies account for 4.9% and 16% of the empirical literature, respectively. Many of these studies have heavily relied on statistical information obtained from secondary sources that include survey data from census reports (Kaplan, 1997), publicly available datasets and document reviews (Fass, 1986; Kaplan, 1997; Wauters & Lambrecht, 2008), and government data repositories (Miyares, 1998). Only a few studies have primarily obtained large-scale quantitative data directly from refugee entrepreneurs through surveys (Crush & Tawodzera, 2017; Johnson, 2000; Obschonka & Hahn, 2018; Wauters & Lambrecht, 2006).

The systematic review also shows the distribution of authorship in refugee entrepreneurship research. The analysis is conducted to uncover if scholars collaborate in authorship or not and whether they collaborate across universities, countries and continents. The data indicates that about 49% of the scholarly contribution comes from solitary authorship. There seems to be a slight change in the trend of authorship during the last few years, with a relatively small number of initiatives within the scholarly community demonstrating the work by teams. The collaborative climate is marked by a few efforts among scholars to collaborate across universities (27%); whereas the cross-country (13%) and cross-continent (10%) collaboration of researchers remains insignificant, notwithstanding the benefits of comparing refugee entrepreneurship across different contexts (Table 3.1).

Theoretical approaches

The systematic review provides information on the extent and type of theoretical application in refugee entrepreneurship research. Data indicates that 52 papers included some form of theoretical framework or concepts in their research design. About 39% of these papers drew on perspectives from immigrant/ethnic minority entrepreneurship research. The remaining publications drew their conceptual point of departure from sociological and related theories (17.3%), economic theories (11.5%), globalisation, migration and integration theories (9.6%) and development (5.8%) and institutional theories (3.8%). The overall implication is that research on refugee entrepreneurship still remains under the influence of 'ethnic minority entrepreneurship'. Scholars routinely based perspectives from the latter to explain the entrepreneurial motivations and activities of refugees in their host environment. The application of concepts from mainstream entrepreneurship (9.6%), despite being initially limited, shows a rise in recent years as the phenomenon has captured the academic interest of management scholars. Of particular concern is that only two papers (3.8%) applied a conceptual framework designed in the context of refugee entrepreneurship (Meyer, 2018; Rashid, 2018).

Table 3.1 Review of refugee entrepreneurship literature (articles in descending order of year)

Author, Year	Research orientation on the different aspects of refugee entrepreneur/ship				Main theoretical perspectives	Main research focus	Research method	Data Source	Host country	Refugee groups
	Characteristics	Potential	Practice	Impact						
Shneikat & Alrawadieh (2019)				X	Exploratory	Role of refugee entrepreneurship in integration	Qualitative	Interviews with 29 Syrian refugees	Turkey	Syrian
Sandberg et al. (2019)	X				Social network view	Characteristics of refugee entrepreneurs and their social networks	Qualitative	Interviews with 4 refugee entrepreneurs	Sweden	Palestinian, Iraqi, Iranian & Vietnamese
Mawson & Kasem (2019)		X			Entrepreneurial intention models	Entrepreneurial intentions of recently arrived Syrian refugees in the UK	Qualitative	In-depth interviews with 9 refugees	UK	Syrian
Heilbrunn (2019)			X		Institutional void and bricolage	Refugee entrepreneurship under institutionally void context	Qualitative	Interviews with refuge entrepreneurs, official reports and observations	Israel	East African
Hartmann & Schilling (2019)			X		Exploratory	Enablers and constraints of refugee entrepreneurship	Qualitative	Interviews with a refugee entrepreneur, consultants, and secondary materials	Germany	Syrian
Plak & Lagarde (2019)			X		Exploratory	Refugee entrepreneurship by unaccompanied minors	Qualitative	Multiple interviews with a refugee entrepreneur	France	Afghan
Freudenberg (2019)			X		Exploratory	Refugee social entrepreneurship	Qualitative	Multiple interviews with a refugee entrepreneur	Germany	Syrian
Abebe & Moog (2019)			X		Exploratory	Factors affecting refugee entrepreneurship	Qualitative	Interviews with refugee entrepreneur	Germany	Ethiopian

Ruparanganda et al. (2019)		X		Exploratory	Factors that influence refugee entrepreneurship	Qualitative	Interviews with a refugee entrepreneur	Australia	Congolese
de la Chaux (2019)		X		Exploratory	Refugee entrepreneurship in extreme environments	Qualitative	Interviews with a refugee entrepreneur	Kenya	Somalian
Tengeh (2019)		X		Exploratory	Determinants of refugee entrepreneurship in hostile and xenophobic context	Qualitative	Interviews with refugee entrepreneur	South Africa	Cameroonian
Alkhaled (2019)		X		Exploratory	Entrepreneurial experiences of a refugee woman in a socio-political and economically restrictive host context.	Qualitative	Interviews with refugee entrepreneur	Jordan	Syrian
Iannone (2019)		X		Exploratory	Determinants of refugee entrepreneurship	Qualitative	Interviews and participant observations	Luxembourg	Iranian
Palalić et al. (2019)		X		Refugee theories	Determinants of refugee entrepreneurship	Qualitative	Interviews with a refugee entrepreneur	Oman	Iraqi
Maalaoui et al. (2019)		X		Exploratory	Entrepreneurial life of refugees	Qualitative	Interviews with a refugee entrepreneur	France	Iranian
Nayır (2019)		X		Exploratory	Social capital and refugee entrepreneurship	Qualitative	Interviews with a refugee entrepreneur	Turkey	Syrian
Kolb (2019)			X	Exploratory	Refugee social entrepreneurship	Qualitative	Interviews with a refugee entrepreneur and stakeholders, and secondary sources	Ireland	Malawian
Freiling & Harima (2019)	X			Exploratory	Characteristics of refugee entrepreneur/ship	Qualitative	16 qualitative case studies	Multiple	Multiple

(Continued)

Author, Year	Research orientation on the different aspects of refugee entrepreneur/ship				Main theoretical perspectives	Main research focus	Research method	Data Source	Host country	Refugee groups
	Characteristics	Potential	Practice	Impact						
Harima et al. (2019)			X		Exploratvory	Characteristics as well as enablers and constraints of refugee entrepreneurship	Qualitative	Interviews with a refugee entrepreneur	Germany	Syrian
Mehtap & Al-Saidi (2019)			X		Exploratory	Informal women refugee entrepreneurship in a patriarchal, collectivist and conservative host context	Qualitative	Interviews with 5 women refugee entrepreneurs	Jordan	Syrian
Ritchie (2018)			X		Institutional change	Women refugee entrepreneurship in fragile settings	Qualitative	Participant observation, semi-structured interviews and focus groups	Kenya & Jordan	Somalian & Syrian
Iannone & Geraudel (2018)			X		Social capital theory	Social capital formation process of nascent refugee entrepreneurs	Qualitative	Interviews with 6 refugee entrepreneurs	Sweden	Syrian
Meister & Mauer (2018)			X		Mixed embeddedness and social network theories	Impact of business incubation on entrepreneurial development and embeddedness of refugee entrepreneurs	Qualitative	Focus groups and interviews with refugee entrepreneurs and incubator stakeholders	Germany	Middle Eastern & Asian
Alrawadieh et al. (2018)			X		Ethnic entrepreneurship and integration theories	Characteristics of and challenges faced by refugee entrepreneurs in tourism and hospitality, as well as the potential role of refugee entrepreneurship as a tool for an effective integration	Qualitative	Interviews with 20 refugee entrepreneurs in tourism and hospitality	Turkey	Syrian

Study				Theoretical lens	Focus	Method	Data	Country	Refugee origin
Omorede & Axelsson (2018)	X			Ethnic minority entrepreneurship concepts	Entrepreneurial self and opportunity identification strategies across the entrepreneurial process	Qualitative	Semi-structured interviews with 11 refugees	Sweden	N/A
Refai et al. (2018)	X			Bourdieu's habitus	Contextualisation of the entrepreneurial identity and activities of refugees	Qualitative	Interviews with 7 aid agency workers and two focus groups with refugees	Jordan	Syrian
Freudenberg & Halberstadt (2018)			X	Concepts on social entrepreneurship	Relevant (social) entrepreneurial concepts for fostering the integration of refugees into workforce and society	Qualitative	N/A	N/A	N/A
Marchand & Dijkhuizen (2018)		X		Exploratory	Effects of entrepreneurship training programme on refugees	Qualitative	Interviews with 8 refugee participants and observations	Netherlands	Syrian & Iranian
Obschonka & Hahn (2018)	X			Entrepreneurial intentions, alertness and career adaptability	The role of personal agency in the early integration process of newly-arrived refugees	Quantitative	Survey data from 267 refugees	Germany	Syrian
Lee (2018)			X	Concepts on activism and social entrepreneurship	Refugee entrepreneurship in the context of social entrepreneurship	Qualitative	Interviews with 30 refugees and participant observation	South Korea	Burmese
Harb et al. (2018)			X	Exploratory	Economic contribution of Syrian refugee entrepreneurs to urban landscapes	Qualitative	Interviews with 12 refugee entrepreneurs	Lebanon	Syrian
Louise & Jiang (2018)			X	Integration framework	Integration of refugees through entrepreneurship	Qualitative	Narrative interviews with 6 refugees	Germany & France	Syrian, Bangladeshis and Iranian

(Continued)

Author, Year	Research orientation on the different aspects of refugee entrepreneur/ship				Main theoretical perspectives	Main research focus	Research method	Data Source	Host country	Refugee groups
	Characteristics	Potential	Practice	Impact						
Rashid (2018)			X		Refugee entrepreneurship barrier framework	Challenges refugee entrepreneurs face across different scenarios	Conceptual	142 studies identified through systematic literature search	N/A	N/A
Eimermann & Karlsson (2018)				X	Social network theory and embeddedness	A relational approach to rural migrant entrepreneurs with refugee background in the restaurant sector	Qualitative	Interviews with 12 refugee restaurateurs	Sweden	Middle Eastern & Algerian
Meyer (2018)			X		Refugee entrepreneurship barrier framework	Challenges facing refugee entrepreneurs while engaging in entrepreneurial activities	Qualitative	17 in-depth interviews with refugee entrepreneurs	Germany	Syrian, Afghan, Iraqi and Eritrean
Trisha (2018)			X		Exploratory	Challenges facing Jewish refugee entrepreneurs in establishing new lives and livelihoods in Ireland at the end of 19th and early 20th centuries	Qualitative	Historiography	Ireland	Lithuanian
Omata (2018)			X		Exploratory	The nexus between refugee mobility, entrepreneurship and socio-economic status in West Africa	Qualitative	Interviews with 300 refugee households and 40 non-refugee stakeholders	Ghana	Liberian
Kong et al. (2018)				X	Social enterprise concept	Social enterprises and their role in the integration of culturally and linguistically diverse (CALD) refugee settlers	Qualitative	Storytelling narrative interviews	Australia	Diverse

Study						Theory	Focus	Method	Data	Country	Nationality
Bizri (2017)		X				Social capital theory and mixed embeddedness	Characteristics of refugee-entrepreneurial start-ups	Qualitative	Interviews with a refugee entrepreneur and employees, observation, official documents and printed materials	Lebanon	Syrian
Betts et al. (2017)					X	Refugee economies	Variation in the economic outcomes for refugees	Mixed	Interviews, and survey among 2, 213 refugee households	Uganda	Somalian, Congolese, and Rwandan
Meyer & Pilkova (2017)				X		UN integration model and entrepreneurial development stages	Entrepreneurial activities by prospective migrant entrepreneurs with the focus on refugees, the challenges they face and their specific needs for promoting migrant entrepreneurship	Qualitative	20 interviews with refugees	Germany	Diverse
Baltaci (2017)			X			The concept of entrepreneurial tendency	Comparison of Syrian refugees' entrepreneurial tendencies and career expectations designation in Turkey and Germany	Qualitative	Interviews with 12 Syrian refugees in Turkey, and 13 Syrian refugees in Germany	Turkey and Germany	Syrian
Predojević-Despić & Lukić (2017)				X		Exploratory	Entrepreneurial motives, and multilevel factors affecting the business practices of long-term settled refugees and returnees in Serbia	Qualitative	15 interviews, 47 online questions and 3 focus groups, and census data	Serbia	Balkan
Gürsel (2017)	X					Exploratory	Emergence of the enterprising refugee discourse in Turkey	Qualitative	Secondary sources	Turkey	Syrian

(Continued)

Author, Year	Research orientation on the different aspects of refugee entrepreneur/ship				Main theoretical perspectives	Main research focus	Research method	Data Source	Host country	Refugee groups
	Characteristics	Potential	Practice	Impact						
Crush et al. (2017b)			X		Exploratory	Understanding the policy and regulatory framework for refugee entrepreneurship in the informal sector	Qualitative	Secondary sources, and interviews with public officials and relevant stakeholders	South Africa	N/A
Crush et al. (2017)			X		Exploratory	Comparison of urban refugee entrepreneurial economies	Mixed	Survey data from over 1000 respondents, and in-depth interviews	South Africa	Diverse
Crush & Tawodzera (2017)			X		The notion of refugee economies	Informal refugee economies in large urban cities and smaller towns	Mixed	Enterprise survey with 1,008 refugee entrepreneurs, interviews with 50 refugee entrepreneurs, and 3 focus groups with refugees	South Africa	Diverse
Crush & McCordic (2017)			X		Exploratory	Comparison of enterprises established by refugees and internal migrants in the urban informal sector	Quantitative	Comparative analysis of quantitative data from over 2000 respondents	South Africa	Diverse
Jiang et al. (2017)			X		Dual embeddedness approach	How refugees become entrepreneurs to reconstruct their career in the host countries	Qualitative	Interviews with 11 refugees	Germany	Unspecified
Villares-Varela et al. (2017)	X				Capabilities approach and mixed embeddedness	The capacity to aspire to become entrepreneur and the capabilities to accomplish these aspirations among recently arrived refugees	Qualitative	Biographical interviews with 44 refugees	England	East African Iranian & Sudanese

Bristol-Faulhammer (2017)	X	Ethnic entrepreneurship concepts	The role of start-up programs in capturing the needs of refugee entrepreneurs	Mixed	Online surveys with 5 start-up program providers and interviews with 12 refugee entrepreneurs	Austria	Armenian, Azerbaijani, Syrian, and Iranian
Katis (2017)	X	Ethnic entrepreneurship theories	The dynamics of entrepreneurship within Vietnamese refugee and migrant communities	Qualitative	35 in-depth interviews	Australia	Vietnamese
Kachkar et al. (2016)	X	Exploratory	Key challenges facing humanitarian organisations and relief NGOs in supporting refuge microenterprises	Qualitative	6 interviews with experts from the aid and relief organisations	Malaysia	Unspecified
Collins (2016)	X	The social ecology framework	The impact of business incubation initiatives on refugee entrepreneurship	Mixed	Data from the incubator database, interviews with 39 refugee entrepreneurs	Australia	Diverse
Barak-Bianco & Raijman (2015)	X	Mixed embeddedness	Entrepreneurship among refugees and asylum seekers in a hostile socio-economic and political environment	Qualitative	Interviews with refugee and asylum seeker entrepreneurs	Israel	Sudanese and Eritrean
Northcote & Dodson (2015)	X	Exploratory	Informal business activities of refugees	Qualitative	Interviews with 32 refugee entrepreneurs	South Africa	Diverse
Tawodzera et al. (2015)	X	Exploratory	International migrant and refugee entrepreneurs engaged in informal economy in	Mixed	Survey data from 518 respondents, 30 interviews and 2 focus groups	South Africa	Diverse

(Continued)

Author, Year	Research orientation on the different aspects of refugee entrepreneur/ship				Main theoretical perspectives	Main research focus	Research method	Data Source	Host country	Refugee groups
	Characteristics	Potential	Practice	Impact						
Gonzales et al. (2013)				X	Social enterprise model	Experiences and perceptions of diverse and marginalised refugees in the process of building a cooperative social enterprise	Qualitative	Participatory observation, semi-structured interviews, and primary source documents	US	Diverse
Dana (2012)			X		Exploratory	Refugee self-employment and entrepreneurship in pre-modern and pre-revolutionary Egyptian economy and beyond	Qualitative	Secondary sources and memoirs	US	Syrian Jew
Sepulveda et al. (2011)			X		Mixed embeddedness	Empirical and conceptual understanding of the recent dramatic growth in migrants and refugee enterprises in London	Qualitative	Reports and interviews with 50 migrant and refugee entrepreneurs	UK	Diverse
Ayadurai (2011)			X		Exploratory	The plight of women refugees in initiating entrepreneurial ventures in an adverse environment	Qualitative	Interviews with 51 refugees	Malaysia	Diverse
Price & Chacko (2009)			X		Mixed embeddedness	The role of local context in influencing entrepreneurial strategies and outcomes, and contrast the entrepreneurial strategies of a refugee group and economic migrants	Mixed	Census data, in-depth interviews and focus groups	US	Ethiopian

Lambrecht (2008)		X	Interactive model of ethnic business development and mixed embeddedness	Barriers towards refugee entrepreneurship in Belgium as a host context	Mixed	Interviews with refugee entrepreneurs and business advisors, and data sets from the Social Security Services for the self-employed (RSVZ)	Belgium	Diverse
Tömöry (2008)	X		Interactive model of ethnic business development	Entrepreneurship among the 1956 Hungarian refugees in Canada	Qualitative	Secondary sources	Canada	Hungarian
Kupferberg (2008)		X	Exploratory	The challenge of entrepreneurial creativity among migrant men with a refugee background	Qualitative	Biographical narrative interviews	Denmark	Pakistanis, Iranian and Turkish
Campbell (2007)	X		Economic globalisation and transnationalism	Somali refugees' business activities in the local context, within the specific history and development of Nairobi, and globally	Qualitative	Secondary sources	Kenya	Somalian
Lyon et al. (2007)		X	Exploratory	Varied local impacts of refugee enterprises within deprived areas of London	Qualitative	Qualitative interviews and focus groups with refugee entrepreneurs, business advisors and refugee community organisations	England	East African & West Asian
Werker (2007)	X		Camp economies and livelihood concepts	Dynamics of refugee camp economy	Qualitative	Interviews and secondary information from government and NGO sources	Uganda	Diverse

(Continued)

Author, Year	Research orientation on the different aspects of refugee entrepreneur/ship				Main theoretical perspectives	Main research focus	Research method	Data Source	Host country	Refugee groups
	Characteristics	Potential	Practice	Impact						
Garnham (2006)		X			Integration and human capability framework	Refugees as potential entrepreneurs and small business owners	Qualitative	N/A	New Zealand	Not specified
Wauters & Lambrecht (2006)		X			Cultural theory, integration model and demographic approach	The potential and practice of refugee entrepreneurship in Belgium	Quantitative	Survey data from refugees and asylum seekers and official data sets from the Social Security Services for Self-employed (RSVZ)	Belgium	Diverse countries, see the refugee groups section
Campbell (2005)			X		Economic globalisation and transnational migration	Contextualisation of informal refugee entrepreneurship in urban areas locally and globally	Qualitative	Secondary sources	Kenya	Somalian
Grey et al. (2004)			X		Immigrant entrepreneurship theories	Refugee and immigrant small business development	Mixed	Survey and ethnographic interviews	Canada	Former Yugoslavian
Johnson (2000)	X				Culture and disadvantage theory	Differences in self-employment among three distinct groups of Southeast Asian refugees in British Columbia, Canada	Mixed	Survey data from the third wave longitudinal study, and interviews with self-employed refugees	Canada	Indochinese
Miyares (1998)			X		Ethnic enclave, human capital theory, disadvantage theory and cultural theory	Business activities of former Soviet refugees in New York city	Quantitative	Quantitative data from local government authorities.	US	Former Soviet Union

Author			Theory	Focus	Method	Data	Country	Population
Kaplan (1997)		X	Ethnic enclave theory	How the growth of Indo-Chinese refugee population in Saint Paul spurred an ethnic sub-economy?	Mixed	Survey data from the 1990 US census and special data set containing records of businesses by location, type, and size for 1981 and 1991	US	Indochinese refugees
Halter (1995)		X	Ethnic entrepreneurship concepts	Self-employment among former Soviet Jewish refugees in Boston	Qualitative	Ethnographic research	US	Soviet Jews
Smith-Hefner (1995)		X	Ethnic entrepreneurship concepts	Culture and patterns of entrepreneurship among Khmer refugees	Qualitative	35 interviews with refugee entrepreneurs and 75 interviews with community members	US	Cambodian
Singh (1994)		X	Exploratory	Emergence, growth and performance of refugee businesses in the bicycle industry	Qualitative	Statistical data from authorities, and review of government reports	India	Pakistani
Latowsky & Grierson (1992)		X	Exploratory	Impact of supervised apprenticeships on refugees' micro-enterprise activities	Qualitative	Qualitative data from a two-year pilot project	Somalia	N/A
Gold (1992)	X		Ethnic economic enclave	Characteristics of self-employed refugees and their resources	Qualitative	Interviews with refugee entrepreneurs, resettlement staff, bankers, city officials, commercial landlords and non-refugee entrepreneurs	US	Soviet Jews & Vietnam

(*Continued*)

Author, Year	Research orientation on the different aspects of refugee entrepreneur/ship				Main theoretical perspectives	Main research focus	Research method	Data Source	Host country	Refugee groups
	Characteristics	Potential	Practice	Impact						
Basok (1989)			X		Petty production framework	Survival and success of small urban enterprises run by Salvadoran refugees in Costa Rica	Qualitative	Interviews with 75 Salvadorian small urban business owners and labourers	Costa Rica	Salvadorian
Gold (1988)	X				Cultural and disadvantage theories	Small business activities of the Soviet Jews and Vietnamese refugees	Qualitative	Interviews with refugee entrepreneurs.	US	Soviet Jews & Vietnamese
Fass (1986)				X	Self-reliance concept	The process of becoming self-reliant through refugee entrepreneurship	Mixed	Statistical data from authorities and document reviews	US	Hmong

Source: Author's own table.

Research orientation

Refugee entrepreneurship literature lacks straightforward and single research orientation. Many of the researchers address more than one research issues in their studies. However, four broad categories have emerged from the analysis. These constitute articles dealing with (1) the characteristics of refugee entrepreneur/ship, (2) the potential of refugee entrepreneurship, (3) the practice of refugee entrepreneurship and (4) the impact of refugee entrepreneurship.

Category (1): characteristics of refugee entrepreneur/ship

The papers (n = 7) in this category focus on individual and group characteristics of refugee entrepreneurs, the nature of their resources and entrepreneurial start-ups that make them distinct, often in comparison with other types of immigrant entrepreneurs. Some articles discuss how refugees' demographic and socio-economic characteristics and migration experiences affect their entrepreneurial motivations, networks and sources of financial capital (Freiling & Harima, 2019; Gold, 1988; 1992; Gursel, 2017). Two recent articles have drawn on social network/capital theories to differentiate the nature of refugee businesses from immigrant-driven entrepreneurial ventures (Bizri, 2017; Sandberg et al., 2019). Johnson (2000), in particular, assessed the unique entrepreneurial behaviour, features and experiences within Southeast Asian refugees and immigrants settled in Canada during the same period to understand their differences in self-employment.

Category (2): potential of refugee entrepreneurship

Entrepreneurial potential and potential entrepreneurs within refugee communities are another line of research in refugee entrepreneurship. The set of publications in this category (n = 8) primarily discuss antecedents of such potential in light of entrepreneurial intentions/tendencies as well as aspirations and capabilities. Three articles (Mawson & Kasem, 2019; Obschonka & Hahn, 2018; Wauters & Lambrecht, 2006) have sought to explore the issue of entrepreneurial intentions within refugees to understand why they self-select into business activities in their host countries. Another similar research (Baltaci, 2017) compares the effect of the host country's culture, values, beliefs and norms on the entrepreneurial tendencies of Syrian refugee students in Turkey and Germany. Additional set of articles (Garnham, 2006; Villares-Varela et al., 2017) draw on capabilities' frameworks (Tipples, 2004; Sen, 1985; 1999) to investigate the levels of entrepreneurial aspirations, skills, positive entry motivations and growth plans of refugees as precursors for the potential of refugee entrepreneurship.

Category (3): practice of refugee entrepreneurship

Articles on the practice of refugee entrepreneurship (n = 61) constitute the bulk of research in the field and can be further grouped into four categories based on

44 *Solomon Akele Abebe*

their specific research orientation. The first set of publications predominantly explore factors for the emergence, survival and success of refugee enterprises (Campbell, 2007; Halter, 1995; Miyares, 1998; Singh, 1994; Smith-Hefner, 1995; Tömöry, 2008). Another segment of the publication in this category explores the dynamics of refugee entrepreneurship in multiplicity of legal, political and social complexities (Ayadurai, 2011; Barak-Bianco & Raijman, 2015; Werker, 2007). These papers analyse how refugees with marginal and precarious status initiated and operated their entrepreneurial ventures in hostile socio-economic and political context. Similarly, additional set of papers focus on entrepreneurial activities of refugees under dynamic, xenophobic, constantly shifting and dangerous urban spaces in Africa (Crush & Tawodzera, 2017; Northcote & Dodson, 2015; Omeje & Mwangi, 2014). Another significant body of articles investigate the barriers refugees face in starting up and running entrepreneurial ventures together with their manoeuvring and coping mechanisms (Ayadurai, 2011; Barak-Bianco & Raijman, 2015; Garnham, 2006; Lyon et al., 2007; Meyer & Pilkova, 2017; Wauters & Lambrecht, 2008). The last corpus of articles discusses the role of host country policies, local opportunity structures and institutional environment in refugee entrepreneurship. These articles specifically highlight the role of enterprise support networks (Kachkar et al., 2016; Latowsky & Grierson, 1992), business support policies (Lyon et al., 2007) and entrepreneurial training programs/projects (Fass, 1986) on successful entrepreneurship for refugees.

Category (4): impact of refugee entrepreneurship

The final category of articles (n = 14) have indicated important impacts of refugee entrepreneurship on different levels. Speaking of levels of analysis, some studies investigate micro- or individual-level impact in terms of income generation and livelihood strategy (Betts et al., 2017), creating a sense of new identity, self-esteem and independence satisfaction of personal development (Kupferberg, 2008) and achieve psychological, sociocultural and economic aspects of integration (Freudenberg & Halberstadt, 2018; Kong et al., 2018; Louise & Jiang, 2018; Shneikat & Alrawadieh, 2019). Other studies deal with the impact of refugee venturing at meso or community level in terms of community building (Lyon et al., 2007), enhancement of local communities (Eimermann & Karlsson, 2018; Gonzales et al., 2013; Kolb, 2019; Lee, 2018) and creating opportunities for local development (Harb et al. 2018). Finally, one publication focuses on the impact derived from refugee's involvement in entrepreneurial self-employment at macro or country level with respect to contributing to the overall national economy (Moore, 1990).

Geographical context for research

Based on the geographical context for empirical research, the publications are grouped under five belts: North and Central America, Europe, Oceania, Asia

Taking stock and moving forward 45

and Africa. However, the discussion in this section only focuses on the regions that contribute a significant body of knowledge on the phenomenon.

Earlier research on refugee entrepreneurship comes from North and Central America. However, the research in the region shows signs of US dominance in the scientific output. It is not surprising that the research tradition has its roots in the country, given its long experience with ethnic minority entrepreneurship in which foreign-born people have been over-represented in small business ownership since the end of the 19th century (Light, 1984). Despite United States' primacy, Canada is also featured in research (Grey et al., 2004; Johnson, 2000; Tömöry, 2008). Much of the literature from the region focuses on the small businesses of Soviet Jews (Halter, 1995; Miyares, 1998) and Indo-Chinese such as Hmong, Vietnamese and Khmer refugees (Fass, 1986; Johnson, 2000; Kaplan, 1997; Smith-Hefner, 1995), who were the largest groups to enter the region since the mid-1970s. Gold (1988; 1992) sought to create a separate research field by highlighting the distinctive features of refugee entrepreneurs in terms of their resources, motivations and challenges compared with immigrants. Nevertheless, as the research tradition in the region was highly influenced by 'ethnic minority entrepreneurship', his efforts did not mobilise a large number of scholars. Most of the discussions have centred on entrepreneurial entry motivations with strong reliance on orthodox and reactive cultural theories (Light, 1980) as well as disadvantage theory (Light, 1979) and the related blocked mobility thesis.

Refugee entrepreneurship research in Europe is a fairly recent phenomenon compared to North America. The empirical focus on East African, West Asian and Middle Eastern refugee groups indicates that research follows the recent refugee immigration trends towards the region. The earliest scholarly effort emerged from the work of Moore (1990), who studied the experiences of German Jewish refugee entrepreneurs in the 1930s recession-hit Netherlands. As anticipated, a fair share of initial contributions comes from the UK. However, refugee entrepreneurship has not been widely recognised as a scientific discipline of its own, notwithstanding the long history of refugee migration and research on ethnic minority business ownership since the 1980s (Ram & Jones, 2008). The UK scholars have studied different categories of migrants in aggregate under the umbrella of 'migrant entrepreneurship' (Edwards et al., 2016). The first systematic empirical examination of refugee entrepreneurs in Europe occurred in Belgium. Wauters and Lambrecht (2006; 2008) did the initial pioneering exercises to provide strong arguments for undertaking refugee entrepreneurship as a separate field of scholarship. In recent years, Germany has featured a lot in recent research endeavours due to its open-door policy for refugees. Research mainly focuses on entrepreneurial potential (Meyer & Pilkova, 2017; Obschonka & Hahn, 2018), challenges (Harima et al., 2019) and the business incubation process (Harima & Freudenberg, 2018) of refugees, in response to the growing concern about their economic adaptation in the country.

In general, what makes refugee entrepreneurship research in Europe different from North American tradition is its theoretical focus. In the former, research focuses on the demand side of refugee entrepreneurship; with the emphasis

46   *Solomon Akele Abebe*

on how political and structural conditions in the host environment determine refugees' entrepreneurial engagement, whereas in the latter, research provides supply-side explanations of refugee entrepreneurship through highlighting the role of cultural characteristics and group resources for self-employment. Refugee entrepreneurship research across Europe has significantly benefited from the growing popularity of the mixed embeddedness perspective (Kloosterman, 2010).

Scholars in Asia and Africa have also contributed to the research field. Except for Singh's (1994) analysis of Pakistani refugee entrepreneurs in India, all articles are published after 2007. This suggests that refugee entrepreneurship is at its infancy stage in these regions. In Asia, and particularly the Middle East, research has seen a rapid increase during the last few years due to the contemporary massive refugee movement(s). A great deal of empirical research features Syrian refugee entrepreneurs in neighbouring countries such as Turkey, Lebanon and Jordan. Research in Africa focuses on the informal business activities of diverse refugee groups from Eastern and Central parts of Africa in the relatively developed urban contexts of the continent such as Nairobi (Campbell, 2005; 2007), Cape Town and Johannesburg (Crush et al., 2017a; 2017b; 2017; Tawodzera et al., 2015). The later groups of scholars particularly devoted their effort to understand the policy and regulatory framework within which refugee entrepreneurs establish and operate their enterprises. Most importantly, research from Asia and Africa, with its highly explorative and descriptive orientation, lacks significant theoretical contribution. The primary focus has been to understand the entrepreneurial motives (Mehtap & Al-Saidi, 2019; Shneikat & Alrawadieh, 2019), experiences (Alkhaled, 2019), challenges and survival mechanisms (Heilbrunn, 2019) of refugee entrepreneurs in the context of highly conservative and institutionally absent host environments.

Discussion

This section deliberates on the principal issues observed from existing research on refugee entrepreneurship. The systematic analysis shows that the current state of research is characterised by its (1) strong theoretical reliance on ethnic minority entrepreneurship, (2) qualitative and descriptive nature and (3) lack of scope and boundaries. As these factors have potential implications for its future development, each of them is deliberated later.

Theoretical reliance on ethnic minority entrepreneurship

The first issue in the current refugee entrepreneurship literature relates with the strong reliance on theoretical frameworks developed in the context of immigrants. Many researchers have applied cultural and disadvantage theories (Campbell, 2007; Gold, 1988; 1992; Johnson, 2000; Miyares, 1998; Omeje & Mwangi, 2014), ethnic enclave thesis (Kaplan, 1997; Miyares, 1998), mixed embeddedness framework (Bizri, 2017; Barak-Bianco & Raijman, 2015; Price & Chacko, 2009; Sepulveda et al., 2011), Waldinger and colleagues' (1990) interactive model of ethnic business development (Price & Chacko, 2009; Tömöry, 2008) and broad conceptual discussions on ethnic entrepreneurship (Halter, 1995; Smith-Hefner, 1995; Wauters & Lambrecht, 2008). However, as refugee entrepreneurs represent a special case of migrant entrepreneurs, perspectives designed in the contexts of immigrant and ethnic entrepreneurs – particularly cultural, structural and mixed embeddedness perspectives – provide limited insights on their unique characteristics.

The logical coherence on ethnic resource perspective promoted by cultural theory and enclave hypothesis lacks relevance to refugee entrepreneurs, due to their limited access to chain-like ethnic networks compared with immigrant and ethnic minority entrepreneurs (Gold, 1992; Wauters & Lambrecht; 2006). The perspectives' problematic process of ethnicisation based on the assumption for the existence of homogeneous communities of origin (Mitchell, 2015) is another concern. This is because refugee communities are diverse groups not only in terms of their countries of origin, but also in terms of ethnic origin, class, tastes, preferences, experiences and more (Gold, 1992).

The structural perspective's explanation of necessity-driven refugee entrepreneurship does not fully capture refugees' business entry decision. The fact that all refugees facing economic disadvantage do not opt for entrepreneurship suggests the existence of an additional set of factors that attract certain groups of refugees more than others (Basu, 2006). Even though labour market discrimination may play a significant role, higher personal ambitions, positive entry motivations and self-efficacy propel the leap into entrepreneurship (Kupferberg, 2008; Mawson & Kasem, 2019; Villares-Varela et al., 2017; Wauters & Lambrecht, 2006).

Finally, the structuralist nature of the mixed embeddedness perspective with its viscous focus on the deterministic aspects of opportunity structure limits an understanding of the entrepreneurial decision-making and actions of refugees in responding to opportunity structures (Mitchell, 2015). The mixed embeddedness helps to capture the complexities of refugee entrepreneurship by accounting the multiple levels of context, but needs to be combined with perspectives that flag up the role of refugees' entrepreneurial agency. For instance, a fairly recent research (Villares-Varela et al., 2017) has coalesced into the mixed embeddedness perspective with Sen's capabilities approach (Sen, 2005). This synthesis has provide due weight to agency in the analysis of refugee entrepreneurship while considering the structural context where agency operates.

Nature of the research and disciplinary approach

The second issue for refugee entrepreneurship stems from the descriptive nature of research. Many researchers have produced a research agenda focusing on rich empirical descriptions, practical orientations and policy concerns. This inexorably leads to a strong reliance on ethnographic methods and secondary information obtained from governmental databases and reports. The scholarly works in this line of research lack any specific theoretical contribution, notwithstanding their richly descriptive analysis and insights. The use of rigorous and

48　*Solomon Akele Abebe*

sophisticated statistical techniques drawing on larger sample sizes and longitudinal study designs are non-existent. The practical research orientation partly explains the limited efforts of theorisation and methodological development. For the field to gain higher levels of academic legitimacy requires methodological upgrading and theoretical sophistication.

The other related issue concerns with the type of academic disciplines involved in research. The analysis shows that much of the literature is contributed by researchers with disciplinary roots in social and behavioural sciences as well as humanities. Entrepreneurship scholars have been largely absent from the research scene. This has affected much of the research focus, direction and what we know about the phenomenon. Research focuses on the ethnic and cultural characteristics of refugee entrepreneurs (Freiling & Harima, 2019; Gold, 1988; 1992; Johnson, 2000), their businesses (Bizri, 2017) and resources (Sandberg et al., 2019). Little is known about issues related with entrepreneurial cognitions and behaviour of refugees. Besides, current research on the topic is disconnected from recent advances in entrepreneurship theory. Contemporary entrepreneurship research has shown a systematic shift from the focus on the traits of the entrepreneur to understanding the entrepreneurial processes and behaviour. To date, much of the refugee entrepreneurship research has focused on the cultural and structural determinants of refugees' entrepreneurial entry and outcomes.

The analysis also shows that entrepreneurship and management journals have played insignificant roles as primary outlets for the scholarship on refugee entrepreneurship, and this can be attributed to the following reasons. First, the academic community specifically interested in self-employment and small business activities within the refugee communities has already recognised a distinct subfield by using existing forums in migration and refugee studies for knowledge exchange. Second, the limited application of entrepreneurship and management theories or concepts in refugee entrepreneurship research has reduced the interest of their journals. Third, Boyacigiller and Adler (1991) have long noted that mainstream management journals suffer from bias and limited openness towards theoretical perspectives from other disciplines. And finally, the qualitative and descriptive nature of much of the research also makes it easier to publish in social science journals than those in the areas of business and management.

Lack of scope and boundary

The third issue from the literature analysis is a lack of any scholarly attempt to demarcate the scope and boundary of refugee entrepreneurship. Confusion and uncertainty are constantly floated about (1) who exactly are refugee entrepreneurs? (2) how are their entrepreneurial behaviour and processes distinct from immigrant entrepreneurs? and (3) what is the scope of refugee entrepreneurship? The term 'refugee entrepreneur/ship' is not well defined and research is highly fragmented without any coherent body of literature, agreed upon research focus and questions. Clear demarcations of the field from other closely related research domains such as immigrant/ethnic minority entrepreneurship have not been clearly drawn.

Lack of scope and boundary has inevitably created at least two problems. One, researchers have been working independently without building on each other's work. Hence, the knowledge in the field is not accumulated. Two, theoretical concerns have been observed regarding the conceptualisation of the phenomenon. For instance, a recent article (Sandberg et al., 2019) has placed refugee entrepreneurship at the intersection of immigrant, transnational and diaspora entrepreneurship. The study has conceptualised refugee entrepreneurs as a subcategory of immigrant entrepreneurs in which their businesses benefit from transnational networks involving their country of residence, country of origin and third-party country. However, the authors' conclusion is primarily influenced by the nature of their research sample. The fact that the study drew on a sample of well-established participants (three of them created their ventures after nine to fifteen years of residence in the host country) has led them to argue that refugee entrepreneurs share similar characteristics with transnational, diaspora and immigrant entrepreneurs. However, refugees manifest distinct entrepreneurial behaviour and characteristics at the early stage of their settlement in the host country. The argument here is that there is a need to strictly define 'Who is a refugee entrepreneur'?, 'When does one stop being a refugee entrepreneur'? and 'What should be the domain of refugee entrepreneurship research'? These questions move the discussion in the next section with possible responses to such inquiries.

The path for future development

Calls for future directions have been widely made by scholars in the hope of moving refugee entrepreneurship research towards its next stages of development. Based on the findings from the review and to respond to growing request for establishing a separate research field, this chapter endeavours to demarcate the domain of refugee entrepreneurship and outline some thoughts that have potential to guide future directions of research on the phenomenon.

The domain of refugee entrepreneurship

Delineating the domain of refugee entrepreneurship primarily requires a coherent definition of entrepreneurship. By following Gartner (1985), this chapter conceptualises entrepreneurship as the process of new venture creation that entails planning, organising and establishing new organisations (Gartner, 1985). Gartner's definition is relevant for refugee entrepreneurship due to its broader conceptualisation focusing on the individuals involved in starting new ventures, processes and actions taken, the type of firms started and the influence of the surrounding environment. Understanding refugee entrepreneurship in this way helps to build on the already existing literature; there is a stock of knowledge on the characteristics of refugee entrepreneurs and their businesses and the impact of the host countries' institutional and economic environment. Gartner (1985) specifically argues that the most fruitful path to study entrepreneurship is to view it as a process that includes a series of activities and behaviours towards the creation of new ventures. Refugee entrepreneurship research accordingly needs to shift from the current preoccupation on cultural and structural determinants towards the process, behavioural and cognitive aspects of the phenomenon.

Conceptualisation of refugee entrepreneur/ship needs to emerge from an understanding of what constitutes refugees and how they inherently differ from immigrants. Literature shows that the difference between immigrants and refugees originates from the fundamental nature of their movement (Bernard, 1977; Gold, 1988; 1992). The term immigrants refers to individuals who move to another country voluntarily in search of better economic opportunities based on their eligibility for permanent residence in terms of academic merits and professional qualifications (Anderson & Blinder, 2011). The term 'refugee', on the other hand, applies to a very specific and defined set of people forcibly displaced from their country of origin due to armed conflict, prosecution and natural catastrophe. Despite the enormous diversity within refugees, the forceful nature of their migration creates certain collective characteristics that affect their subsequent economic behaviour in a way different from immigrants. Figure 3.3 indicates the idiosyncratic features that differentiate refugees from immigrants. Therefore, following from this and based on an understanding of entrepreneurship (Gartner, 1985), refugee entrepreneurship entails the process by which individual or groups of refugees create new ventures in their host countries.

Refugee entrepreneurs are specifically distinct from different migrant entrepreneur categories due to their unique demographic, social and economic

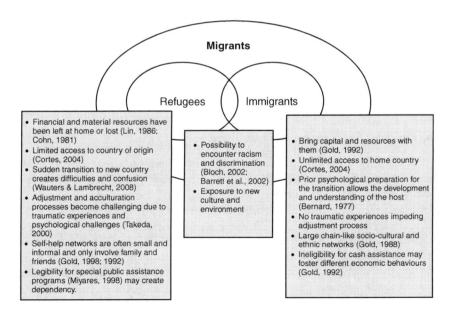

Figure 3.3 Characteristics of refugees versus immigrants.[3]
Source: Author's own figure.

Taking stock and moving forward 51

characteristics, migration experiences and legal situations in their host country. They enter their host countries with different intentions and level of resources (Bernard, 1977; Garnham, 2006; Gold, 1992). Their main differences, with immigrant, transnational and ethnic minority entrepreneurs, are in terms of the type and extent of their resources and the scope of their activities (Table 3.2).

Refugee entrepreneurs, due to their diverse origins and the uncontrolled nature of their movements, are unable to form large chain-like socio-cultural and

Table 3.2 Differences between refugee entrepreneurs and other categories of migrant entrepreneurs*

Type of entrepreneurs	*Sources of resources*	*Business Location*	*Types of businesses*	*Characteristics of the entrepreneurs*
Refugee entrepreneurs	Informal small social circle of family and close friends, bricolage, aid agencies	Host country	Small businesses which are extensions of the family itself	Displaced individuals/ families, with high levels of resilience, risk-taking propensity and ambition
Immigrant entrepreneurs	Large-scale, chain-like networks and ethno-cultural institutions for mutual support	Host country	Small- to medium-sized businesses located in vacancy chains and sectors marked by cut-throat competition	Individual immigrants/ groups with distinct language and customs in the host country
Ethnic minority entrepreneurs	Co-ethnic networks tied to a common cultural heritage and ethnic identity and structure	Host country	Small businesses mainly catering to co-ethnic clientele	Ethnic individuals and racial minorities who maintain a distinctive level of attachment to a community
Transnational entrepreneurs	Global networks and connections	Cross-national	Family businesses	Immigrants engaged in two or more socially embedded environments
Returnee entrepreneurs	Personal or group fund	Home country	Internationally export-oriented and often high-tech	Immigrants; individuals or team, who are experts
Diaspora entrepreneurs	Personal, ethnic and structural	Home and host country	Micro and primarily small scale in the service sector	Expatriates engaged in entrepreneurial activities in their home country

Source: Author's own table.

* This typology draws on Drori et al. (2009).

52   Solomon Akele Abebe

ethnic networks based on kinship and common ethnic camaraderie that are present among ethnic minority and immigrant entrepreneurs. Literature shows how these networks enhance the competitive advantage of immigrant and ethnic entrepreneurs through facilitating the provision of co-ethnic labour supply, crucial business information, capital markets, mutual aid and assistance and financial arrangements (Masurel et al., 2002). The fact that bounded solidarity in refugee communities are formed within localised subgroups than in the entire population makes their entrepreneurial resources limited to small and informal circles of family and close friends (Gold, 1988; 1992).

Besides, immigrant entrepreneurs (including diaspora and transnational entrepreneurs) can individually or in groups maintain advantageous trading relationships between their home and host countries, in order to arrange deals, recruit suppliers and raise capital. Research shows the positive impact of this dual embeddedness on the entrepreneurial-opportunity-creation process of immigrant entrepreneurs in their host countries (Evansluong, 2016). Access to home country provides unique entrepreneurial inspiration, opportunities, social networks, resources and access to human and financial capitals. In contrast, refugee entrepreneurs have limited access to their home countries to acquire funds, capital and labour force for their businesses (Wauters & Lambrecht, 2008).

Another feature of refugee entrepreneurship is the scope of their business activities. Ethnic minority entrepreneurship (also, in many cases applies to immigrant entrepreneurship) focuses primarily on satisfying the needs and preferences of co-ethnic customers in the host nation, as it is often conducted in regions with dense ethnic population (Fong & Ooka, 2002). The business activities of refugee entrepreneurs are directed to the wider population due to limited embeddedness in ethnic networks.

Finally, the definition of refugee entrepreneur/ship requires a temporal breadth to maintain its distinctiveness from the other entrepreneur/ship categories. Refugees manifest distinct economic behaviour during their early years of residency when they suffer most from their liabilities of foreignness and refugeeness. However, their entrepreneurial characteristics and behaviour may not significantly differ from immigrants with better embeddedness in their new social, economic and institutional environment. There exists no universally accepted time frame and yardsticks to determine the termination of 'refugeehood'. Few indicators that mark the end of a 'refugee' include acquisition of new nationality, access to home country and full participation in the social, economic and political spheres of the host society. Anecdotal evidences from Sweden show that it takes on average up to ten years for refugees to achieve these benchmarks (Riksrevisionen, 2015). However, this is not to argue that refugees immediately lose the whole refugee experience as typical behaviours related with psychological traumas can remain through their lifetime (Silove et al., 2017). However, the argument in this section is that the scope of refugee entrepreneurship needs to be bounded by the time of their early period of settlement. When refugees eventually build up access to social and financial resources, both in their host and home countries, their entrepreneurial characteristics and behaviour may not

Taking stock and moving forward 53

significantly differ from immigrants. Henceforward, based on the this discussion, the definition of refugee entrepreneurs takes up individuals and refugee groups engaged in the processes of new venture creation activities from their arrival in the host context up to the first ten years of residency.

Future research directions

The systematic analysis shows that the omnipresent paradigm in refugee entrepreneurship research overlooks the agency of refugee entrepreneurs. Much of the earlier research focuses on the role of cultural characteristics and traits, country of origin effects and ethnocultural resources (Gold, 1988; 1992; Halter, 1995; Moore, 1990; Singh, 1994; Smith-Hefner, 1995; Wauters & Lambrecht, 2006) for refugees' entrepreneurial actions. Another section of literature addresses how structural disadvantages, opportunity structures and institutional environments impact refugees' leap into entrepreneurial activities and their outcomes (Fass, 1986; Latowsky & Grierson, 1992; Werker, 2007). The prevailing research in general considers refugee entrepreneurship as group level phenomenon enabled and constrained by refugees' cultural characteristics and macrostructural conditions in the host environment. There exists a lack of knowledge about how refugees act in the face of these circumstances, and the absence of individual analyses obscures the heterogeneity of refugee entrepreneurs and their entrepreneurial strategies, actions, outcomes and experiences.

Hence, future research needs to acknowledge the agentic properties of refugee entrepreneurs, with equal emphasis on the context. The embedded agency approach is relevant for refugee entrepreneurship research, as it resonates well with a call to understand the nexus between the entrepreneurial agent and the embedding context (Garud et al., 2007). By considering the entrepreneurial phenomenon of refugees in the context where it unfolds, the understanding of its nature, dynamics and specificity is enriched. The role of embeddedness and context is amplified in the specific case of refugees due to their liability of foreignness and sensitivity to institutional frameworks. However, refugees possess the agency to aspire to become entrepreneurs and accomplish their goals as they manoeuvre through their new host surroundings (Mawson & Kasem, 2019; Obschonka & Hahn, 2018; Villares-Varela et al., 2017).

Refugee entrepreneurship research lags behind contemporary theoretical shift towards the process view of new venture creation (Davidsson, 2015). Existing research has identified several cultural and structural determinants that influence the phenomenon. The literature predominantly explains why refugees leap into entrepreneurial self-employment in their host countries through highlighting the various aspects of the individual-, community- and environment-level determinants as sources of their advantages and disadvantages. However, these explanations only provide an understanding of the factors that influence the entrepreneurial motivation and success of refugee entrepreneurs, but do not provide an understanding of how they become entrepreneurs in their host environment. The process through which refugee entrepreneurs actively take part

54 *Solomon Akele Abebe*

and influence the perquisites for venture creation has been missing in the literature. There are extant process models in entrepreneurship literature that can be applicable to refugee entrepreneurship research (see Moroz & Hindle, 2012). However, the application of process models needs to build on previously known refugee specific multilevel factors and their interaction with and effect on each stage of the entrepreneurial process.

Conclusion

This chapter provides one of the pioneering exercises to systematically review the research on refugee entrepreneurship. The analysis shows that the existing body of knowledge has built the cornerstones for future empirical and theoretical works. Scholars have specifically proposed valid arguments about the ontological differences of refugees from immigrants to strengthen credence in the existence of distinct entrepreneurial characteristics and behaviour. The seemingly rising consensus among scholars has contributed to an interest to legitimise the quest for separate consideration of refugee entrepreneurship.

Results of the analysis, however, demonstrate that certain factors characterise the nature of refugee entrepreneurship research with some potential implications for its future development. First, the field relies strongly on theoretical frameworks developed in the context of immigrant entrepreneurs. However, these theoretical frameworks do not help to capture the specificities of refugee entrepreneurship, even though they serve as points of departure. Thus, the field needs empirically grounded theory that provides the conceptual ground for future studies. Second, a significant body of research has been driven by practical and policy issues, where the focus has been on rich empirical descriptions using ethnographic methods and secondary reports. The practical research orientation, in part, has contributed to the limited efforts of theorisation and methodological development. Besides, much of the scholarly contributions come from the works of social scientists such as sociologists and anthropologists. This has affected the research focus, direction and what is known about the phenomenon. In particular, the absence of entrepreneurship researchers from the research scene may well have disconnected the field from the contemporary developments in entrepreneurship in terms of advances in modern theory and methodological rigour. Third, the field lacks common criterion to univocally define its domain and potentially overcome the incongruity arising from the different meanings and measurements provided to conceptualise the phenomenon. Since the term 'refugee entrepreneurship' appeared for the first time in academic context in the work of Gold (1992), there have not been any attempts to demarcate its domain and scope even though the topic has also been featured a lot in current research.

Importantly, this chapter suggests few potential avenues in the hope of overcoming some of the limitations and moving the field towards its next stage of development. First, the domain of refugee entrepreneurship needs to be delimited to understanding the new venture creation of refugees from their arrival in the host country to the first ten years of residency. This is based on the evidence that liabilities experienced during this period in terms of their foreignness and refugeeness are what make refugees' entrepreneurial behaviour distinct from immigrant, diaspora, transnational and returnee entrepreneurs. Second, future research needs conceptual orientations that acknowledge the agency of refugee entrepreneurs, with equal attention provided to the embedding structures. Analysis of the review shows that the omnipresent paradigm, with its overwhelming focus on cultural and structural determinants of entrepreneurship, disregards agential discretion of refugee entrepreneurs. The embedded agency approach resonates well with the call to understand the nexus between the entrepreneurial agent and the embedding structural context. Third, future research needs to drift from its overwhelming focus on the characteristics of refugee entrepreneur/ship towards the processes leading to the creation of new venture. However, any adoption of entrepreneurial process models needs to build on the effect and interaction of previously known refugee specific factors within each entrepreneurial phase.

Notes

1 The search included publications up to February 2019.
2 These include Babson College Entrepreneurship conference (BCERC), Nordic Conference on Small Business Research (NCSB), Research in Entrepreneurship and Small Business Conference (RENT), International Conference Innovation Management, Entrepreneurship and Sustainability (IMES) and International Council for Small Business (ICSB).
3 This figure is based on the typology made by the Calgary Board of Education, "Teaching Refugees with Limited Formal Learning", http://teachingrefugees.com/student-background/106-2/.

References

References marked by an **asterisk** (*) are included in the systematic literature review
*Abebe, B. Y., & Moog, P. (2019). A Case Study of an Ethiopian Refugee in Germany. In: Heilbrunn, S., Freiling, J., & Harima, A. (eds) *Refugee Entrepreneurship* (pp. 115–125). Palgrave Macmillan, Cham.
*Alkhaled, S. (2019). The Resilience of a Syrian Woman and Her Family Through Refugee Entrepreneurship in Jordan. In: Heilbrunn, S., Freiling, J., & Harima, A. (eds) *Refugee Entrepreneurship* (pp. 241–253). Palgrave Macmillan, Cham.
*Alrawadieh, Z., Karayilan, E., & Cetin, G. (2018). Understanding the challenges of refugee entrepreneurship in tourism and hospitality. *The Service Industries Journal*, 39, 1–24.
Anderson, B., & Blinder, S. (2011). Who counts as a migrant? Definitions and their consequences. *Migration Observatory Briefing*, 4th Revision, 1–9. COMPAS, University of Oxford, UK.
Aubry, M., Bonnet, J., & Renou-Maissant, P. (2015). Entrepreneurship and the business cycle: The "Schumpeter" effect versus the "refugee" effect—a French appraisal based on regional data. *The Annals of Regional Science*, 54(1), 23–55.
Arnould, E. J., & Thompson, C. J. (2005). Reflections twenty years of research. *Journal of Consumer Research*, 31(4), 868–882. doi: 10.1086/426626
*Ayadurai, S. (2011). Challenges faced by women refugees in initiating entrepreneurial ventures in a host country: Case study of UNHCR women refugees in Malaysia. *Asian Journal of Business and Management Sciences*, 1(3), 85–96.

56 Solomon Akele Abebe

*Baltaci, A. (2017). A comparison of Syrian migrant students in Turkey and Germany: Entrepreneurial tendencies and career expectations. *European Journal of Educational Research*, 6(1), 15–27.

*Barak-Bianco, A., & Raijman, R. (2015). Asylum seeker entrepreneurs in Israel, economic sociology. *The European Electronic Newsletter*, ISSN 1871–3351, 16(2), 4–13.

*Basok, T. (1989). How useful is the "petty commodity production" approach? Explaining the survival and success of small Salvadorian urban enterprises in Costa Rica. *Labour, Capital and Society/Travail, capital et société*, 22(1), 41–64.

Basu, A. (2006). Ethnic Minority Entrepreneurship. In: Casson, M., Yeung, B., Basu, A., & Wadeson, N. (eds.) *The Oxford Handbook of Entrepreneurship* (pp. 580–600). Oxford University Press, Oxford.

Beehner, L. (2015). Are Syria's do-it-yourself refugees outliers or examples of a new norm? *Journal* of International Affairs, 68(2), 157–175.

Bernard, W. S. (1977). Immigrants and refugees: Their similarities, differences and needs. *International Migration*, 14(4), 267–281.

*Betts, A., Omata, N., & Bloom, L. (2017). Thrive or survive: Explaining variation in economic outcomes for refugees. *Journal on Migration & Human Security*, 5, 716.

*Bizri, R. M. (2017). Refugee-entrepreneurship: A social capital perspective. *Entrepreneurship & Regional Development*, 29(9–10), 847–868.

Boyacigiller, N. A., & Adler, N. J. (1991). The parochial dinosaur: Organizational science in a global context. *Academy of management Review*, 16(2), 262–290.

*Bristol-Faulhammer, M. (2017). How Does Start-Up Assistance Capture the Challenges, Barriers, and Successes for Refugee Entrepreneurs in Austria? (Doctoral dissertation, Saybrook University).

Cacciotti, G., & Hayton, J. C. (2015). Fear and entrepreneurship: A review and research agenda. *International Journal of Management Reviews*, 17(2), 165–190.

*Campbell, E. H. (2007). Economic Globalization from Below: Transnational Refugee Trade Networks in Nairobi. In: Murray, M. J.,& Myers, G. A. (eds.) *Cities in Contemporary Africa* (pp. 125–148). Palgrave Macmillan, New York.

*Campbell, E. H. (2005). 'Formalizing the informal economy: Somali refugee and migrant trade networks in Nairobi.' *Global Migration Perspectives* No. 47, Geneva. Report for the Global Commission on International Migration.

Carree, M., Congregado, E., Golpe, A., & van Stel, A. (2015). Self-employment and job generation in metropolitan areas, 1969–2009. *Entrepreneurship & Regional Development*, 27(3–4), 181–201.

*Collins, J. (2016). *From Refugee to Entrepreneur in Sydney in Less Than Three Years*, UTS Business School, Sydney.

Cortes, K. E. (2004). Are refugees different from economic immigrants? Some empirical evidence on the heterogeneity of immigrant groups in the United States. *Review of Economics and Statistics*, 86(2), 465–480.

Costa, E., Soares, A. L., & de Sousa, J. P. (2016). Information, knowledge and collaboration management in the internationalisation of SMEs: A systematic literature review. *International Journal of Information Management*, 36(4), 557–569.

*Crush, J., Skinner, C., & Stulgaitis, M. (2017a). Rendering South Africa Undesirable: A Critique of Refugee and Informal Sector Policy (rep. i-35). Waterloo, ON: Southern African Migration Programme. SAMP Migration Policy Series No. 79.

*Crush, J., Skinner, C., & Stulgaitis, M. (2017b). Benign neglect or active destruction? A critical analysis of refugee and informal sector policy and practice in South Africa. *African Human Mobility Review*, 3(2), May–August 2017 – Special Issue.

Taking stock and moving forward 57

*Crush, J., Tawodzera, G., McCordic, C., Ramachandran, S., & Tengeh, R. (2017). Refugee entrepreneurial economies in urban South Africa. *African Human Mobility Review*, 3(2), May–August 2017 – Special Issue.

*Crush, J., & McCordic, C. (2017). Comparing refugee and South African migrant enterprise in the urban informal sector. *African Human Mobility Review*, 3(2), May–August 2017 – Special Issue.

*Crush, J., & Tawodzera, G. (2017). *Refugee Entrepreneurial Economies in Urban South Africa* (No. 76). Southern African Migration Programme.

*Dana, L. P. (2012). Learning from Lagnado about self-employment and entrepreneurship in Egypt. *International Journal of Entrepreneurship & Small Business*, 17(1), 140–153.

Davidsson, P. (2015). Entrepreneurial opportunities and the entrepreneurship nexus: A re-conceptualization. *Journal of Business Venturing*, 30(5), 674–695.

*De la Chaux, M. (2019). Entrepreneurship in Extreme Environments: Businesses in the Dadaab Refugee Camp in Kenya. In: Heilbrunn, S., Freiling, J., & Harima, A. (eds) *Refugee Entrepreneurship* (pp. 221–229). Palgrave Macmillan, Cham.

Drori, I., Honig, B., & Wright, M. (2009). Transnational entrepreneurship: An emergent field of study. *Entrepreneurship Theory and Practice*, 33(5), 1001–1022.

Edwards, P., Ram, M., Jones, T., & Doldor, S. (2016). New migrant businesses and their workers: Developing, but not transforming, the ethnic economy. *Ethnic and Racial Studies*, 39(9), 1587–1617.

*Eimermann, M., & Karlsson, S. (2018). Globalising Swedish countryside? A relational approach to rural immigrant restaurateurs with refugee backgrounds. *Norsk Geografisk Tidsskrift-Norwegian Journal of Geography*, 72(2), 82–96.

Evansluong, Q. V. D. (2016). Opportunity creation as a mixed embedding process: A study of immigrant entrepreneurs in Sweden. (Doctoral dissertation, Jönköping: Jönköping University, Jönköping International Business School).

*Fass, S. (1986). Innovations in the struggle for self-reliance: The Hmong experience in the United States. *International Migration Review*, 20, 351–380.

*Fong, R., Busch, N. B., Armour, M., Cook Heffron, L., & Chanmugan, A. (2007). Pathways to self-sufficiency: Successful entrepreneurship for refugees. *Journal of Ethnic and Cultural Diversity in Social Work*, 16(1–2), 127–159.

Fong, E., & Ooka, E. (2002). The social consequences of participating in the ethnic economy. *International Migration Review*, 36(1), 125–146.

*Freiling, J., & Harima, A. (2019). Refugee Entrepreneurship: Learning from Case Evidence. In: Heilbrunn, S., Freiling, J., & Harima, A. (eds) *Refugee Entrepreneurship* (pp. 255–277). Palgrave Macmillan, Cham.

*Freudenberg, J. (2019). "FlüchtlingMagazin" (Refugee Magazine): A Syrian Social Business in Hamburg, Germany. In: Heilbrunn, S., Freiling, J., & Harima, A. (eds) *Refugee Entrepreneurship* (pp. 83–100). Palgrave Macmillan, Cham.

*Freudenberg, J., & Halberstadt, J. (2018). How to integrate refugees into the workforce – different opportunities for (social) entrepreneurship. *Problemy Zarządzania*, (1/2018 (73), t. 2), 40–60.

*Garnham, A. (2006). Refugees and the entrepreneurial process. *Labour, Employment and Work in New Zealand*, 156–165.

Gartner, W. B. (1985). A conceptual framework for describing the phenomenon of new venture creation. *Academy of Management Review*, 10(4), 696–706.

Garud, R., Hardy C., & Maguire, S. (2007). Institutional entrepreneurship as embedded agency. *Organisation Studies*, 28, 957–969.

*Gold, S. J. (1992). The employment potential of refugee entrepreneurship: Soviet Jews and Vietnamese in California. *Review of Policy Research*, 11(2), 176–186.

58 *Solomon Akele Abebe*

*Gold, S. J. (1988). Refugees and small business: The case of Soviet Jews and Vietnamese. *Ethnic and Racial Studies*, 11(4), 411–438.

*Gonzales, V., Forrest, N., & Balos, N. (2013). Refugee farmers and the social enterprise model in the American Southwest. *Journal of Community Positive Practices*, 13(4), 32.

Gough, D., Thomas, J., & Oliver, S. (2012). Clarifying differences between review designs and methods. *Systematic Reviews*, 1(1), 28.

*Grey, M. A., Rodríguez, N., & Conrad, A. (2004). *Immigrant and refugee small business development in Iowa: A research report with recommendations.* Cedar Falls, IA: University of Northern Iowa New Iowans Program/Iowa Centre for Immigrant Leadership and Integration.

Gusenbauer, M. (2019). Google scholar to overshadow them all? Comparing the sizes of 12 academic search engines and bibliographic databases. *Scientometrics*, 118, 1–38.

*Gürsel, D. (2017). The emergence of the enterprising refugee discourse and differential inclusion in Turkey's changing migration politics. *Movements*, 3(2), 133–146.

Halter, M. (1995). Ethnicity and the entrepreneur: Self-employment among former Soviet Jewish refugees. In: Halter, M. (ed) *New Migrants in the Marketplace: Boston's Ethnic Entrepreneurs* (pp. 43–58). University of Massachusetts Press/AMHERST, Boston, MA.

*Harb, M., Kassem, A., & Najdi, W. (2018). Entrepreneurial refugees and the city: Brief encounters in Beirut. *Journal of Refugee Studies*, 32(1), 23–41.

*Harima, A., & Freudenberg, J. (2018). Determinants of Refugee Business Incubator: Organisation and Embeddedness, RENT Conference on Sustainable Entrepreneurship: A win-win strategy for the future, Toledo (Spain), (14) 15–16 November 2018.

*Harima, A., Haimour, M., & Freiling, J. (2019). Umayyad: A Syrian Refugee Business in Bremen, Germany. In: Heilbrunn, S., Freiling, J., & Harima, A. (eds) *Refugee Entrepreneurship* (pp. 27–37). Palgrave Macmillan, Cham.

*Hartmann, C., & Schilling, K. (2019). Cham Saar: The First Syrian-German Cheese Manufacturer. In: Heilbrunn, S., Freiling, J., & Harima, A. (eds) *Refugee Entrepreneurship* (pp. 39–53). Palgrave Macmillan, Cham.

Hauff, E., & Vaglum, P. (1993). Integration of Vietnamese refugees into the Norwegian labour market: The impact of war trauma. *International Migration Review*, 27(2), 388–405.

*Heilbrunn, S. (2019). Against all odds: Refugees bricoleuring in the void. *International Journal of Entrepreneurial Behavior & Research.* doi: 10.1108/IJEBR-10-2017-0393.

*Heilbrunn, S., & Rosenfeld, A. (2019). The Story of Jonny, an Eritrean Entrepreneur in Tel Aviv, Israel. In: Heilbrunn, S., Freiling, J., & Harima, A. (eds) *Refugee Entrepreneurship* (pp. 101–113). Palgrave Macmillan, Cham.

Holmes, S. M., & Castañeda, H. (2016). Representing the "European refugee crisis" in Germany and beyond: Deservingness and difference, life and death. *American Ethnologist*, 43(1), 12–24.

Hutchinson, M., & Dorsett, P. (2012). What does the literature say about resilience in refugee people? Implications for practice. *Journal of Social Inclusion*, 3(2), 55–78.

Hägg, G., & Gabrielsson, J. (2017). Evolution of Pedagogy in Research on Entrepreneurship Education: Reviewing Achievements and Addressing Challenges. In: Hägg, G. (ed) *Experiential Entrepreneurship Education: Reflective Thinking as a Counterbalance to Action for Developing Entrepreneurial Knowledge* (141 ed., pp. 113–151). Lund: MediaTryck Lund.

*Iannone, R. L. (2019). Refuge to Centre Stage: The Story of Arash. In: Heilbrunn, S., Freiling, J., & Harima, A. (eds) *Refugee Entrepreneurship* (pp. 141–161). Palgrave Macmillan, Cham.

*Iannone, R. L., & Geraudel, M. (2018). In refugees we trust: Exploring social capital formation from scratch. ICSB Conference Paper.

*Jiang, Y., Straub, C., & Klyver, K. (2017). Refugee Entrepreneurship as a Career Re-Construction: A Dual Embeddedness Perspective. Babson Entrepreneurship Conference paper.

*Johnson, P. J. (2000). Ethnic differences in self-employment among Southeast Asian refugees in Canada. *Journal of Small Business Management*, 38(4), 78.

*Kachkar, O., Mohammed, M. O., Saad, N., & Kayadibi, S. (2016). Refugee microenterprises: Prospects and challenges. *Journal of Asian and African Social Science and Humanities*, 2(4), 55–69.

*Kaplan, D. H. (1997). The creation of an ethnic economy: Indo-Chinese business expansion in Saint Paul. *Economic Geography*, 73(2), 214–233.

*Katis, J. (2017). The Dynamics of Ethnic Entrepreneurship: Vietnamese Small Business in Victoria. (Doctoral dissertation, Victoria University).

Kloosterman, R. (2010). Matching opportunities with resources: A framework for analysing (migrant) entrepreneurship from a mixed embeddedness perspective. *Entrepreneurship and Regional Development*, 22(1), 25–45.

*Kolb, J. (2019). "Our Table": Between Activism and Business in Dublin, Ireland. In: Heilbrunn, S., Freiling, J., & Harima, A. (eds) *Refugee Entrepreneurship* (pp. 56–69). Palgrave Macmillan, Cham.

*Kong, E., Bishop, S., & Iles, E. (2018). Social Enterprise and CALD Refugee Settlement Experience. In: *Social Capital and Enterprise in the Modern State* (pp. 203–225). Palgrave Macmillan, Cham.

*Kupferberg, F. (2008). Migrant Men and the Challenge of Entrepreneurial Creativity. In: Apitzsch, U., & Kontos, M. (eds) *Self-Employment Activities of Women and Minorities* (pp. 145–157). VS Verlag für Sozialwissenschaften.

*Latowsky, R. J. I., & Grierson, J. P. (1992). Traditional apprenticeships and enterprise support networks. *Small Enterprise Development*, 3(3), 42–48.

*Lee, S. K. (2018). From political activists to social entrepreneurs: Burmese refugees in South Korea. *Journal of Refugee Studies*.

Light, I. (1984). Immigrant and ethnic enterprise in North America. *Ethnic and Racial Studies*, 7(2), 195–216.

Light, I. (1980). Ethnic entrepreneurship in America.

Light, I. (1979). Disadvantaged minorities in self-employment. *International Journal of Comparative Sociology*, 20, 31.

*Louise, B., & Jiang, Y. (2018). Refugee Integration through Entrepreneurship – Empirical Evidence from Refugees in Germany and France, Entrepreneurship: A win-win strategy for the future, Toledo (Spain), (14) 15–16 November 2018.

*Lyon, F., Sepulveda, L., & Syrett, S. (2007). Enterprising refugees: Contributions and challenges in deprived urban areas. *Local Economy*, 22(4), 362–375.

*Maalaoui, A., Razgallah, M., Picard, S., & Leloarne-Lemaire, S. (2019). From Hell To … An Entrepreneurial Life: An Iranian Refugee in France. In: Heilbrunn, S., Freiling, J., & Harima, A. (eds) *Refugee Entrepreneurship* (pp. 163–173). Palgrave Macmillan, Cham.

Mamgain, V., & Collins, K. (2003). Off the boat, now off to work: Refugees in the labour market in Portland, Maine. *Journal of Refugee Studies*, 16(2), 113–143. doi: 10.1093/jrs/16.2.113.

*Marchand, K., & Dijkhuizen, J. (2018). Entrepreneurship as a Tool for a New Beginning – Entrepreneurship Training for Refugees in a New Homeland. *Contemporary Issues in Entrepreneurship Research*, 8, 135–149. doi:10.1108/S2040-724620180000008013

Masurel, E., Nijkamp, P., Tastan, M., & Vindigni, G. (2002). Motivations and performance conditions for ethnic entrepreneurship. *Growth and Change*, 33(2), 238–260.

60 Solomon Akele Abebe

*Mawson, S., & Kasem, L. (2019). Exploring the entrepreneurial intentions of Syrian refugees in the UK. *International Journal of Entrepreneurial Behaviour and Research.* doi: 10.1108/IJEBR-02-2018-0103.

*Mehtap, S., & Al-Saidi, A. G. (2019). Informal Refugee Entrepreneurship: Narratives of Economic Empowerment. In: Ramadani, V., Dana, L. P., Ratten, V., & Bexheti, A. (eds) *Informal Ethnic Entrepreneurship* (pp. 225–242). Springer, Cham.

*Meister, A. D., & Mauer, R. (2018). Understanding refugee entrepreneurship incubation – An embeddedness perspective. *International Journal of Entrepreneurial Behavior & Research.* doi:10.1108/IJEBR-02-2018-0108

*Meyer, H. H. (2018). Analysis of Entrepreneurial Eco-System for Refugee Entrepreneurial Activities in Germany. *Proceedings of the 6th International Conference on Innovation Management, Entrepreneurship and Sustainability (IMES 2018),* 669–682. Vysoká škola ekonomická v Praze.

*Meyer, H., & Pilkova, A. (2017). Challenges in Promoting Migrant Entrepreneurship: First Empirical Evidence from Germany. In: Dvouletý, O., Lukeš, M., & Mísa, J. (eds), *IMES Conference 2017: Innovation Management, Entrepreneurship and Sustainability* (pp. 606–617). University of Economics, Prague.

Mitchel, C. (2015). *Immigrant Entrepreneurship and Firm Growth: Building an Integrated Approach to Understand Firm Growth in Immigrant Owned Firms.* Lund: Lund University, Department of Business Administration.

*Miyares, I. M. (1998). "Little Odessa"—Brighton beach, Brooklyn: An examination of the former soviet refugee economy in New York city. *Urban Geography,* 19(6), 518–530.

*Moore, B. (1990). Jewish Refugee Entrepreneurs and the Dutch Economy in the 1930s. *Immigrants & Minorities,* 9(1), 46–63.

Moroz, P. W., & Hindle, K. (2012). Entrepreneurship as a process: Toward harmonizing multiple perspectives. *Entrepreneurship Theory and Practice,* 36(4), 781–818.

*Nayır, D. Z. (2019). From Refugee to Trader: In the Footsteps of Marco Polo. In: Heilbrunn, S., Freiling, J., & Harima, A. (eds) *Refugee Entrepreneurship* (pp. 175–194). Palgrave Macmillan, Cham.

*Northcote, M., & Dodson, B. (2015). Refugees and Asylum Seekers in Cape Town's Informal Economy. In Crush J., Chikanda, A., & Skinner, C. (eds) *Mean streets: Migration, xenophobia and informality in South Africa* (pp. 145–161). South African Migration Programme (SAMP), Ontario, Canada.

*Obschonka, M., & Hahn, E. (2018). Personal agency in newly arrived refugees: The role of personality, entrepreneurial cognitions and intentions, and career adaptability. *Journal of Vocational Behavior,* 105, 173–184.

*Omata, N. (2018). Who takes advantage of mobility? Exploring the nexus between refugees' movement, livelihoods and socioeconomic status in West Africa. *African Geographical Review,* 37(2), 98–108.

Omata, N. (2012). *Refugee livelihoods and the private sector: Ugandan case study.* Refugee Studies Centre.

*Omeje, K., & Mwangi, J. (2014). Business travails in the diaspora: The challenges and resilience of Somali refugee business community in Nairobi, Kenya. *Journal of Third World Studies,* 31(1), 185–217.

*Omorede, A., & Axelsson, K. (2018). To Exist or To Persist: Exploring the Entrepreneurial Phases for Immigrant Entrepreneurs. In: *20th Nordic Conference on Small Business Research – Entrepreneurship and Collaboration,* May 23–25, 2018, Luleå University of Technology, Luleå, Sweden.

*Palalić, R., Dana, L. P., & Ramadani, V. (2019). Refugee Entrepreneurship: A Case Study from the Sultanate of Oman. In: Heilbrunn, S., Freiling, J., & Harima, A. (eds) *Refugee Entrepreneurship* (pp. 207–219). Palgrave Macmillan, Cham.

*Plak, C., & Lagarde, V. (2019). The Story of an Adolescent Afghan Refugee Who Became an Entrepreneur in France. In: Heilbrunn, S., Freiling, J., & Harima, A. (eds) *Refugee Entrepreneurship* (pp. 71–81). Palgrave Macmillan, Cham.

*Predojević-Despić, J., & Lukić, V. (2017). Migration, Integration and Entrepreneurship: Insights from the Serbian Experience. In: *International Scientific Conference on Sustainable Growth in Small Open Economies, Belgrade, Serbia.*

*Price, M., & Chacko, E. (2009). The mixed embeddedness of ethnic entrepreneurs in a new immigrant gateway. *Journal of Immigrant & Refugee Studies*, 7(3), 328–346.

Pulla, V., & Kharel, P. (2014). The carpets and karma: The resilient story of the Tibetan community in two settlements in India and Nepal. *Space and Culture, India*, 1(3), 27–42. doi: 10.20896/saci.v1i3.33.

Ram, M., & Jones, T. (2008). Ethnic-minority businesses in the UK: A review of research and policy developments. *Environment and Planning C: Government and Policy*, 26(2), 352–374.

*Rashid, L. (2018). "Call Me a Business Owner, Not a Refugee!" Challenges of and Perspectives on Newcomer Entrepreneurship. World Refugee Council Research Paper No. 7. Centre for International Governance Innovation.

Rauch, A., & Frese, M. (2007). Let's put the person back into entrepreneurship research: A meta-analysis on the relationship between business owners' personality traits, business creation, and success. *European Journal of work and organizational psychology*, 16(4), 353–385.

*Refai, D., Haloub, R., & Lever, J. (2018). Contextualizing entrepreneurial identity among Syrian refugees in Jordan: The emergence of a destabilized habitus? *The International Journal of Entrepreneurship and Innovation*, 19(4), 250–260.

Riksrevisionen. (2015). Hur kan nyanlända snabbare bli ekonomiskt etablerade?

*Ritchie, H. A. (2018). Gender and enterprise in fragile refugee settings: Female empowerment amidst male emasculation—a challenge to local integration? *Disasters*, 42, S40–S60.

Roth, W. D., Seidel, M. D. L., Ma, D., & Lo, E. (2012). In and out of the ethnic economy: A longitudinal analysis of ethnic networks and pathways to economic success across immigrant categories 1. *International Migration Review*, 46(2), 310–361.

*Ruparanganda, J., Ndjoku, E. N., & Vemuri, R. (2019). The Blessing African Boutique and City Market Food: A Congolese Refugee Business in Darwin, Australia. In: Heilbrunn, S., Freiling, J., & Harima, A. (eds) *Refugee Entrepreneurship* (pp. 127–140). Palgrave Macmillan, Cham.

Samuel, T. J. (1984). Economic adaptation of refugees in Canada: Experience of a quarter century. *International Migration*, 22(1), 45–55.

Sen, A. (2005). Human rights and capabilities. *Journal of Human Development*, 6(2), 151–166.

*Sandberg, S., Immonen, R., & Kok, S. (2019). Refugee entrepreneurship: Taking a social network view on immigrants with refugee backgrounds starting transnational businesses in Sweden. *International Journal of Entrepreneurship and Small Business*, 36(1–2), 216–241.

Sen, A. (1990). Development as capability expansion. *The Community Development Reader*, 41–58.

62 Solomon Akele Abebe

Sen, A. (1985). Well-being, agency and freedom: The Dewey lectures 1984. *The Journal of Philosophy*, *82*(4), 169–221.

*Sepulveda, L., Syrett, S., & Lyon, F. (2011). Population superdiversity and new migrant enterprise: The case of London. *Entrepreneurship & Regional Development*, 23(7–8), 469–497.

Shneikat, B., & Alrawadieh, Z. (2019). Unravelling refugee entrepreneurship and its role in integration: Empirical evidence from the hospitality industry. *The Service Industries Journal*, 39(9–10), 741–761.

Silove, D., Ventevogel, P., & Rees, S. (2017). The contemporary refugee crisis: An overview of mental health challenges. *World Psychiatry*, 16(2), 130–139.

*Singh, S. (1994). Refugees as entrepreneurs: The case of the Indian bicycle industry. *The Journal of Entrepreneurship*, 3(1), 81–96.

*Smith-Hefner, N. J. (1995). The culture of entrepreneurship among Khmer refugees. In: Halter, M. (ed) *New Migrants in the Marketplace: Boston's Ethnic Entrepreneurs* (pp. 141–158). University of Massachusetts Press/AMHERST, Boston, MA.

Takeda, J. (2000). Psychological and economic adaptation of Iraqi adult male refugees: Implications for social work practice. *Journal of Social Service Research*, 26(3), 1–21.

*Tawodzera, G., Chikanda, A., Crush, J., & Tengeh, R. (2015). International Migrants and Refugees in Cape Town's Informal Economy (rep., pp. i-57). Waterloo, ON: Southern African Migration Programme. SAMP Migration Policy Series No. 70.

*Tengeh, R. K. (2019). From Cameroon to South Africa: From Refugee to Successful Businessman. In: Heilbrunn, S., Freiling, J., & Harima, A. (eds) *Refugee Entrepreneurship* (pp. 231–240). Palgrave Macmillan, Cham.

Thurik, A. R., Carree, M. A., Van Stel, A., & Audretsch, D. B. (2008). Does self-employment reduce unemployment? *Journal of Business Venturing*, 23(6), 673–686.

Tipples, R. (2004). The human capability framework-an important and useful framework for understanding the labour market? *New Zealand Journal of Employment Relations*, 29(1), 3.

Tranfield, D., Denyer, D., & Smart, P. (2003). Towards a methodology for developing evidence-informed management knowledge by means of systematic review. *British Journal of Management*, 14(3), 207–222.

*Trisha, O. K. (2018). In search of Jewish footprints in the West of Ireland. *Jewish Culture and History*, 19(2), 191–208. doi: 10.1080/1462169X.2018.1478216.

*Tömöry, E. (2008). Immigrant Entrepreneurship: How the '56-ers Helped to Build Canada's Economy. *Hungarian Studies Review*, 35(1–2), 125–142.

Valtonen, K. (1999). The societal participation of Vietnamese refugees: Case studies in Finland and Canada. *Journal of Ethnic and Migration Studies*, 25(3), 469–491.

*Villares-Varela, M., Ram, M., & Jones, T. (2017). Thwarted or facilitated? The entrepreneurial aspirations and capabilities of new migrants and refugees in the UK. RENT Conference paper.

Waldinger, R. D., Aldrich, H., & Ward, R. (1990). *Ethnic entrepreneurs: Immigrant business in industrial societies* (Vol. 1). Sage Publications, Inc.

*Wauters, B., & Lambrecht, J. (2008). Barriers to refugee entrepreneurship in Belgium: Towards an explanatory model. *Journal of Ethnic and Migration Studies*, 34(6), 895–915.

*Wauters, B., & Lambrecht, J. (2006). Refugee entrepreneurship in Belgium: Potential and practice. *International Entrepreneurship and Management Journal*, 2(4), 509–525.

Webster, J., & Watson, R. T. (2002). Analysing the past to prepare for the future: Writing a literature review. *MIS Quarterly*, 26, xiii–xxiii.

*Werker, E. (2007). Refugee camp economies. *Journal of Refugee Studies*, 20(3), 461–480.

*Williams, N., & Krasniqi, B. A. (2018). Coming out of conflict: How migrant entrepreneurs utilise human and social capital. *Journal of International Entrepreneurship*, 16(2), 301–323.

4 International research on social entrepreneurship

Looking for an operational definition of the concept

Giorgi Jamburia and Jean-Marie Courrent

Introduction

Social entrepreneurship (SE) has been quite often regarded as a field in a pre-paradigmatic state (Nicholls, 2010). Certain leitmotif of scepticism has also been noticed about the legitimacy of SE as a separate and distinctive area of research (Trexler, 2008). Yet, some researchers argue that SE is emerging from this pre-paradigmatic condition of the field development (Kay et al., 2016). Social enterprises are important in several terms. First, they usually employee underserved segments of society. Second, they innovate to create new goods and services to tackle pressing social and environmental problems. Third, they create social capital. Finally, they contribute to equality around the world (Nagler, 2007). According to Bacq and Janssen (2011), SE has a unique objective of creation of a double – social and economic – value through the innovative solution of social problems.

SE is a worldwide phenomenon, but the variety in definition and approach does not facilitate theory building and international comparative studies in the field. Defining SE and social enterprises has been a problematic issue for researchers and practitioners for the last two decades, and the problem remains actual to date (Choi and Majumdar, 2014; Conway Dato-on and Kalakay, 2016; Halberstadt and Kraus, 2016; Hossain et al., 2017; Kay et al., 2016; Kee, 2017; Rey-Martí et al., 2016; Scheuerle et al., 2015; Young and Lecy, 2014). The paper of Kraus and colleagues (2014), based on the bibliometric citation analysis, outlines that definitions and conceptual approaches represent one of the five major topic clusters in SE literature. Peattie and Morley (2008) note that there is a problem of a definition of SE as well as small sample sizes and small-scale research. It is argued that a lack of universally agreed definition makes it difficult to conduct quantitative research on social enterprises (Lyon and Sepulveda, 2009), particularly based on cross-country surveys. Moreover, that research is usually carried out on small sample sizes, limiting the generalisability of the findings.

Furthermore, SE research is mostly 'phenomenon-driven' and built up on specific case studies (Bacq and Janssen, 2011; Mair and Marti, 2006). In addition, the focus of the research has been on personality traits of the social entrepreneurs. However, the researchers claim that studying a set of activities that form SE as a process can be a more productive approach (Mair and Marti, 2006).

64   *Giorgi Jamburia and Jean-Marie Courrent*

Several authors also see the location of SE in only economic or business fields as one of the possible limitations in the SE research and assert that such approaches may affect the broader understanding of the phenomenon (Nicholls and Cho, 2006). It is also notable that most of the researchers of SE are entrepreneurship scholars and therefore, use respective theories of their field, although applying a more multidisciplinary perspective could be more useful for SE research (Lehner and Kansikas, 2013).

Lehner and Kansikas (2013) conducted a systematic literature review to determine the current status and tendencies that characterise the research field. The authors have found that research methodology and paradigms in SE literature are different from the commercial entrepreneurship ones. As the percentage of conceptual publications is quite high and the majority of the authors use qualitative methods instead of quantitative and mixed ones, the authors who had performed systematic bibliometric analyses concluded that the SE research is still in its initial stages and more quantitative studies have to be conducted in order to contribute to the legitimacy of the research field (Granados et al., 2011; Lehner and Kansikas, 2013; Short et al., 2009).

Similarly, Haugh (2012) suggests that generalisability of findings to a larger number of organisations and different country contexts will be a valuable contribution to the field. Thus, the aim of this paper is to address both these theoretical and methodological issues from a systematic analysis of academic literature. We can suggest that the major underlying problem behind most of the difficulties in SE research is a lack of operating definition of the field. Therefore, in order to achieve an inclusive definition of SE relevant for theory building and international research projects, this paper has three objectives related to three main questions:

- Does the research have to focus on social entrepreneurial processes, social entrepreneurs or social enterprises?
- Can this definition overcome the differences in national representations of SE?
- How could this definition be operationalised through indicators and items that would be workable both in quantitative and qualitative approaches?

The paper will first cover the nature of SE as opposed to other types of entrepreneurship. Next, several SE paradigms will be presented. The section will be followed by the analysis of heterogeneity of the conceptions by distinguishing the legal differences relating to public policies and the conceptual differences relating to academic debates. Finally, a common definition will be proposed from the common core of these approaches.

The nature of social entrepreneurship

In order to define SE, first we have to see the commonalities and differences with entrepreneurship, a field that 'seeks to understand how opportunities to bring into existence "future" goods and services are discovered, created, and exploited,

Research on social entrepreneurship 65

by whom, and with what consequences' [Venkataraman, (1997), p. 120]. Furthermore, an entrepreneur is characterised as an innovator implementing an entrepreneurial change (Schumpeter, 1934). Meanwhile, Hill and colleagues (2010, p. 21) define SE as 'a disciplined, innovative, risk tolerant entrepreneurial process of opportunity recognition and resource assembly directed toward creating social value by changing underlying social and economic structures'. Thus, as we see, SE shares some of the major characteristics of entrepreneurship such as innovativeness, risk taking, opportunity recognition and resource endowment. Halberstadt and Kraus (2016) also find that social and commercial entrepreneurship are highly interrelated concepts and cannot be considered distinct fields.

Sustainable, Environmental and Institutional Entrepreneurship. To formulate a clear operating definition of SE, it may be argued that we also must consider the related sustainability focused fields such as sustainable entrepreneurship, environmental entrepreneurship and institutional entrepreneurship, since there are certain common aspects among the areas. For instance, sustainable entrepreneurship has a description similar to SE being defined as a field:

> focused on the preservation of nature, life support, and community in the pursuit of perceived opportunities to bring into existence future products, processes, and services for gain, where gain is broadly construed to include economic and non-economic gains to individuals, the economy, and society.
>
> [Shepherd and Patzelt, (2011), p. 142]

However, there are still observable differences. To illustrate, SE is focused on achieving social goals and securing its funding; environmental entrepreneurs are focused on creating economic and ecological values; sustainable entrepreneurs are oriented towards a triple bottom line, thus creating social, environmental and economic values; and finally, institutional entrepreneurship aims to change existing institutions or create new ones (Schaltegger and Wagner, 2011; Thompson et al., 2011).

Schaltegger and Wagner (2011) suggest that despite the differences, all these fields can be considered under the same umbrella. Furthermore, social, environmental and institutional types of entrepreneurship can be included in the subdomain of sustainable entrepreneurship. Although the historical development paths of these fields are different from one another, underlying motivations are similar and therefore, authors call for converging the rather independent literatures. Dean and McMullen (2007) suggest that sustainable entrepreneurship can be considered a subset of SE. However, Thompson and colleagues (2011, p. 211) disagree, since SE focuses on resolving social issues while sustainable entrepreneurship is aimed towards 'balancing social, economic, and environmental benefits in their venture'. Several sustainable enterprises may intend to solve social issues, though it is not regarded as their only concentration. There are several characteristics that make SE different from sustainable entrepreneurship. First, social entrepreneurs are trying to find alternative ways to accomplish positive social goals, namely 'social intrapreneurship, community-based enterprises,

66 *Giorgi Jamburia and Jean-Marie Courrent*

and non-profit organizations' (Thompson et al., 2011, p. 205). Next, altruistic motivation is common in this subfield of entrepreneurship. And finally, social ventures prioritise social agenda over financial goals (Thompson et al., 2011).

Likewise, SE should not be considered a part of the sustainable entrepreneurship field since not all social missions are sustainable. For example, some social enterprises may struggle financially with the will to achieve their primary social mission. Furthermore, social ventures may be driven by altruistic motivations. And finally, they may focus more on social benefits than on other competing dimensions. All in all, in such cases, social enterprises may not belong to the sustainable entrepreneurship domain. Moreover, a 'whole enterprise design' that is the foundation of sustainable entrepreneurship suggests that focus must be placed on long-term goals rather than short-term ones. However, it may not always be the case for social entrepreneurs (Thompson et al., 2011). Furthermore, economic gains are stated to be the main motivation for opportunity recognition in sustainable entrepreneurship, as motivations coming from altruistic views for society and environment will not be effective since institutional changes require proper financing. Thus, we can see the difference from SE where economic motivations are not primary (Pacheco et al., 2010).

Consequently, in this section we will focus on the aspects that make SE different or like the general entrepreneurship domain. In order to demonstrate the nature of SE, we are going to structure our discussion around the four main paradigms of entrepreneurship: value creation, business opportunity, innovation and organisation building.

Value creation

Entrepreneurial process involves value creation, value delivery and value capture (Osterwalder and Pigneur, 2010). In the commercial context, it may be more appropriate to use the concepts of value creation and value capture; but in SE, the focus is mostly on value creation as the market exchange of the value would not be an accurate measure of the social value (Ormiston and Seymour, 2011). It is also noteworthy that social entrepreneurs find it more difficult to capture the value created, since they may be targeting the very basic needs of underprivileged groups who have very limited purchasing power (Mair and Marti, 2006). The main distinctive factor between SE and entrepreneurship is that the concept of wealth is broadened, including social value (Hill et al., 2010) that is the defining characteristic of SE (Di Domenico et al., 2010) and can be described as what 'benefits people whose urgent and reasonable needs are not being met by other means' (Young, 2006, p. 56).

Nevertheless, commercial entrepreneurship also has an indirect social impact such as economic growth, employment and reduction of poverty, although created social value can be considered a 'by-product' of economic value creation (Ormiston and Seymour, 2011). Some researchers also argue that the social nature of opportunities influences the entrepreneurial process and creates social value in different forms such as self-realisation, community development and broader social impact (Korsgaard and Anderson, 2011). In this regard, several authors suggest that there should not be any distinctions made between economic and social values (Lautermann, 2013; Santos, 2012). As Santos (2012) notes, economic value creation improves the welfare of society. Furthermore, considering social value creation non-measurable makes the theory development more difficult. Finally, defining certain types of value creation as 'social' is subjective and relative to the researcher. The author argues that the main distinction from commercial entrepreneurship is between value creation and value capture and therefore, it is the trade-off between the two that matters. According to the researcher, social entrepreneurs mainly operate in the areas characterised with high levels of value creation and low levels of value capture.

Although SE involves both the social and economic aspects, the focus is still on social value creation, whereas economic value creation is regarded as a necessity for achieving financial self-sufficiency and commercial entrepreneurship posits economic value creation as its main goal (Mair and Marti, 2006; Ormiston and Seymour, 2011). Prioritising social value creation is embedded in the organisational mission of social enterprises. Neck and colleagues (2009) propose the venture typology by the combination of mission and primary market impact and argue that, although a primary impact of the venture may involve positive social consequences, a primary social mission is what qualifies a venture as a social enterprise, even though hybrid forms do also exist. However, Mueller and colleagues (2011) underline that the social enterprises should not be considered superior to commercial enterprises in terms of social value creation. In certain situations, social venture initiatives may be unintentionally harmful while commercial enterprises can be contributing to social development. The authors suggest that SE research may benefit from the case studies that focus on how traditional commercial enterprises succeed or fail in the creation of a social value.

Dees (1998) claims that a profit motive is not a necessary precondition for social entrepreneurial pursuits. Therefore, it is another original characteristic of social entrepreneurs. Thompson and colleagues (2011) suggest that most economic models that are designed to study entrepreneurship do not take into consideration such kind of motives and intentions. Therefore, researchers have problems in comparing SE to commercial entrepreneurship. However, when it comes to the distinction of SE from a larger entrepreneurship domain, Mair and Marti (2006) argue that it is not about profit motive versus altruism. On the one hand, SE may be based on non-altruistic drivers such as personal fulfilment, and on the other, commercial entrepreneurship can also have significant social aspects. The researchers agree that what distinguishes SE is its creative combination of resources that are used to address social problems and change existing social structures.

Furthermore, simultaneous aim of social and economic value creation can be a source of tensions for social enterprises (Austin et al., 2006). Although social entrepreneurs do not always have to face a trade-off between social and economic goals as financial returns may be necessary for further social value creation, still there is an existing dilemma of balancing these two missions (Bosma et al., 2016;

68 *Giorgi Jamburia and Jean-Marie Courrent*

Santos, 2012). Some researchers state that social enterprises can successfully balance both missions and be successful in social and economic value creation (Bellostas et al., 2016; Teasdale, 2012; Wilson and Post, 2013), while other authors cast doubt on this opinion and approach SE from a single value creation perspective (Pirson, 2012; Stevens et al., 2015; Thompson and Doherty, 2006). Therefore, performance measurement becomes a clear challenge for social enterprises. While commercial ventures have clear measurable indicators such as financial ratios, market share and more, it is not the case for social enterprises since the field involves the element of social value creation that is not always easily quantifiable (Austin et al., 2006; Certo and Miller, 2008).

In conclusion, it is the consideration of social value creation as a central goal in SE that distinguishes SE from commercial entrepreneurship.

Business opportunity

Opportunity is a central concept in entrepreneurship. There is a critical mass of literature on opportunities in the scientific field of entrepreneurship (Short et al., 2010). Schumpeter (1934) proposes a process of 'creative destruction' where new opportunities replace existing ones. Meanwhile, Kirzner (1973) views entrepreneurs as agents with special alertness to opportunities that can address inefficiencies on the market. Short and colleagues (2010, p. 55) define an opportunity as 'an idea or dream that is discovered or created by an entrepreneurial entity and that is revealed through analysis over time to be potentially lucrative'.

Austin and colleagues (2006) note that the main distinctive factor between commercial and SE is the type of opportunities: while market failures can be a danger to commercial enterprises, social entrepreneurs may view market failures as opportunities. Although traditional entrepreneurs may also consider certain market failures opportunities, social entrepreneurs usually address neglected problems with positive externalities, frequently dealing with local issues and powerless segments of society through building sustainable solutions based on empowerment logic rather than seeking sustainable advantages based on logic of control (Santos, 2012). However, it does not mean that all kinds of social problems can be solved by social entrepreneurs (Mueller et al., 2011). Neck and colleagues (2009, p. 15) also agree that what distinguishes SE from traditional entrepreneurship are 'sources of opportunity and the founding mission'". Researchers argue that social issues such as health, education, poverty alleviation, water, energy and environment represent a natural domain for SE. Furthermore, the embedded social mission makes SE unique in this regard.

Korsgaard (2011) notes that in contrast to commercial entrepreneurship, SE is characterised more with opportunity creation rather than with opportunity discovery. Moreover, there is no evidence in SE that opportunity discovery precedes resource mobilisation. On the contrary, resource mobilisation in certain cases is a predecessor to the opportunity discovery process. Similar viewpoint is shared by Corner and Ho (2010), who argue that the opportunity recognition process in SE is not like the one in commercial entrepreneurship that follows the traditional process of 'opportunity identification and exploitation' and is more recursive. However, there is a contrasting view that opportunity recognition in SE cannot be regarded as a part of only discovery or creative views as both approaches characterise the process in SE (Lehner and Kansikas, 2012; Short et al., 2010).

Furthermore, Zahra and colleagues (2008) distinguish the following attributes of SE opportunity recognition: pervasiveness, relevance, social urgency, accessibility to others and radicalness of solution sought. The authors conclude that while relevance of opportunities is also integral to commercial entrepreneurship, pervasiveness and social urgency may or may not be a characteristic of opportunities in more business-oriented entrepreneurship and accessibility to others and radicalness of solution sought are more common in SE.

However, it is notable that the specificity of SE relies more on the nature of the opportunity rather than the opportunity recognition process. As Lehner and Kansikas (2012) argue, opportunity recognition in SE is different from the main entrepreneurship domain because of the different context and the final objective of SE itself. Furthermore, studying opportunity recognition only among heroic social entrepreneurs may cause biases. But the comparison of findings regarding the opportunity recognition seems to be problematic, as one must consider the context of social entrepreneur and the approach of the author towards SE. Besides, differing legal structures in different countries can have an impact on the way social enterprises operate and consequently limit opportunity recognition and exploitation in certain ways.

Gawell (2013) states that social entrepreneurial actions are grounded in perceived necessities and facilitated by favourable events or opportunities. Namely, social entrepreneurs are alert to respond to opportunities. Furthermore, social entrepreneurs are successful in the creation of opportunities by convincing resource owners to provide resources. However, it is also argued that opportunities facilitate SE, though they may not be the main reasons of engagement. Instead, the author proposes a concept of perceived necessities, since most social entrepreneurs engage in SE activities so far as they believe that it is meaningful and necessary. As Grassl (2012) also underlines, social entrepreneurs are personally committed to a cause and opportunity recognition is an obvious process for them unlike their commercial counterparts. It is even argued that inefficiencies that social entrepreneurs address are also recognised by many other individuals compared to commercial entrepreneurial opportunities (Lumpkin et al., 2013). Nevertheless, it should be noted that even though detecting problems may be easier for social entrepreneurs, it does not automatically mean that it is equally easy to create feasible solutions to those social problems.

The recent research by Yitshaki and Kropp (2016) shows that pull factors such as present or past life events and ethical/moral orientation as well as push factors such as job dissatisfaction motivate social entrepreneurs. The researchers propose a conceptual framework where pull and push factors serve as motivation to become aware of unmet social needs that lead to opportunity recognition and consequently social venture creation through purposeful actions. This model

70   *Giorgi Jamburia and Jean-Marie Courrent*

differs from the commercial entrepreneurship process models, as different antecedents precede opportunity recognition in SE. The opportunity recognition in SE is associated with solving a social problem rather than a gap between needs and demands. The model of opportunity recognition is also provided by Guclu and colleagues (2002), who argue that social needs and social assets serve as antecedents to promising ideas and that a successful realisation of a business model is needed to transform promising ideas into attractive opportunities.

To conclude, SE shares many characteristics with the commercial entrepreneurship in terms of opportunity search, recognition and exploitation. However, there are notable differences such as the sources and nature of opportunities that distinguish SE from conventional entrepreneurship.

Innovation

Innovation is more than just 'invention', since it is a tool for social change that can be viewed as an 'ultimate value created by innovation' (Mair and Ganly, 2008, p. 80). Schumpeter (1934) considers innovation to be an integral part of entrepreneurship involving 'creative destruction' of existing structures and systems and their replacement. However, for Kirzner (1973), innovation is not a main distinctive element of entrepreneurship; rather, it must fill inefficiencies on the market.

Similarly, several authors have different views on the importance of innovation for social enterprises. There exist *Social Innovation* and *Social Enterprise* schools of thought that have different approaches to the presence of innovation in social entrepreneurial processes (Bacq and Janssen, 2011). The Social Innovation School views innovativeness as a key criterion, whereas the Social Enterprise School as well as the EMES Network and the UK approaches do not emphasise the centrality of innovation (Hoogendoorn et al., 2011). Continuous innovation is considered an integral part of SE by some researchers (Austin et al., 2006; Chell et al., 2010; Dees, 2001; Haugh, 2005). Innovativeness along with proactiveness and risk taking, similar to the entrepreneurship field, have been named a key characteristic of social entrepreneurs (Peredo and McLean, 2006; Sullivan Mort et al., 2003; Weerawardena and Sullivan Mort, 2006). Even more, innovativeness has been traced in all stages of value creation among social enterprises (Weerawardena and Sullivan Mort, 2006).

However, it must be noted that innovation in commercial entrepreneurship is driven by the motivation of increasing profits and gaining a competitive advantage, while social innovations are motivated by the well-being of society, though it may have complementary commercial, technological or other aims (Dawson and Daniel, 2010). As El Ebrashi (2013) notes, business entrepreneurs try to defend their innovations through economic barriers (Porter, 1980), while social entrepreneurs seek to replicate their ideas even outside their organisations.

Furthermore, there is a disagreement on the type of changes that are facilitated by social entrepreneurs. While some researchers state that social entrepreneurs cause fundamental social changes, others suggest that SE is all about incremental innovations (Hill et al., 2010). Some SE researchers characterise the field as a playground for revolutionary social innovations (Di Zhang and Swanson,

Research on social entrepreneurship 71

2014) and argue that what makes social ventures entrepreneurial is Schumpeterian 'creative destruction' (Kee, 2017; Ormiston and Seymour, 2011) through involvement in processes that completely change the existing social equilibria in non-standard ways (Hill et al., 2010). However, Gawell (2013) maintains that the innovative role of SE should not be overrated as the roles of both innovative challengers and adjustable followers have been observed in social enterprises. Therefore, some social enterprises fall in the category of alert individuals within established systems and some can be regarded as radical innovators challenging the existing equilibria (Gawell, 2013; Short et al., 2009).

It is also important to understand the conceptual differences between SE and social innovation. Mulgan (2006, p. 146) defines social innovation as a set of 'innovative activities and services by the goal of meeting a social need and that are predominantly developed and diffused through organisations whose primary purposes are social'. Social innovation is distinguished from SE as social innovation may occur in social enterprises, government and commercial sector, or as a result of intersection and collaboration among these parties (Salim Saji and Ellingstad, 2016). 'Shared value creation' between corporate and social stakeholders (Porter and Kramer, 2011) is a notable example. However, innovation may not be an integral part of SE, even though SE may lead to social innovation (Salim Saji and Ellingstad, 2016). In contrast, some authors consider social innovation one of the major characteristics of SE (Choi and Majumdar, 2014) and others argue that social entrepreneurs are more radical innovators (Huysentruyt, 2014).

Nevertheless, it is notable that international studies on SE have become more inclusive through the years. For instance, the 2015–2016 study Global Entrepreneurship Monitor (GEM) has dropped the compulsory requirement of innovation in social enterprises for inclusion that was present in the GEM 2009 study, thus becoming more inclusive through the years. Though Lepoutre and colleagues (2013), based on prior research on SE, considered innovativeness in delivery of products and services a key criterion in the GEM 2009 study and innovation was expected in terms of product, production process, delivery, promotion or unattended customer niche. The GEM 2015–2016 study on SE proposed two questions in order to map innovative activities in social enterprises: first, regarding the provision of new products or services, and second about offering a new approach to producing a product/service. Those social entrepreneurs who self-reported as being value creators prioritising social value creation over value capture (Santos, 2012) tended to classify themselves as more innovative (Bosma et al., 2016).

In short, innovation is an important component of SE as in commercial entrepreneurship, though sources of innovation as well as more openness of innovation in case of SE are distinctive characteristics.

Organisation building

Parrish (2010) distinguishes five major requirements for organisation design – purpose for justifying existence, efficiency (for achieving synergies), trade-offs in balancing competing objectives, criteria for prioritising decision choices and

72 *Giorgi Jamburia and Jean-Marie Courrent*

inducements (allocating benefits). In response to organisation design requirements, two types of reasoning are outlined, namely 'perpetual' and 'exploitative'.
On the one hand, 'exploitative' reasoning calls for resource exploitation to generate the highest possible financial profits in the short term. It also reduces inputs
without a simultaneous reduction in outputs. In addition, this approach focuses
on maximisation of a single objective while using quantity as a major decision
criterion. In the end, allocations of benefits are dictated by the claims of power.
On the other hand, 'perpetual' reasoning considers resource perpetuation by
producing benefits through 'enhancing and maintaining quality of human and
natural resources' in the long term (Parrish, 2010, p. 517). Besides, this approach
supports achievement of synergies and balance of conflicting goals while the
focus is on assessing quality of outcomes for decision-making. Finally, alloca-
tion of benefits involves directing benefits towards worthy recipients by offering
possibilities to contribute to the enterprise. Thus, resource perpetuation, benefit
stacking, strategic satisficing, qualitative management and worthy contribution
are the subsequent major principles of perpetual reasoning. Sustainability-driven
enterprises are keen to employ the 'perpetual' reasoning in order to build an
organisation that will be in line with their subsequent missions – achieving economic, social and environmental goals (Parrish, 2010). It is argued that the motivation to create social value drives social entrepreneurs to build organisations
differently compared to commercial entrepreneurs (Dorado, 2006).

The integration of social and business goals and perpetual reasoning make
SE a hybrid phenomenon. According to Grassl (2012), hybridity in business can
bridge different poles in several criteria, mainly ultimate ends, societal sector,
type of integration, goods produced, product status, agents of value creation and
ownership. In the case of SE, mixes of ultimate ends (for-profit and non-profit),
societal sector (market, civil society and state) and type of integration (external,
integrated and embedded) are more common (Grassl, 2012). Battilana and Lee
(2014, p. 397) propose that social enterprise can be considered an ideal type of
hybrid organisation where the authors define hybrid organising as 'the activities, structures, processes and meanings by which organizations make sense of
and combine multiple organizational forms'. Hybridity may occur through the
combinations of multiple organisational identities, organisational forms or institutional logics (Battilana and Lee, 2014). For instance, the findings of Moss and
colleagues (2011) show that social enterprises are characterised by dual identities
– a utilitarian organisational identity that is more entrepreneurial and product
oriented and a normative organisational identity that is social/people oriented.
Using Thompson's (1967) notions of organisational core and periphery, Battilana and Lee (2014) suggest that social enterprises have both business and charity missions at its core. The researchers note that hybridity is a source of tensions
between different dimensions, though the success depends on the advancement
of both missions. Tensions may occur both at the external level such as organisational environment as well as at the internal level, for example, in balancing
organisational identity, resource distribution and decision-making. The authors
distinguish five dimensions of hybrid organising, namely, inter-organisational

relationships, culture, organisational design, workforce composition and organisational activities.

Resource Mobilisation. Austin and colleagues (2006) note that resource mobilisation is a considerable challenge for social entrepreneurs as they do not have access to the same capital markets as commercial entrepreneurs. Same is true for human resources, since social enterprises are not able to pay compensations comparable to the ones of commercial enterprises. Similarly, the study that Bacq and colleagues (2013) conducted in Belgium and the Netherlands shows that social enterprises are inferior to commercial ones in terms of employment growth and advancements in entrepreneurial processes. However, there are contrasting views on social enterprises and their use of resources. According to Hoogendoorn and colleagues (2011), it is easier for commercial enterprises to complete the foundation stage, while after establishment social ventures are less likely to fail. One of the reasons is that social ventures are more resource dependent. Though this factor may seem to be a threat for social enterprise survival, SEs can benefit from the relationships created through the much-needed social networks (Burt, 2000).

The concepts of creative combination of resources that is considered central to entrepreneurial value creation (Moran and Goshal, 1999) and resourcefulness link to the notion of bricolage resource mobilisation. Bricolage is defined as making do with resources at hand and recombination of resources for new products and services (Baker and Nelson, 2005; Lévi-Strauss, 1967). Several authors find bricolage to be a useful concept for studying social enterprises (Desa, 2012; Desa and Basu, 2013; Di Domenico et al., 2010; Owusu and Janssen, 2013). According to Desa (2012), bricolage in SE covers material bricolage, labour bricolage and skills bricolage. Furthermore, Di Domenico and colleagues (2010) propose that besides the main constructs of *making do, a refusal to be constrained by limitations* and *improvisation,* SE-related constructs such as *social value creation, stakeholder participation* and *persuasion* are the components of social bricolage.

To sum up, SE is built on perpetual reasoning and hybrid organising principles, while creative resource mobilisation is a challenging though critical aspect of SE.

As we have seen, SE shares some of the key characteristics of entrepreneurship in all dimensions; however, SE is distinguished in terms of the primacy of social value creation, source of opportunities, social nature of innovation and hybrid organising among others. It is notable that it is the embeddedness of central social mission that results in all these differences.

Social entrepreneurship paradigms

As noted, defining the field is one of the distinctive 'research paths' (Desa, 2010; Kraus et al., 2014) in SE literature. Grassl (2012) suggests that terminological disagreement about SE can be mainly explained by the fact that social enterprises are structural hybrids in various terms. The author argues that social

74 *Giorgi Jamburia and Jean-Marie Courrent*

ventures must be categorised according to the real distinguishing factors rather than just conceptual abstractions. In the following section, we will approach SE through individual, process and organisational dimensions, analyse different typologies, distinguish respective schools of thought and review subsequent definitional debates.

Individual, process and organisational dimensions

When characterising SE, the researchers usually focus on individual, process and organisational aspects of the field (Alegre et al., 2017; Bacq and Janssen, 2011; Conway Dato-on and Kalakay, 2016).

The authors and organisations that apply an individual-centred approach on SE research describe a social entrepreneur as a change agent who 'acts boldly' (Dees, 2001) and 'revolutionises industries' (Ashoka, 2015). The small-scale research conducted by Spear (2006) illustrates that unlike the general 'heroic' view of an entrepreneur, the collective nature of SE is more common in cooperatives, one of the forms of social enterprises. The author notes that it might seem natural that a cooperative form of an organisation is selected for collective initiatives, however, the key managers of socially minded cooperatives can be also described as 'individualistically entrepreneurial'. Furthermore, social entrepreneurs are mostly dependent on collective experience rather than personal competences and they put higher emphasis on long-term goals rather than short-term financial profit (Thalhuber, 1998 in Bacq and Janssen, 2011). However, as Haugh (2012) underlines, actor-centred papers rarely suggest new approaches to explain the emergence and activities of social entrepreneurs.

Other researchers describe SE as a process of combination of necessary resources for achieving social goals (Mair and Marti, 2006). Those authors who focus on entrepreneurial processes discuss such topics as social commitment, social capital, human capital, social networks, social construction of SE roles, social relations, social exclusion/inclusion and more. In addition, social ownership, social, economic and institutional processes and the impact of social/economic policy are some more themes (Hill et al., 2010).

Organisational aspects are another area of discussion and debates. Some researchers limit the definition of SE only to not-for-profit organisations that also engage in business operations to increase self-sustainability by revenue generation streams (Hill et al., 2010). However, Grassl (2012) does not agree to this viewpoint, as it is the use of profits that distinguishes social enterprises, not the generation itself. However, it is a highly debatable topic in the scientific literature (Bacq and Janssen, 2011). Nevertheless, Lynch and Walls (2009) assert that if the organisations have both social and business goals embedded in their missions, they can be considered social enterprises despite their legal status. Di Zhang and Swanson (2014) note that the definition of SE has become more 'inclusive' in recent years. According to the authors, the reason is that more organisations have included both social and business goals in their missions. Porter and Kramer (2011) also argue that shared value creation blurs the

Research on social entrepreneurship 75

borders between for-profit and non-profit establishments. Similarly, Austin and colleagues (2006, p. 2) state that SE 'can occur within or across the non-profit, business, or government sectors', stretching the field to three different sectors, including 'non-profits, social-purpose for-profits, cooperatives, community-led organizations and intrapreneurial efforts within public organizations' (Hill et al., 2010, p. 22). Furthermore, it is notable that SE is not limited to founding new organisations, as SE processes can occur both in new and established organisations where it may be called 'social intrapreneurship' (Mair and Marti, 2006), facilitated by 'corporate social entrepreneurs' who act entrepreneurially to integrate social agenda into corporate strategy (Hemingway, 2005). All in all, SE has a dual goal – to work on projects that address certain social needs at the microeconomic level and promote a civil economy at the macroeconomic level, where the market is seen more as a cooperative area rather than a competitive one (Grassl, 2012).

Organisational aspects represent one of the key differentiators in SE and in most cases, the basis of different typologies and categorisations of social entrepreneurial organisations.

Focus on typologies

As SE is a hybrid phenomenon (Battilana and Lee, 2014; Grassl, 2012), SE researchers tend to propose typologies that illustrate the characteristics of the different types of social enterprises. For instance, Alter (2006) considers social enterprises part of the hybrid spectrum that ranges from non-profits with income-generating activities and social enterprises to socially responsible businesses and corporations practicing social responsibility. Similarly, Swanson and Di Zhang (2010) propose the concept of a SE zone, where the researchers map the domain of SE according to the planned approach to implementing social change and level of business practices applied to support social change, placing SE in the social improvement and social transformation regions. Several categorisations and typologies of social enterprises developed by different researchers that illustrate the hybridity in SE are summarised in Table 4.1.

Many researchers categorise social enterprises based on an organisational form (non-profit, hybrid and for-profit) (Dorado, 2006; Lepoutre et al., 2013; Mair and Marti, 2006), while others focus on the place of social goals within an enterprise (Peredo and McLean, 2006), type of integration of a social programme (Alter, 2006), nature of problems addressed by SE (Zahra et al., 2009) and combinations of automatic/contingent value spillovers with overlap/difference between clients and beneficiaries (Santos et al., 2015), among others. As we see from these typologies, there are some of the subsets of social enterprises the 'legitimacy' of which are often debatable. For example, social enterprises with a non-profit status that solely depend on fundraising income usually fall out from some of the typologies. Same can be also true for the commercial end of the hybrid spectrum. It is usually a debatable topic what level of social orientation classifies an organisation as a social enterprise.

Table 4.1 Different categorisations/typologies of social enterprises

Year	Author	Typology
2006	Alter	External social enterprise – the relationship is one-sided and resembles the interaction between a charity and a recipient. External social enterprises are created in order to finance the social programmes. The not-for-profit client indirectly benefits from the revenues of the external social enterprise.
		Integrated social enterprise – there are certain commonalities between the social programmes and an enterprise. Social programmes and business activities often share costs, assets and resources. Social services are usually commercialised for new markets or existing customers. The not-for-profit client may or may not be part of the enterprise's operations.
		Embedded social enterprise – social programmes and enterprise activities are united at the strategy and execution layers. Social programmes are self-financed by the enterprise revenues. An enterprise strives to achieve both financial and social benefits at the same time. The not-for-profit target population is directly served by the enterprise either as the target market, beneficiary, owner or employee.
2006	Dorado	Non-profit social entrepreneurial ventures – Non-profit organisations adopting business models.
		For-profit social entrepreneurial ventures – For-profit initiatives for whom social goals are central to their business model.
		Cross-sector social entrepreneurial ventures – Inter-organisational arrangements created to solve complex social problems.
2006	Mair and Marti	Non-profit organisations that complement business principles to undertake social campaigns.
		For-profit commercial businesses that use socially responsible practices via partnering across sectors.
		Ventures that are involved in innovative activities to find solutions to social and environmental problems.
2006	Peredo and McLean	Enterprises with exclusively social goals.
		Enterprises with mainly social goals, but not exclusively.
		Enterprises with social goals that are important among other goals.
		Enterprises with social goals subordinate to other goals.
2008	Elkington and Hartigan	Leveraged non-profit – the economic sustainability is achieved by fundraising activities.
		Hybrid non-profit – the enterprise covers a part of its costs through commercial activities. However, fundraising is still needed to ensure economic sustainability.
		Social business venture – the enterprise that functions as a for-profit business with the mission to achieve social and environmental changes. It includes social business and inclusive business models.
2009	Zahra et al.	Social bricoleur – the theoretical inspiration coming from Hayek. This type of social entrepreneurs addresses small-scale local needs.
		Social constructivist – the theoretical inspiration coming from Kirzner. This breed of social entrepreneurs addresses social problems in the existing social structures at small to large and local to international scales.
		Social engineer – the theoretical inspiration coming from Schumpeter. Social Engineers create new systems to replace existing ineffective structures at a very large scale and national to international in scope.

2013	Lepoutre et al.	Social entrepreneurship spectrum (GEM Study 2009).

2013 Lepoutre et al.
Social entrepreneurship spectrum (GEM Study 2009).
Non-governmental organisations – only those not-for-profit organisations that have an explicit social mission, innovative approach to addressing social problems and less than 5% of market revenues. Such entities were given the name of not-for-profit social enterprises. The NGOs that are dependent on more traditional practices were not taken into consideration.
Hybrid social enterprises – this subset of the SE spectrum includes the organisations that have both social and economic goals. They had to have at least 5% of earned income. Two subcategories were distinguished – 'economically oriented hybrids' and 'socially oriented hybrids', depending on whether they were paying primary attention to either their economic or social goals.
Socially committed regular enterprises – this component of the spectrum includes 'socially committed regular enterprises' and 'for-profit social enterprises'. The latter are regular enterprises for which social/environmental objectives are more important than the economic ones. In contrast, those organisations that rated social/environmental objectives twice as important as the economic ones are 'for-profit social enterprises'.

2014 Jäger and Schröer
'Enterprising non-profits with activities supporting solidarity by selling in markets.
Social innovation (social entrepreneurship) with planned social value and income-generating activities.
Hybrid organisations (social businesses/social enterprises) with activities supporting functional solidarity.
Socially responsible enterprises (corporate social responsibility) with market activities and additional social-value generating activities'(p. 1294).

2015 Dohrmann et al.
Social enterprises differentiated based on social mission.
One-sided social mission – Social investors subsidise the social target group on the consumption side.
Two-sided social mission – two social target groups: one on production and one on consumption side.
Market-oriented social mission – a social target group on the production side and a focus on a market target group on the consumption side.
Commercially utilised social mission – a social target group attracted by a social mission and later used as a resource input to meet specific consumption needs of a different market target group.

2015 Santos et al.
Market hybrid – Clients and beneficiaries are the same and value spillovers are automatic.
Blending hybrid – Clients and beneficiaries are the same, but value spillovers are contingent.
Bridging hybrid – Clients and beneficiaries are not the same, but value spillovers are automatic.
Coupling hybrid – Clients and beneficiaries are not the same and value spillovers are contingent.

2017 Defourny and Nyssens
Entrepreneurial non-profit – non-profit organisations with income-generating activities focused on supporting their social mission.
Public sector SE – public sector spin-offs.
Social cooperative – resulting from a move of mutual interest organisations towards more general interest-seeking behaviours.
Single stakeholder – all members sharing mutual interest.
Multiple stakeholder – different stakeholders becoming members of social cooperatives.
Social business – involves the move of for-profits towards general interest.
SME – hybrid economic model involving shared value creation.
Yunus type – non-dividend social business, profits are fully reinvested to achieve the social mission.

Source: Author's own table.

78 *Giorgi Jamburia and Jean-Marie Courrent*

To add an additional discourse to the this discussion, in Appendix A1 we summarise the SE typologies outlined by the SE researchers according to the International Comparative Social Enterprise Models (ICSEM) Project Working papers (available at www.iap-socent.be/icsem-working-papers) and the summary shows a vast array of social enterprise types in more than 30 countries, each characterised with a different set of aspects.

It is noteworthy that different schools of thought 'recognise' the legitimacy of different types of social enterprises and focus on specific aspects characterising SE.

Schools of thought

Through a meta-analysis of the SE literature, Hill and colleagues (2010) determined influential words and word pairs in the field and consequently detected four schools of thought, namely entrepreneurship, social, governance and for-profit/non-profit. The entrepreneurship school is focused on how entrepreneurs create social ventures based on management/entrepreneurship theories. The authors in this school frequently employ a quantitative approach studying such variables as individual values, size of the enterprise, social capital and relations. The social school is directed towards building an organisation that meets social needs. The governance school is interested in community-influenced governance of social enterprises. The for-profit/non-profit school is concentrated on commercial/non-profit hybrids and business-like non-profit organisations. The authors conclude that the social school is characterised by the social roots of entrepreneurial opportunities; the entrepreneurship school is concerned with how entrepreneurs manage resources to create social ventures and the governance school deals with the management of stakeholder involvement (Hill et al., 2010).

Similarly, Bacq and Janssen (2011) have identified three schools of thought in the SE research. The Social Innovation School focuses on the individual characteristics of a social entrepreneur. The followers of Social Enterprise School argue that SEs must conduct profit-generating activities to fund the social mission. Finally, European approaches are characterised by the creation of specific legal frameworks for SEs. The Social Innovation School and European approaches require a direct link between the social mission and profit-generating activities; whereas the Social Enterprise School does not require such kind of link. According to the Social Innovation School, the organisational form of a social enterprise can be either non-profit or for-profit. This approach has led to the emergence of hybrid organisations. In contrast, the Social Enterprise School first considered only non-profits that used earned income strategies. However, it later included any business that trades for achieving a social mission. Finally, Europe has been characterised by the creation of new types of legal forms for SEs, though most social enterprises still adopt common legal forms. Profit distribution has often been connected to the legal form of a social enterprise. The Social Innovation School does not impose strict limits on profit

Research on social entrepreneurship 79

distribution. In contrast, the Social Enterprise School forbids any profit distribution as all profit must be reinvested for achieving the social mission, though recent trend accepts some profit distribution to owners or workers, whereas the European approach recommends a limited profit distribution (Bacq and Janssen, 2011).

Furthermore, in Europe, social enterprises are seen more as a part of the third sector (Bacq and Janssen, 2011). According to the EMES network, social enterprises must bear a significant level of economic risk, which depends both on market performance and its ability to mobilise public and voluntary resources (Defourny and Nyssens, 2006). The US is characterised more with the domination of the 'earned income' school that defines a social enterprise as an organisation that trades for achieving a social mission. According to the representatives of this school of thought, the more productive activity the social purpose organisation has, more it deserves to be called a social enterprise. Several European countries such as the UK and Finland share this approach. However, even in the US there is the Social Innovation School that focuses more on innovative capabilities of social enterprises (Bacq and Janssen, 2011).But the EMES approach accepts that social enterprises may depend on a combination of business, public and voluntary resources (Defourny and Nyssens, 2006). Furthermore, several researchers focus on differentiating *social entrepreneurs* from *social enterprise managers*. The Social Innovation School stresses on several key characteristics of a social entrepreneur such as visionary and innovative approach, strong ethical fibre, special ability to detect opportunities, a role of a change agent and resourcefulness. For the Social Enterprise School, the initiative must come from a non-governmental organisation (NGO) or a state; hence, social entrepreneur plays a secondary role here. Similarly, although the European school does not exclude leadership in the field, the focus is still more on 'collective governance mechanisms' (Bacq and Janssen, 2011).

Nevertheless, Alegre and colleagues (2017) argue that despite general perceptions that there is a disagreement among different schools of thought, detected clusters of *Social and Financial, Innovation, Community, Sustainability and Change* reveal that there is a certain overlap among them; however, it is the relative priority of certain conceptions that differentiates the clusters.

These different approaches to characterising SE, including individual, process and organisational dimensions, focus on typologies and promotion of different schools of thought are reflected in subsequent definitional debates.

Definitional debates

In order to illustrate the variety of SE definitions, we provide a table of some of the selected definitions from the various papers and systematic reviews among others (Bacq and Janssen, 2011; Conway Dato-on and Kalakay, 2016; Dacin et al., 2010; Zahra et al., 2009) (Table 4.2). Key characteristics of SE are italicised.

Table 4.2 Definitions of social entrepreneurship, social enterprise and social entrepreneur

Year	Author	Definition	Page(s)
1997	Leadbeater	'Social entrepreneurs identify *under-utilised resources* – people, buildings, equipment – and find ways of putting them to use to satisfy *unmet social needs*'.	p. 2
2000	Fowler	'Social Entrepreneurship is the creation of viable socio-economic structures, relations, institutions, organizations and practices that yield and sustain *social benefits*'.	p. 649
2001	Dees	'Social entrepreneurs play the role of *change agents* in the social sector, by: Adopting a mission to *create and sustain social value* (not just private one), Recognizing and relentlessly *pursuing new opportunities* to serve that mission; Engaging in a process of *continuous innovation, adaptation, and learning*, Acting boldly *without being limited by resources currently at hand*, and exhibiting *heightened accountability* to the constituencies served and the outcomes created'.	p. 4
2002	Drayton	'Social entrepreneurs focus their entrepreneurial talent on solving social problems. ... [W]hat defines a leading social entrepreneur? First, there is no entrepreneur without a powerful, new, *system change idea*.... There are four other necessary ingredients: *creativity, widespread impact, entrepreneurial quality, and strong ethical fibre*'.	pp. 123–124
2002	Department of Trade and Industry (DTI)	'[A social enterprise] is defined as a business with *primarily social objectives*, whose *surpluses are principally reinvested* for that purpose in the business or in the community, rather than being driven by the need to maximize profits for shareholders and owners'.	p. 13
2004	Alvord et al.	'Social entrepreneurship ... creates *innovative solutions* to immediate social problems and mobilizes the ideas, capacities, *resources*, and social arrangements required for *sustainable social transformations*'.	p. 262
2004	Harding	'Entrepreneurs motivated by *social objectives* to instigate some form of new activity or venture'.	p. 41
2005	Roberts and Woods	'Social entrepreneurship is the construction, evaluation and pursuit of *opportunities* for *transformative social change* carried out by visionary, passionately dedicated individuals'.	p. 49
2005	Seelos and Mair	'Social entrepreneurship creates *new models for the provision of products and services* that cater directly to *basic human needs that remain unsatisfied by current economic or social institutions*'.	pp. 243–244
2006	Austin et al.	'*Innovative, social value creating activity* that can occur within or across the nonprofit, business, or government sectors'.	p. 2
2006	Mair and Marti	'First, we view social entrepreneurship as a process of *creating value* by *combining resources in new ways*. Second, these resource combinations are intended primarily to explore and exploit opportunities to create *social value* by stimulating *social change* or meeting *social needs*. And third, when viewed as a process, social entrepreneurship involves the offering of services and products but can also refer to the creation of new organizations'.	p. 37

2006	Peredo and McLean	'Social entrepreneurship is exercised where some person or persons (1) *aim either exclusively or in some prominent way to create social value* of some kind, and pursue that goal through some combination of (2) recognizing and exploiting *opportunities* to create this value, (3) employing *innovation*, (4) *tolerating risk* and (5) *declining to accept limitations in available resources*'.	p. 56
2007	Martin and Osberg	'We define social entrepreneurship as having the following three components: (1) identifying a stable but inherently *unjust equilibrium* that causes the exclusion, marginalization, or suffering of a segment of humanity that lacks the financial means or political clout to achieve any transformative benefit on its own; (2) *identifying an opportunity* in this unjust equilibrium, developing *a social value proposition*, and bringing to bear inspiration, creativity, direct action, courage, and fortitude, thereby *challenging the stable state's hegemony*; and (3) *forging a new, stable equilibrium* that releases trapped potential or alleviates the suffering of the targeted group, and through imitation and the creation of a stable ecosystem around the new equilibrium ensuring a better future for the targeted group and even society at large'.	p. 35
2008	Defourny and Nyssens	'Social enterprises are not-for-profit private organizations providing goods or services directly related to their explicit aim to benefit the community. They generally rely on a collective dynamics involving various types of stakeholders in their governing bodies, they place a high value on their autonomy and they bear economic risks related to their activity'.	p. 204
2008	Nicholls	'Social entrepreneurship is a set of *innovative* and *effective* activities that focus strategically on *resolving social market failures* and *creating new opportunities* to add social value systemically by using a range of *resources* and organizational formats to maximize social impact and bring about change. Simply put, social entrepreneurship is defined by its two constituent elements: a prime strategic focus on *social impact* and an *innovative approach* to achieving its mission'.	p. 23
2009	Zahra et al.	'Social entrepreneurship encompasses the activities and processes undertaken to discover, define, and exploit *opportunities* in order to enhance *social wealth* by creating new ventures or managing existing organizations in an *innovative manner*'.	p. 522
2010	Hill et al.	'A *disciplined, innovative, risk tolerant* entrepreneurial process of *opportunity recognition and resource assembly* directed toward creating *social value* by *changing* underlying social and economic *structures*'.	p. 21
2011	Bacq and Janssen	'The process of identifying, evaluating and exploiting *opportunities* aiming at *social value creation* by means of *commercial, market-based activities* and of the use of a *wide range of resources*'.	p. 376
2013	Lepoutre et al.	'[T]here seem to be a number of characteristics that distinguish social entrepreneurs from "regular" entrepreneurs and/or traditional charities. In particular, three selection criteria seem to stand out from extant literature: the predominance of a *social mission*, the importance of *innovation*, and the role of *earned income*'.	p. 694
2016	Bosma et al.	'Any kind of activity, organisation or initiative that has a particularly *social, environmental or community objective*'.	p. 5

Source: Author's own table.

82   *Giorgi Jamburia and Jean-Marie Courrent*

A majority of the researchers agree that a dominant social value creation is a defining characteristic of SE (Austin et al., 2006; Bacq and Janssen, 2011; Conway Dato-On and Kalakay, 2016; Dees, 2001; Di Domenico et al., 2010; Hill et al., 2010; Mair and Marti, 2006; Nicholls, 2008; Peredo and McLean, 2006; Weerawardena and Sullivan Mort, 2006). Market orientation is another key aspect of SE (Boschee and McClurg, 2003; Bosma et al., 2016; Dart, 2004; Guclu et al., 2002; Lepoutre et al., 2013; Mair and Schoen, 2007; Robinson, 2006; Thompson, 2002; Thompson and Doherty, 2006; Tracey and Phillips, 2007), though not all schools of thought, especially the Social Innovation School, have the similar approach.

Innovativeness is an integral component for the other group of researchers who view social transformation and radical innovation as crucial components of SE. As mentioned, different researchers and schools of thought have different views on the required presence of innovation in social entrepreneurial activities. Many authors consider innovation a key characteristic of SE (Alvord et al., 2004; Austin et al., 2006; Conway Dato-on and Kalakay, 2016; Dees, 2001; Lepoutre et al., 2013; Mair and Marti, 2006; Mair and Noboa, 2006; Nicholls, 2008; Peredo and McLean, 2006; Zahra et al., 2009). However, there are definitions that do not stress on the aspect of innovativeness, especially among the group of researchers not belonging to the Social Innovation School of thought; though, as mentioned, the boundaries between the schools of thought are blurring (Bacq and Janssen, 2011; Lehner and Kansikas, 2012).

Opportunity discovery or creation is also central to SE and many definitions focus on this aspect (Hill et al., 2010; Roberts and Woods, 2005; Weerawardena and Sullivan Mort, 2006; Zahra et al., 2009). However, most of these definitions do not cover the opportunity creation aspect of SE. Similarly, creative resource mobilisation is a characteristic encountered in most of the reviewed definitions (Austin et al., 2006; Bacq and Janssen, 2011; Dees, 2001; Defourny and Nyssens, 2006; Hill et al., 2010; Leadbeater, 1997; Mair and Marti, 2006; Mair and Noboa, 2006).

However, it can be suggested that the definitions do not show the signs of convergence through the years (Conway Dato-on and Kalakay, 2016). Choi and Majumdar (2014) even argue that SE is an essentially contested concept and reaching a universally agreed definition seems almost impossible. Even though there exists a problem of SE definition, some authors note that research on different types of social enterprises would contribute to the field more rather than the new definitions (Conway Dato-on and Kalakay, 2016; Defourny and Nyssens, 2017). Defourny and Nyssens (2017) also argue of the impossibility of a unified definition. Instead, the authors suggest that the list of EMES criteria across economic/entrepreneurial, social and governance dimensions may serve as a guide to locate social enterprises. The researchers distinguish general, capital and mutual interest and dominant non-market, hybrid and dominant market resources, and by the combinations of interest principles and resource mix arrive at a typology consisting of the entrepreneurial non-profit model, the social cooperative model (single stakeholder and multiple stakeholders), the social business model (Yunus type and SME type) and the public sector social enterprise model.

Finally, we argue that the proposed definition must be inclusive and represent the 'common denominator' of the existing definitional debates. Thus, as suggested by several researchers (Defourny and Nyssens, 2017), the focus can be forwarded towards studying different subtypes of social enterprises and testing the generalisability of findings.

To conclude, different approaches, typologies and schools of thought exist in the SE literature. In most of the cases, they conflict each other. It is important to characterise all these different perspectives for developing a definition of the field.

The heterogeneity of social enterprise conceptions

Mapping of social enterprises

In order to detect a sample of social enterprises, a special mapping strategy must be developed. There are many different aspects that must be taken into consideration before setting the mapping criteria.

Lyon and Sepulveda (2009) review the previous approaches to mapping social enterprises in the UK. According to the authors, none of the surveys are totally perfect. For instance, the IFF (2005) survey excludes several forms of social enterprises, including charities with trading income and companies limited by shares, though several highly inclusive definitions may wrongly categorise types of organisations that are not generally considered social enterprises. In addition, some regional studies have asked organisations if they classified themselves as social enterprises while others did not. Similarly, some approaches focused on social aspects of enterprises, while others emphasised on the trading orientation of organisations. Therefore, the authors explain that researchers should have more detailed information about potential social ventures under study (Lyon and Sepulveda, 2009).

DTI (2004) has outlined the following categories of social ownership: 'community interest companies, companies limited by guarantee, industrial and provident societies, housing associations, and registered charities with trading income' (Lyon and Sepulveda, 2009, p. 87). The Annual Small Business Survey sets 50% as the threshold amount that must be used for social aims by an organisation in order to be considered a social enterprise (DTI, 2006). Yunus (2011), however, has a radical stance on this issue and advocates for social business model where no dividend must be paid to the investors and all profits must be reinvested towards achieving social goals, although the requirement of full profit distribution would drop the share of social entrepreneurs (Bosma et al., 2016). Lyon and Sepulveda (2009) also find it important to make a distinction between independent social enterprises and branches of larger organisations, as many companies register their branches as separate entities.

84 *Giorgi Jamburia and Jean-Marie Courrent*

There is also no general agreement on the minimum percentage of the trading income that a socially focused organisation has to be classified as a social venture. Some studies use a 25% barrier, while others tend to a 50% threshold. However, such kind of cut-offs may leave out those organisations that considerably contribute to the social sector, but their trading income falls short of the established barrier (Lyon and Sepulveda, 2009). Community Interest Company (CIC) guidance also states that social benefits should extend beyond a limited membership group to a broader population, if the group does not include socially disadvantaged people, for example. The difference also must be understood between the organisations that contribute to social goals using the trading profit and the organisations that achieve social aims via trading (Lyon and Sepulveda, 2009).

Teasdale and colleagues (2013) relate the issue of mapping of social enterprises with the social enterprise growth myth. As the authors note, though the definition of social enterprises has remained the same in the UK, underlying criteria for mapping SEs have changed several times. Thus, it resulted in an unrealistically high-growth statistics of social ventures in the UK. The researchers demonstrate that the political agenda has influenced the changes in mapping criteria. The changes applied through the years included the following modifications: decrease in the minimum level of earned income from 50% to 25%; allowance of self-reporting on being a social enterprise and good fit with the DTI definition instead of reporting to have a primary social mission instead of a financial one; changing the element of reinvestment of at least 51% of surplus for the social mission with just limitation of stakeholder profit sharing up to 50%; and modifying sampling of organisations that have a clear social ownership with all registered businesses. Consequently, the number of social enterprises has 'increased' from 5,300 in 2003 to 62,000 in 2007. Furthermore, Ipsos MORI's narrow definition was based on reinvesting surplus. Therefore, 35% of the respondents were not mistakenly considered social enterprises simply because of making loss. This example shows how important it is to have a unified definition that will reflect the reality.

Dart and colleagues (2010) also point out some of the serious problems in mapping of social enterprises. According to the authors, all operational definitions considered by them turned out to be unworkable. Creating both social and economic value was thought to be an initial approach for selection. However, as most of the businesses and NGOs create both values, the researchers had to limit the definition to the 'organisations which deliberatively cultivate both social and economic value' (Dart et al., 2010, p. 188). However, many NGOs that are concerned with economic development and many businesses with corporate social responsibility policies fell into the sample. Therefore, the researchers decided to limit the definition to those organisations that have embedded social and economic value creation as a central component of their organisational strategy; although finding out the level of earned income or social focus that a non-profit or a business should have to be considered a social enterprise turned out to be a remarkable difficulty. In addition, contrasting SE from green businesses, triple

Research on social entrepreneurship 85

bottom line and quadruple bottom line organisations seemed to be a serious obstacle. Later, the authors suggested researching those organisations that identify themselves as social enterprises. However, the major intention was to map the organisations that 'behaved differently and innovatively' (Dart et al., 2010, p. 189) and not the ones that simply label themselves in one way or another. Finally, the researchers decided to limit their study to work integration social enterprises. But most of such organisations turned out to be part of non-profit parent organisations, either as a programme, department or a project. And there were few social purpose businesses employing excluded people.

Defourny and Nyssens (2010, 2012) propose the criteria for the EMES ideal type of social enterprise across economic/entrepreneurial, social and governance dimensions. The economic and entrepreneurial dimension consists of a continuous activity of producing goods and/or selling services, a significant level of economic risk and at least a minimum level of paid work. The social dimensions cover an explicit aim to benefit society, an initiative launched by a group of citizens or NGOs and a limited profit distribution. Finally, participatory governance of social enterprises can be achieved through a high degree of autonomy, a decision-making power not proportional to capital and a participatory nature through involving various actors affected by the activity. As argued by Defourny and Nyssens (2017), these criteria can be utilised for locating different forms of social enterprises and checking their conformity in relation to the 'ideal' criteria.

Lepoutre and colleagues (2013) discuss the issue of developing a global standardised methodology for mapping and measuring SE activity. The research was conducted in collaboration with GEM. According to the authors, current SE research lacks studies on generalisability of theoretical propositions, preconditions and results of SE activities and statistical differences among social enterprises based on large-scale quantitative dataset. The questionnaire developed by the researchers was included in the GEM survey, the largest initiative that measures entrepreneurship activity around the globe. Lepoutre and colleagues (2013) distinguish three major criteria that differentiate SE from regular entrepreneurship or traditional charities: 'the predominance of a social mission, the importance of innovation and the role of earned income' (Lepoutre et al., 2013, p. 694). However, there are controversial understandings of SE – for a part of researchers an organisation must use innovative approaches in achieving a social mission to be considered a social enterprise, while following the market logic is enough for the others.

Lepoutre and colleagues (2013) have considered several factors during the design process of the research study. First, researchers avoided using the word 'social entrepreneur', as it may have different interpretations in different countries. Instead, a series of indirect questions were asked to identify social entrepreneurs. On the one hand, the respondents had to state whether their organisation had a particular social, environmental or community objective, and on the other, individuals who identified themselves as founders, owners or managers of companies had to allocate 100 points among three organisational goals: economic, social and environmental. In addition, to be considered social enterprises,

86   Giorgi Jamburia and Jean-Marie Courrent

organisations had to have at least 5% of an earned income. Finally, interviewees had to state whether their organisation was innovative in at least one of the following six aspects: product, production, process, delivery, promotion and unattended customer niche (Lepoutre et al., 2013).

GEM has produced another special topic report on SE in 2015–2016. For the purposes of the research and a broad measure, the authors have defined social entrepreneurial activity (SEA) as:

> any kind of activity, organisation or initiative that has a particularly social, environmental or community objective. This might include providing services or training to socially deprived or disabled persons, activities aimed at reducing pollution or food-waste, organising self-help groups for community action, etc.
>
> [Bosma et al., (2016), p. 2]

The researchers have looked at the following parameters: '(i) an explicit social mission, (ii) offering products or services in the market, (iii) offering an innovative solution, (iv) reinvesting profits and (v) making an effort to measure the social impact of their activities' (Bosma et al., 2016, p. 2). In order to make the SE definition more compatible with the scientific literature, the researchers have introduced two compulsory criteria for the narrow definition: first that the organisation prioritises value creation over value capture and second that the organisation is more market based than non-market based (Bosma et al., 2016). As mentioned, more inclusiveness by dropping the innovation requirement for classifying as a social enterprise is evident.

The given examples illustrate that mapping of social enterprises is a clear challenge with several complex issues that must be carefully addressed in order to have accurate research results.

International and legal specificities

Understanding international and legal specificities is also indispensable when it comes to conducting valid national and international research. According to Desa (2012), SE can exist everywhere and not only in underdeveloped or emerging economies; there are six variables that characterise social enterprises internationally: outcome emphasis, programme area focus, common organisational type, legal framework, societal sector and strategic development base (Kerlin, 2009).

International Specificities. Although terminological confusions may be common in every emerging field of social science, Grassl (2012) points out two major reasons that complicate the situation in SE research even more; first, the ones who determine the development of the field are not the researchers, but managers and entrepreneurs; and second, there are vast differences in the world in terms of 'socio-economical values and systems'. The researcher mentions that definitions of SE vary from country to country. For example, SE definition in the US stresses on solving social problems by private initiatives. However, in

European definitions, profit, funding and governance statuses are not usually strictly specified. Looking for a common working definition becomes even more difficult when developing countries are taken into consideration (Grassl, 2012). It is noteworthy that the same type of activities may or may not be considered social entrepreneurial in different countries. For example, in Western Europe, social cooperatives are considered under the social enterprise domain, which is not the case in the US (Kerlin, 2010). Some researchers even categorise small businesses that operate in rural areas as social ventures since they contribute to the well-being of local inhabitants (Poon et al., 2009). This is especially true of the rural areas in the developing or transitional economies where existence of small businesses may have a particularly significant importance for the social welfare of local communities. Furthermore, according to Bacq and Janssen (2011), governmental actions may influence the nature of social entrepreneurial activities. For example, European states are better against mobilising their resources to deal with exclusion and poverty, among others, while in the US, poverty is more of a charity than a governmental issue. That is why, in the US, SE can be considered as a substitute to social security (Bacq and Janssen, 2011).

Bacq and Janssen (2011) have analysed North American and European literatures using Gartner's (1985) four differentiating aspects: the individual, the process, the organisation and the environment. At first sight, there seems to be a difference between the American and European conceptions of SE. However, the analysis shows that there is no distinctive difference between the continents, and different definitions coexist. It is notable that several European governments have created new organisational frameworks to support SE. Besides, several organisations facilitating social entrepreneurial initiatives have emerged both in Europe and North America (Bacq and Janssen, 2011).

Kerlin (2010) compares the context of social enterprises across seven regions and countries of the world: Western Europe, East-Central Europe, Japan, the US, Zimbabwe and Zambia, Argentina and Southeast Asia. The author uses social origins theory, recent comparative research on social enterprises and socioeconomic contexts to distinguish the factors that influenced the emergence of social enterprise in these regions. Uses of social enterprise, its organisational forms, legal structures and supportive environment are the factors that may vary across different regions. According to Kerlin (2009), social enterprise is most commonly associated with the following elements: civil society, state capacity, market functioning and international aid. The general unifying theme about the emergence of social enterprise in almost all regions has been linked to weak state social programmes and/or funding. In the US, non-profits started generating market income after losing access to government funds. In Western Europe, the social enterprise movement was a response to the unemployment problem. As a result, work integration of unemployed through social cooperatives and provision of human services became some of the most common activities of SEs. In East-Central Europe, social enterprise initiatives had to tackle the problems created by the withdrawal of the state as a result of the fall of communism. In addition, transition to market economy led to high levels of unemployment.

88   *Giorgi Jamburia and Jean-Marie Courrent*

In Argentina, various cooperatives and mutual benefit societies were created to solve problems of unemployment and social exclusion. In Zimbabwe and Zambia, because of the poor state support and economies, international aid has mainly focused on microcredit schemes for small enterprises. In Southeast Asia, social enterprises are addressing poverty, unemployment and environmental issues. Finally, social ventures in Japan are focused on social integration (Kerlin, 2009).

The research study of Lepoutre and colleagues (2013) showed that there was higher SEA in innovation-driven countries, followed by efficiency-driven and factor-driven economies. Although it might be predicted that developing countries that have severe social problems and state failures would have more social enterprises, the reverse turned out to be true. One of the reasons can be that there are other objectives that must be achieved in developing countries. In addition, the US and Western Europe were characterised with higher number of NGOs while Latin America and the Caribbean countries were dominated by hybrid organisations. A high level of pure regular entrepreneurship was also a good predictor for high rates of SE activity.

The recent GEM Special Report on SE of 2015–2016 has found that, according to the broad definition, the average rate of SEA at the start-up phase across 58 economies is 3.2%, ranging from 0.3% in South Korea to 10.1% in Peru. In contrast, the average prevalence rate of the start-up commercial entrepreneurship is 7.6% around the globe. When it comes to the operating SEA, the average rate is 3.7%, ranging from 0.4% in Iran to 14% in Senegal. In case of applying the narrow definition of SEA, the rates go down considerably by almost two-third and total 1.1% for the nascent entrepreneurs and 1.2% for currently operating social entrepreneurs (Bosma et al., 2016). According to the GEM 2015–2016 study, almost half the individuals currently involved in operating SEA reinvest their profits for the achievement of social goals. In addition, the gender gap in SEA was considerably smaller, with 55% male and 45% female compared to the commercial entrepreneurial activity where the ratio was around 2:1. When it comes to finance, most of the social entrepreneurs use personal funds; however, the share of own investment varies around the globe – from 30% in sub-Saharan Africa to 60% in Southeast Asia and Middle East and North Africa. More than one-third of the social entrepreneurs use government funds, and family and banks remain key sources of funding for them (Bosma et al., 2016). It is also important to note that Western Europe, Australia and the US had the highest conversion rates of SEA, from the start-up phase to the operational phase. This can be explained by the highest levels of institutional support mechanisms, among others. On the other side, sub-Saharan Africa had the highest rate of overlap between commercial and SE. As it can be assumed, lower levels of economic development facilitate intertwinement between social and business activities, since this region is characterised with leading rates in necessity entrepreneurship. The studies have also shown that the younger generation is more involved in SE (Bosma et al., 2016).

Similarly, Defourny and Nyssens (2010) divide the European countries according to their socio-economic contexts in four parts: corporatist, socio-democratic, liberal and the southern European countries. For example, the corporatist countries (Belgium, France, Germany and Ireland) play a key role in provision of social services. High rates of unemployment in the corporatist countries in the 1980s were addressed by the different associations integrating unemployed people through a productive activity. In order to solve problems both in unemployment and social needs, job creation was encouraged in those areas that needed to satisfy social needs. The socio-democratic countries (Nordic countries such as Sweden, Norway and Denmark) are characterised by a strong cooperative movement. The UK, viewed as an example of the liberal model, is characterised with a lower level of public social spending. However, the government creates a competitive environment for the public sector, third sector and for-profit organisations to win the contracts for the social service provision. As a result, the entrepreneurial dimension of the associations has increased noticeably. The southern European countries such as Spain, Italy and Portugal have a solid tradition of cooperatives. In Italy, such kind of cooperatives became especially active in terms of work integration of the excluded people. In contrast, in the US, the share of the public support decreased significantly while the commercial income has increased (Kerlin, 2006).

Legal Specificities. Haugh (2005) notes that as different legal formats are being adopted by social enterprises in different countries, nowadays it makes national and international comparisons unreliable. In the UK alone, there are many different formats in which social enterprises operate, though valid statistical data has not yet been produced for each type of organisation. Galera and Borzaga (2009, p. 210) propose that 'the legal recognition of social enterprise contributes to conceptual clarification'. Laratta and colleagues (2011) also note that without a specific legal structure, it is difficult to realise the underlying concept of social enterprise. However, there is a contrasting view that the organisational form and the legal structure do not suggest much about the enterprise activities and its impact (Elson and Hall, 2012).

There are several organisational types or legal frameworks in which social enterprises function. These types usually differ according to countries or regions. For example, in Japan, the most common legal forms for social enterprise are non-profit and company. In contrast, in Argentina, cooperative and mutual benefit societies are the most widespread forms. Several countries have also created separate legal frameworks for social enterprises, even though it might not be the organisational form most often used by SEs. Western Europe is an evident leader in this regard (Kerlin, 2010). Furthermore, according to Michelini and Fiorentino (2012), the joint social venture is the form of social enterprise that makes it possible to create more shared value. In this case, for-profit and non-profit organisations form a joint business. The legal entity is then called a social business enterprise. The profits generated by the venture first cover the capital investments and are later reinvested into the enterprise. This kind of cooperation is mutually beneficial – the for-profit company provides economic, managerial and technological resources, while the non-profit organisation contributes by its knowledge of local needs and established networks.

90 *Giorgi Jamburia and Jean-Marie Courrent*

Defourny and Nyssens (2010) make an overview of the development of new legal forms for social enterprises in Europe. As the authors note, Italy was the first country to adopt a law focusing on two types of social cooperatives: the ones delivering social, health and education services and those offering work integration to disadvantaged people. While France, Spain, Portugal and Greece created new legal forms for the cooperative type, Belgium, the UK and Italy decided to pass the bills on more open models of the social enterprise. Despite the creation of the new legal forms, many social enterprises still adopt already existing forms such as association, cooperative, company limited by guarantee or by share and so on. For instance, social enterprises are usually set up as associations if the legal form of an association allows considerable freedom to sell goods/services. Otherwise, social enterprises adopt cooperative or traditional business forms. It is noteworthy that the work integration social enterprise is a dominant form of SEs in Europe. Several European countries such as France, Finland, Poland and Spain have special public schemes targeting such types of social enterprises. However, these schemes serve as official registers for social enterprises and they do not introduce any different legal forms. Having a preference or non-preference attitude towards social enterprises during the selection process for public contracts is another controversial topic. For instance, Italy has a quota of social enterprises for certain public contracts. In certain countries, the legal frameworks regulating the public contracts are neutral or less favourable for social enterprises (Defourny and Nyssens, 2010).

Different legal forms can be appropriate in different cases; 'copying' also needs a careful consideration. For instance, Lan (2014) notes that the UK's CIC model that involves asset lock and dividend cap to ensure the service for community (Liao, 2014) could be more beneficial for China than the US benefit corporation model, since the UK model also operates at the intersection of government and associations, though it would require similar 'light touch' from the side of the government as it is the case in the UK. Furthermore, Reinsch and colleagues (2017) argue that the traditional US legal forms can be as effective in preventing mission drift as socially oriented legal forms, given the fact that social goals are integrated into the legal form of the enterprise.

As we have seen, different historical perspectives have shaped contrasting realities internationally that, in turn, influenced the adoption of differing legal forms by social enterprises and creation of special frameworks by the governments.

Discussion and conclusion

There are many different perspectives on SE and its definition. As we have seen from the literature review, finding a common operating definition is of utmost importance for conducting valid national and international statistical research studies, though there is no consensus on what can be regarded a social enterprise and what not. Furthermore, there seems to be no end to the scientific debate on this issue.

Several researchers (Alter, 2006; Dees, 1998; Lepoutre et al., 2013) view social enterprises as a part of the hybrid spectrum that seems to be a legitimate approach. Our perspective on this topic is to endorse this view and place a social enterprise on the continuum of social value creation. Besides, SE is a field resting on the multidimensional continuum, with the major dimensions of focus on social value creation, market orientation and innovativeness. We suggest that these three factors define the field, as similarly viewed by Lepoutre and colleagues (2013), though several additional dimensions and criteria can be mentioned. However, our aim is to propose an inclusive definition on the common core of the proposed definitions.

Consequently, the definition of the field can be formulated in the following way: *Social entrepreneurship is a process of opportunity discovery or creation and creative resource mobilisation towards predominant social value creation with either certain level of market orientation or innovativeness or a combination of both.*

Therefore, the social enterprise continuum would consist of innovative social enterprises, market-oriented social enterprises and innovative market-oriented social enterprises at the intersection of two types. In this way, our definition will be bridging definitions that focus more on earned income generation and the definitions that articulate on the aspect of innovativeness.

We can go back to the questions posed in the beginning of the paper:

Does the research have to focus on social entrepreneurial processes, social entrepreneurs or social enterprises?

The research must be conducted on all dimensions, despite the fact that the focus on process and organisational dimensions rather than on individual characteristics would further advance the field, making the findings more generalisable and escaping from the illustrations of heroic social entrepreneurs and best practice cases only. The focus on processes will help us see all the elements that combine for a successful social value creation. While focus on organisational dimension is important, outcomes are in the end what matter.

Can this definition overcome the differences in national representations of SE?

The definition can overcome the differences in national representations of SE. The SE can have different forms in different countries though our definition is built on the common core of existing definitions.

How this definition could be operationalised through indicators – items – that would be workable both in quantitative and qualitative approaches?

In order to operationalise this definition, we need a set of tangible and measurable parameters that will make it possible to conduct valid national and international research employing both qualitative and quantitative approaches. For this purpose, first, we must look at the share that is spent on social issues that can be one of the aspects to assess the level of organisational focus on social mission. Besides, distribution of priorities between social and financial goals may also provide a valuable insight (Lepoutre et al., 2013). Next, in order to assess the relative market orientation of social enterprises, we can find it from the percentage of earned income. Finally, innovativeness can be measured on a specific scale through a series of questions, for example, through the types of questions used in GEM 2009 and 2015–2016 studies on social enterprises. For instance,

92 *Giorgi Jamburia and Jean-Marie Courrent*

providing new products or services, offering a new approach to producing a product/service or a new way of delivery and promotion and unattended customer niche can characterise innovations among social enterprises (Bosma et al., 2016; Lepoutre et al., 2013). In the end, the researchers can select the sample that will conform to their preferences. As a result, the research will be valid at least in those specific sample boundaries.

Finally, certainly there are several more dimensions other than focus on social mission, business activities and level of innovativeness that characterise SE. They can be used as complementary criteria. For instance, differentiation of social enterprise business models according to embedded, integrated or external social missions (Alter, 2006) can be beneficial for the process of analysis, among others. Furthermore, researchers can test their hypotheses on different types of social enterprises and later check the generalisability of findings on other forms of social entrepreneurial ventures.

References

Alegre, I., Kislenko, S. and Berbegal-Mirabent, J. (2017) 'Organized Chaos: Mapping the definitions of social entrepreneurship', *Journal of Social Entrepreneurship*, Vol. 8, No. 2, pp. 248–264.

Alter, S.K. (2006) 'Social Enterprise Models and Their Mission and Money Relationships', in Nicholls, A. (Ed.), *Social Entrepreneurship: New Models of Sustainable Social Change*, Oxford University Press, Oxford, pp. 205–232.

Alvord, S.H., Brown, L.D. and Letts, C.W. (2004) 'Social entrepreneurship and societal transformation: An exploratory study', *The Journal of Applied Behavioral Science*, Vol. 40, No. 3, pp. 260–282.

Ashoka. (2015) [online] www.ashoka.org/en/story/planting-seeds-social-startup-success-10-things-remember-when-starting-social-enterprise (Accessed 25 September 2015)

Austin, J., Stevenson, H. and Wei-Skillern, J. (2006) 'Social and commercial entrepreneurship: Same, different, or both?', *Entrepreneurship Theory and Practice*, Vol. 30, No. 1, pp. 1–22.

Bacq, S. and Janssen, F. (2011) 'The multiple faces of social entrepreneurship: A review of definitional issues based on geographical and thematic criteria', *Entrepreneurship & Regional Development*, Vol. 23, Nos. 5–6, pp. 373–403.

Bacq, S., Hartog, C. and Hoogendoorn, B. (2013) 'A quantitative comparison of social and commercial entrepreneurship: Toward a more nuanced understanding of social entrepreneurship organizations in context', *Journal of Social Entrepreneurship*, Vol. 4, No. 1, pp. 40–68.

Baker, T. and Nelson, R.E. (2005) 'Creating something from nothing: Resource construction through entrepreneurial bricolage', *Administrative Science Quarterly*, Vol. 50, No. 3, pp. 329–366.

Battilana, J. and Lee, M. (2014) 'Advancing research on hybrid organizing – Insights from the study of social enterprises', *The Academy of Management Annals*, Vol. 8, No. 1, pp. 397–441.

Bellostas, A.J., López-Arceiz, F.J. and Mateos, L. (2016) 'Social value and economic value in social enterprises: Value creation model of Spanish sheltered workshops', *VOLUNTAS: International Journal of Voluntary and Nonprofit Organizations*, Vol. 27, No. 1, pp. 367–391.

Research on social entrepreneurship 93

Boschee, J. and McClurg, J. (2003) *Toward a Better Understanding of Social Entrepreneurship: Some Important Distinctions.* www.law.berkeley.edu/php-programs/courses/fileDL.php?fID=7289 (Accessed 4 October 2017)

Bosma, N., Schøtt, T., Terjesen, S.A. and Kew, P. (2016) *Global Entrepreneurship Monitor 2015 to 2016: Special Report on Social Entrepreneurship.* [online] Global Entrepreneurship Research Association, London. http://gemconsortium.org/report/49542 (Accessed 5 September 2017)

Burt, R.S. (2000) 'The Network Entrepreneur', in Swedberg, R. (Ed.), *Entrepreneurship: The Social Science View*, Oxford University Press, Oxford, pp. 281–307.

Certo, S.T. and Miller, T. (2008) 'Social entrepreneurship: Key issues and concepts', *Business Horizons*, Vol. 51, No. 4, pp. 267–271.

Chell, E., Nicolopoulou, K. and Karataş-Özkan, M. (2010) 'Social entrepreneurship and enterprise: International and innovation perspectives', *Entrepreneurship & Regional Development*, Vol. 22, No. 6, pp. 485–493.

Choi, N. and Majumdar, S. (2014) 'Social entrepreneurship as an essentially contested concept: Opening a new avenue for systematic future research', *Journal of Business Venturing*, Vol. 29, No. 3, pp. 363–376.

Conway Dato-on, M. and Kalakay, J. (2016) 'The winding road of social entrepreneurship definitions: A systematic literature review', *Social Enterprise Journal*, Vol. 12, No. 2, pp. 131–160.

Corner, P.D. and Ho, M. (2010) 'How opportunities develop in social entrepreneurship', *Entrepreneurship Theory and Practice*, Vol. 34, No. 4, pp. 635–659.

Dacin, P.A., Dacin, M.T. and Matear, M. (2010) 'Social entrepreneurship: Why we don't need a new theory and how we move forward from here', *The Academy of Management Perspectives*, Vol. 24, No. 3, pp. 37–57.

Dart, R. (2004) 'The legitimacy of social enterprise', *Nonprofit Management and Leadership*, Vol. 14, No. 4, pp. 411–424.

Dart, R., Clow, E. and Armstrong, A. (2010) 'Meaningful difficulties in the mapping of social enterprises', *Social Enterprise Journal*, Vol. 6, No. 3, pp. 186–193.

Dawson, P. and Daniel, L. (2010) 'Understanding social innovation: A provisional framework', *International Journal of Technology Management*, Vol. 51, No. 1, pp. 9–21.

Dean, T.J. and McMullen, J.S. (2007) 'Toward a theory of sustainable entrepreneurship: Reducing environmental degradation through entrepreneurial action', *Journal of Business Venturing*, Vol. 22, No. 1, pp. 50–76.

Dees, J.G. (1998) 'Enterprising nonprofits', *Harvard Business Review*, Vol. 76, No. 1, pp. 54–69.

Dees, J.G. (2001) *The Meaning of "Social Entrepreneurship".* https://centers.fuqua.duke.edu/case/wp-content/uploads/sites/7/2015/03/Article_Dees_MeaningofSocial Entrepreneurship_2001.pdf (Accessed 17 September 2015)

Defourny, J. and Nyssens, M. (2006) 'Defining social enterprise', in Nyssens, M. (Ed.), *Social Enterprise. At the Crossroads of Market, Public Policies and Civil Society*, Routledge, London, pp. 3–26.

Defourny, J. and Nyssens, M. (2008) 'Social enterprise in Europe: Recent trends and developments', *Social Enterprise Journal*, Vol. 4, No. 3, pp. 202–228.

Defourny, J. and Nyssens, M. (2010) 'Conceptions of social enterprise and social entrepreneurship in Europe and the United States: Convergences and divergences', *Journal of Social Entrepreneurship*, Vol. 1, No. 1, pp. 32–53.

Defourny, J. and Nyssens, M. (2012) *The EMES approach of social enterprise in a comparative perspective.* EMES Working Paper Series. No. 12/03. www.emes.net/site/wp-content/uploads/EMES-WP-12-03_Defourny-Nyssens.pdf (Accessed 18 March 2018)

94 Giorgi Jamburia and Jean-Marie Courrent

Defourny, J. and Nyssens, M. (2017) 'Fundamentals for an international typology of social enterprise models', *VOLUNTAS: International Journal of Voluntary and Nonprofit Organizations*, Vol. 28, No. 6, pp. 2469–2497.

Department of Trade and Industry. (2002) *Social Enterprise: A Strategy for Success.* [online]. DTI, London. http://webarchive.nationalarchives.gov.uk/20061211103745/http://www.cabinetoffice.gov.uk/third_sector/documents/social_enterprise/se_strategy_2002.pdf (Accessed 19 January 2015)

Department of Trade and Industry. (2004) *Collecting Data on Social Enterprise: A Guide to Good Practice.* [online]. DTI, Social Enterprise Unit, London. http://webarchive.nationalarchives.gov.uk/20060213231110/http://www.sbs.gov.uk/SBS_Gov_files/socialenterprise/guidanceforresearchers.pdf (Accessed 19 January 2015)

Department of Trade and Industry. (2006) *Annual Small Business Survey 2005.* [online]. DTI, London. http://webarchive.nationalarchives.gov.uk/20070108132421/http://www.sbs.gov.uk/SBS_Gov_files/researchandstats/AnnualSurveyOfSmallBus05FullReport.pdf (Accessed 19 January 2015)

Desa, G. (2010) 'Social entrepreneurship: Snapshots of a research field in emergence', in Hockerts K., Mair, J. and Robinson, J. (Eds.), *Values and Opportunities in Social Entrepreneurship*, Palgrave Macmillan, London, pp. 6–28.

Desa, G. (2012) 'Resource mobilization in international social entrepreneurship: Bricolage as a mechanism of institutional transformation', *Entrepreneurship Theory and Practice*, Vol. 36, No. 4, pp. 727–751.

Desa, G. and Basu, S. (2013) 'Optimization or bricolage? Overcoming resource constraints in global social entrepreneurship', *Strategic Entrepreneurship Journal*, Vol. 7, No. 1, pp. 26–49.

Di Domenico, M., Haugh, H. and Tracey, P. (2010) 'Social bricolage: Theorizing social value creation in social enterprises', *Entrepreneurship Theory and Practice*, Vol. 34, No. 4, pp. 681–703.

Di Zhang, D. and Swanson, L.A. (2014) 'Linking social entrepreneurship and sustainability', *Journal of Social Entrepreneurship*, Vol. 5, No. 2, pp. 175–191.

Dohrmann, S., Raith, M. and Siebold, N. (2015) 'Monetizing social value creation – A business model approach', *Entrepreneurship Research Journal*, Vol. 5, No. 2, pp. 127–154.

Dorado, S. (2006) 'Social entrepreneurial ventures: Different values so different process of creation, no?' *Journal of Developmental Entrepreneurship*, Vol. 11, No. 4, pp. 319–343.

Drayton, W. (2002) 'The citizen sector: Becoming as entrepreneurial and competitive as business', *California Management Review*, Vol. 44, No. 3, pp. 120–132.

El Ebrashi, R. (2013) 'Social entrepreneurship theory and sustainable social impact', *Social Responsibility Journal*, Vol. 9, No. 2, pp. 188–209.

Elkington, J. and Hartigan, P. (2008) *The Power of Unreasonable People: How Social Entrepreneurs Create Markets that Change the World*, Harvard Business Review Press, Boston.

Elson, P.R. and Hall, P.V. (2012) 'Canadian social enterprises: Taking stock', *Social Enterprise Journal*, Vol. 8, No. 3, pp. 216–236.

Fowler, A. (2000) 'NGDOs as a moment in history: Beyond aid to social entrepreneurship or civic innovation?' *Third World Quarterly*, Vol. 21, No. 4, pp. 637–654.

Galera, G. and Borzaga, C. (2009) 'Social enterprise: An international overview of its conceptual evolution and legal implementation', *Social Enterprise Journal*, Vol. 5, No. 3, pp. 210–228.

Gartner, W.B. (1985) 'A conceptual framework for describing the phenomenon of new venture creation', *Academy of Management Review*, Vol. 10, No. 4, pp. 696–706.

Gawell, M. (2013) 'Social entrepreneurship: Action grounded in needs, opportunities and/or perceived necessities?', *VOLUNTAS: International Journal of Voluntary and Nonprofit Organizations*, Vol. 24, No. 4, pp. 1071–1090.

Granados, M.L., Hlupic, V., Coakes, E. and Mohamed, S. (2011) 'Social enterprise and social entrepreneurship research and theory: A bibliometric analysis from 1991 to 2010', *Social Enterprise Journal*, No. 7, No. 3, pp. 198–218.

Grassl, W. (2012) 'Business models of social enterprise: A design approach to hybridity', *ACRN Journal of Entrepreneurship Perspectives*, Vol. 1, No. 1, pp. 37–60.

Guclu, A., Dees, J.G. and Battle Anderson, B. (2002) *The Process of Social Entrepreneurship: Creating Opportunities Worthy of Serious Pursuit.* https://centers.fuqua.duke.edu/case/wp-content/uploads/sites/7/2015/02/Article_Dees_TheProcessOfSocial EntrepreneurshipCreatingOppWorthyOfSeriousPursuit_2002.pdf (Accessed 4 October 2017)

Halberstadt, J. and Kraus, S. (2016) 'Social entrepreneurship: The foundation of tomorrow's commercial business models'?, *International Journal of Entrepreneurial Venturing*, Vol. 8, No. 3, pp. 261–279.

Harding, R. (2004) 'Social enterprise: The new economic engine'? *London Business School Review*, Vol. 15, No. 4, pp. 39–43.

Haugh, H. (2005) 'A research agenda for social entrepreneurship', *Social Enterprise Journal*, Vol. 1, No. 1, pp. 1–12.

Haugh, H. (2012) 'The importance of theory in social enterprise research', *Social Enterprise Journal*, Vol. 8, No. 1, pp. 7–15.

Hemingway, C.A. (2005) 'Personal values as a catalyst for corporate social entrepreneurship', *Journal of Business Ethics*, Vol. 60, No. 3, pp. 233–249.

Hill, T.L., Kothari, T.H. and Shea, M. (2010) 'Patterns of meaning in the social entrepreneurship literature: A research platform', *Journal of Social Entrepreneurship*, Vol. 1, No. 1, pp. 5–31.

Hoogendoorn, B., van der Zwan, P. and Thurik, R. (2011) *Social Entrepreneurship and Performance: The Role of Perceived Barriers and Risk.* [online] ERIM Report Series Reference No. ERS-2011-016-ORG. https://ssrn.com/abstract=1910483 (Accessed 2 October 2017)

Hossain, S., Saleh, M.A. and Drennan, J. (2017) 'A critical appraisal of the social entrepreneurship paradigm in an international setting: A proposed conceptual framework', *International Entrepreneurship and Management Journal*, Vol. 13, No. 2, pp. 347–368.

Huysentruyt, M. (2014) *Women's Social Entrepreneurship and Innovation.* [online] OECD Local Economic and Employment Development (LEED) Working Papers, No. 2014/01, OECD Publishing, Paris. doi: 10.1787/5jxzkq2sr7d4-en (Accessed 12 September 2017)

IFF. (2005) *A Survey of Social Enterprises Across the UK.* [online] Research report prepared for the Small Business Service (SBS). Available at http://webarchive.nationalarchives.gov.uk/+/http:/www.cabinetoffice.gov.uk/media/cabinetoffice/third_sector/assets/survey_social_enterprise_across_uk.pdf (Accessed 20 January 2015)

Jäger, U.P. and Schröer, A. (2014) 'Integrated organizational identity: A definition of hybrid organizations and a research agenda', *VOLUNTAS: International Journal of Voluntary and Nonprofit Organizations*, Vol. 25, No. 5, pp. 1281–1306.

Kay, A., Roy, M.J. and Donaldson, C. (2016) 'Re-imagining social enterprise', *Social Enterprise Journal*, Vol. 12, No. 2, pp. 217–234.

Kee, D.M. (2017) 'Defining social entrepreneurship: A Schumpeterian non-solution', *International Journal of Entrepreneurship and Small Business*, Vol. 31, No. 3, pp. 416–433.

Kerlin, J.A. (Ed.), (2009) *Social enterprise: A global comparison*, University Press of New England (UPNE), Lebanon, NH.

Kerlin, J.A. (2006) 'Social enterprise in the United States and Europe: Understanding and learning from the differences', *VOLUNTAS: International Journal of Voluntary and Nonprofit Organizations*, Vol. 17, No. 3, pp. 247–263.

Kerlin, J.A. (2010) 'A comparative analysis of the global emergence of social enterprise', *VOLUNTAS: International Journal of Voluntary and Nonprofit Organizations*, Vol. 21, No. 2, pp. 162–179.

Kirzner, I.M. (1973) *Competition and Entrepreneurship*, University of Chicago Press, Chicago.

Korsgaard, S. (2011) 'Opportunity formation in social entrepreneurship', *Journal of Enterprising Communities: People and Places in the Global Economy*, Vol. 5, No. 4, pp. 265–285.

Korsgaard, S. and Anderson, A.R. (2011) 'Enacting entrepreneurship as social value creation', *International Small Business Journal*, Vol. 29, No. 2, pp. 135–151.

Kraus, S., Filser, M., O'Dwyer, M. and Shaw, E. (2014) 'Social entrepreneurship: An exploratory citation analysis', *Review of Managerial Science*, Vol. 8, No. 2, pp. 275–292.

Lan, G. (2014) 'US and UK social enterprise legislation: Insights for China's social entrepreneurship movement', *International Journal of Innovation and Sustainable Development*, Vol. 8, No. 2, pp. 146–166.

Laratta, R., Nakagawa, S. and Sakurai, M. (2011) 'Japanese social enterprises: Major contemporary issues and key challenges', *Social Enterprise Journal*, Vol. 7, No. 1, pp. 50–68.

Lautermann, C. (2013) 'The ambiguities of (social) value creation: Towards an extended understanding of entrepreneurial value creation for society', *Social Enterprise Journal*, Vol. 9, No. 2, pp. 184–202.

Leadbeater, C. (1997) *The Rise of the Social Entrepreneur*, Demos, London.

Lehner, O.M. and Kansikas, J. (2012) 'Opportunity recognition in social entrepreneurship: A thematic meta analysis', *The Journal of Entrepreneurship*, Vol. 21, No. 1, pp. 25–58.

Lehner, O.M. and Kansikas, J. (2013) 'Pre-paradigmatic status of social entrepreneurship research: A systematic literature review', *Journal of Social Entrepreneurship*, Vol. 4, No. 2, pp. 198–219.

Lepoutre, J., Justo, R., Terjesen, S. and Bosma, N. (2013) 'Designing a global standardized methodology for measuring social entrepreneurship activity: The Global Entrepreneurship Monitor social entrepreneurship study', *Small Business Economics*, Vol. 40, No. 3, pp. 693–714.

Lévi-Strauss, C. (1967) *The Savage Mind*, University of Chicago Press, Chicago.

Liao, C. (2014) 'Disruptive Innovation and the Global Emergence of Hybrid Corporate Legal Structures', *European Company Law*, Vol. 11, No. 2, pp. 67–70.

Lumpkin, G.T., Moss, T.W., Gras, D.M., Kato, S. and Amezcua, A.S. (2013) 'Entrepreneurial processes in social contexts: How are they different, if at all'? *Small Business Economics*, Vol. 40, No. 3, pp. 761–783.

Lynch, K. and Walls Jr, J. (2009) *Mission, Inc.: The Practitioners Guide to Social Enterprise*, Berrett-Koehler Publishers, Oakland, CA.

Lyon, F. and Sepulveda, L. (2009) 'Mapping social enterprises: Past approaches, challenges and future directions', *Social Enterprise Journal*, Vol. 5, No. 1, pp. 83–94.

Mair, J. and Ganly, K. (2008) 'Social entrepreneurship as dynamic innovation (innovations case discussion: Freeplay energy and freeplay foundation)', *Innovations: Technology, Governance, Globalization*, Vol. 3, No. 4, pp. 79–84.

Research on social entrepreneurship 97

Mair, J. and Marti, I. (2006) 'Social entrepreneurship research: A source of explanation, prediction, and delight', *Journal of World Business*, Vol. 41, No. 1, pp. 36–44.

Mair, J. and Schoen, O. (2007) 'Successful social entrepreneurial business models in the context of developing economies: An explorative study', *International Journal of Emerging Markets*, Vol. 2, No. 1, pp. 54–68.

Mair, J. and Noboa, E. (2006) 'Social entrepreneurship: How intentions to create a social venture are formed', in Mair, J., Robinson J. and Hockerts K. (Eds.), *Social Entrepreneurship*, Palgrave Macmillan, London, pp. 121–135.

Martin, R.L. and Osberg, S. (2007) 'Social entrepreneurship: The case for definition', *Stanford Social Innovation Review*, Vol. 5, No. 2, pp. 28–39.

Michelini, L. and Fiorentino, D. (2012) 'New business models for creating shared value', *Social Responsibility Journal*, Vol. 8, No. 4, pp. 561–577.

Moran, P. and Ghoshal, S. (1999) 'Markets, firms, and the process of economic development', *Academy of Management Review*, Vol. 24, No. 3, pp. 390–412.

Moss, T.W., Short, J.C., Payne, G.T. and Lumpkin, G.T. (2011) 'Dual identities in social ventures: An exploratory study', *Entrepreneurship Theory and Practice*, Vol. 35, No. 4, pp. 805–830.

Mueller, S., Nazarkina, L., Volkmann, C. and Blank, C. (2011) 'Social entrepreneurship research as a means of transformation: A vision for the year 2028', *Journal of Social Entrepreneurship*, Vol. 2, No. 1, pp. 112–120.

Mulgan, G. (2006) 'The process of social innovation', *Innovations: Technology, Governance, Globalization*, Vol. 1, No. 2, pp. 145–162.

Nagler, J. (2007) *Is Social Entrepreneurship Important for Economic Development Policies?* www.oscrousse.org/programs/socialno/statii/Is%20SE%20important.pdf (Accessed 25 September 2015)

Neck, H., Brush, C. and Allen, E. (2009) 'The landscape of social entrepreneurship', *Business Horizons*, Vol. 52, No. 1, pp. 13–19.

Nicholls, A. (2010) 'The legitimacy of social entrepreneurship: Reflexive isomorphism in a pre-paradigmatic field', *Entrepreneurship Theory and Practice*, Vol. 34, No. 4, pp. 611–633.

Nicholls, A. (Ed.), (2008) *Social entrepreneurship: New models of sustainable social change*, Oxford University Press, Oxford.

Nicholls, A. and Cho, A.H. (2006) 'Social entrepreneurship: The structuration of a field', in Nicholls, A. (Ed.), *Social Entrepreneurship: New Models of Sustainable Social Change*, Oxford University Press, Oxford, pp. 99–118.

Ormiston, J. and Seymour, R. (2011) 'Understanding value creation in social entrepreneurship: The importance of aligning mission, strategy and impact measurement', *Journal of Social Entrepreneurship*, Vol. 2, No. 2, pp. 125–150.

Osterwalder, A. and Pigneur, Y. (2010) *Business Model Generation: A Handbook for Visionaries, Game Changers, and Challengers*, 1st ed., John Wiley & Sons, Hoboken, NJ.

Owusu, W.A. and Janssen, F. (2013) 'Social Entrepreneurship: Effectuation and Bricolage Approaches to Venture Establishment in West Africa'. Paper Presented at the *4th EMES International Research Conference on Social Enterprise*. 1–4 July 2013. Liege, Belgium.

Pacheco, D.F., Dean, T.J. and Payne, D.S. (2010) 'Escaping the green prison: Entrepreneurship and the creation of opportunities for sustainable development', *Journal of Business Venturing*, Vol. 25, No. 5, pp. 464–480.

Parrish, B.D. (2010) 'Sustainability-driven entrepreneurship: Principles of organization design', *Journal of Business Venturing*, Vol. 25, No. 5, pp. 510–523.

Peattie, K. and Morley, A. (2008) *Social Enterprises: Diversity & Dynamics, Contexts and Contributions: A Research Monograph*. [online] ESRC Centre for Business

98 *Giorgi Jamburia and Jean-Marie Courrent*

Relationships, Accountability, Sustainability and Society (BRASS), Cardiff University, Cardiff. http://orca.cf.ac.uk/30775/1/SE%20Monograph%20Published.pdf (Accessed 20 January 2015)

Peredo, A.M. and McLean, M. (2006) 'Social entrepreneurship: A critical review of the concept', *Journal of World Business*, Vol. 41, No. 1, pp. 56–65.

Pirson, M. (2012) 'Social entrepreneurs as the paragons of shared value creation? A critical perspective', *Social Enterprise Journal*, Vol. 8, No. 1, pp. 31–48.

Poon, P.S., Zhou, L. and Chan, T.S. (2009) 'Social entrepreneurship in a transitional economy: A critical assessment of rural Chinese entrepreneurial firms', *Journal of Management Development*, Vol. 28, No. 2, pp. 94–109.

Porter, M.E. (1980) *Competitive Strategy: Techniques for Analyzing Industries and Competitors*, The Free Press, New York, NY.

Porter, M.E. and Kramer, M.R. (2011) 'Creating shared value', *Harvard Business Review*, Vol. 89, Nos. 1/2, pp. 62–77.

Reinsch, R., Jones, III, R.J. and Skalberg, R. (2017) 'The Hobby Lobby decision: Legal formation for social enterprises made easier', *Social Enterprise Journal*, Vol. 13, No. 1, pp. 4–16.

Rey-Martí, A., Ribeiro-Soriano, D. and Palacios-Marqués, D. (2016) 'A bibliometric analysis of social entrepreneurship', *Journal of Business Research*, Vol. 69, No. 5, pp. 1651–1655.

Roberts, D. and Woods, C. (2005) 'Changing the world on a shoestring: The concept of social entrepreneurship', *University of Auckland Business Review*, Vol. 7, No. 1, pp. 45–51.

Robinson, J. (2006) 'Navigating Social and Institutional Barriers to Markets: How Social Entrepreneurs Identify and Evaluate Opportunities', in Mair, J., Robinson, J. and Hockerts, K. (Eds.), *Social Entrepreneurship*, Palgrave Macmillan, London, pp. 95–120.

Salim Saji, B. and Ellingstad, P. (2016) 'Social innovation model for business performance and innovation', *International Journal of Productivity and Performance Management*, Vol. 65, No. 2, pp. 256–274.

Santos, F., Pache, A.C. and Birkholz, C. (2015) 'Making hybrids work: Aligning business models and organizational design for social enterprises', *California Management Review*, Vol. 57, No. 3, pp. 36–58.

Santos, F.M. (2012) 'A positive theory of social entrepreneurship', *Journal of Business Ethics*, Vol. 111, No. 3, pp. 335–351.

Schaltegger, S. and Wagner, M. (2011) 'Sustainable entrepreneurship and sustainability innovation: Categories and interactions', *Business Strategy and the Environment*, Vol. 20, No. 4, pp. 222–237.

Scheuerle, T., Schmitz, B., Spiess-Knafl, W., Schües, R. and Richter, S. (2015) 'Mapping social entrepreneurship in Germany – A quantitative analysis', *International Journal of Social Entrepreneurship and Innovation*, Vol. 3, No. 6, pp. 484–511.

Schumpeter, J.A. (1934) *Capitalism, Socialism, and Democracy*, Harper & Row, New York, NY.

Seelos, C. and Mair, J. (2005) 'Social entrepreneurship: Creating new business models to serve the poor', *Business Horizons*, Vol. 48, No. 3, pp. 241–246.

Shepherd, D.A. and Patzelt, H. (2011) 'The new field of sustainable entrepreneurship: Studying entrepreneurial action linking "what is to be sustained" with "what is to be developed"', *Entrepreneurship Theory and Practice*, Vol. 35, No. 1, pp. 137–163.

Short, J.C., Ketchen Jr, D.J., Shook, C.L. and Ireland, R.D. (2010) 'The concept of "opportunity" in entrepreneurship research: Past accomplishments and future challenges', *Journal of Management*, Vol. 36, No. 1, pp. 40–65.

Short, J.C., Moss, T.W. and Lumpkin, G.T. (2009) 'Research in social entrepreneurship: Past contributions and future opportunities', *Strategic Entrepreneurship Journal*, Vol. 3, No. 2, pp. 161–194.

Spear, R. (2006) 'Social entrepreneurship: A different model'? *International Journal of Social Economics*, Vol. 33, Nos. 5/6, pp. 399–410.

Stevens, R., Moray, N. and Bruneel, J. (2015) 'The social and economic mission of social enterprises: Dimensions, measurement, validation, and relation', *Entrepreneurship Theory and Practice*, Vol. 39, No. 5, pp. 1051–1082.

Sullivan Mort, G., Weerawardena, J. and Carnegie, K. (2003) 'Social entrepreneurship: Towards conceptualization', *International Journal of Nonprofit and Voluntary Sector Marketing*, Vol. 8, No. 1, pp. 76–88.

Swanson, L.A. and Di Zhang, D. (2010) 'The social entrepreneurship zone', *Journal of Nonprofit & Public Sector Marketing*, Vol. 22, No. 2, pp. 71–88.

Teasdale, S. (2012) 'Negotiating tensions: How do social enterprises in the homelessness field balance social and commercial considerations?' *Housing Studies*, Vol. 27, No. 4, pp. 514–532.

Teasdale, S., Lyon, F. and Baldock, R. (2013) 'Playing with numbers: A methodological critique of the social enterprise growth myth', *Journal of Social Entrepreneurship*, Vol. 4, No. 2, pp. 113–131.

Thalhuber, J. (1998) 'The definition of social entrepreneur'. *National Centre for Social Entrepreneurs*, pp. 1–3. www.socialentrepreneurs.org/entredef.html

Thompson, J. and Doherty, B. (2006) 'The diverse world of social enterprise: A collection of social enterprise stories', *International Journal of Social Economics*, Vol. 33, Nos. 5/6, pp. 361–375.

Thompson, J.D. (1967) *Organizations in Action: Social Science Bases of Administrative Theory*, McGraw-Hill, New York, NY.

Thompson, J.L. (2002) 'The world of the social entrepreneur', *International Journal of Public Sector Management*, Vol. 15, No. 5, pp. 412–431.

Thompson, N., Kiefer, K. and York, J.G. (2011) 'Distinctions not dichotomies: Exploring social, sustainable, and environmental entrepreneurship', in Lumpkin, G.T. and Katz J.A. (Eds.), *Social and Sustainable Entrepreneurship (Advances in Entrepreneurship, Firm Emergence and Growth, Volume 13)*, Emerald Group Publishing, Bingley, pp. 201–229.

Tracey, P. and Phillips, N. (2007) 'The distinctive challenge of educating social entrepreneurs: A postscript and rejoinder to the special issue on entrepreneurship education', *Academy of Management Learning & Education*, Vol. 6, No. 2, pp. 264–271.

Trexler, J. (2008) 'Social entrepreneurship as algorithm: Is social enterprise sustainable'? *Emergence: Complexity and Organization*, Vol. 10, No. 3, [online] https://journal.emergentpublications.com/article/social-entrepreneurship-as-an-algorithm/ (Accessed 19 September 2017)

Venkataraman, S. (1997) 'The distinctive domain of entrepreneurship research', *Advances in Entrepreneurship, Firm Emergence and Growth*, Vol. 3, No. 1, pp. 119–138.

Weerawardena, J. and Sullivan Mort, G. (2006) 'Investigating social entrepreneurship: A multidimensional model', *Journal of World Business*, Vol. 41, No. 1, pp. 21–35.

Wilson, F. and Post, J.E. (2013) 'Business models for people, planet (& profits): Exploring the phenomena of social business, a market-based approach to social value creation', *Small Business Economics*, Vol. 40, No. 3, pp. 715–737.

Yitshaki, R. and Kropp, F. (2016) 'Motivations and opportunity recognition of social entrepreneurs', *Journal of Small Business Management*, Vol. 54, No. 2, pp. 546–565.

Young, D.R. and Lecy, J.D. (2014) 'Defining the universe of social enterprise: Competing metaphors', *VOLUNTAS: International Journal of Voluntary and Nonprofit Organizations*, Vol. 25, No. 5, pp. 1307–1332.

Young, R. (2006) 'For what it is worth: Social value and the future of social entrepreneurship', in Nicholls, A. (Ed.), *Social Entrepreneurship: New Models of Sustainable Social Change*, Oxford University Press, Oxford, pp. 56–73.

Yunus, M. (2011) *Building Social Business: The New Kind of Capitalism that Serves Humanity's Most Pressing Needs*, Public Affairs, New York, NY.

Zahra, S.A., Gedajlovic, E., Neubaum, D.O. and Shulman, J.M. (2009) 'A typology of social entrepreneurs: Motives, search processes and ethical challenges', *Journal of Business Venturing*, Vol. 24, No. 5, pp. 519–532.

Zahra, S.A., Rawhouser, H.N., Bhawe, N., Neubaum, D.O. and Hayton, J.C. (2008) 'Globalization of social entrepreneurship opportunities', *Strategic Entrepreneurship Journal*, Vol. 2, No. 2, pp. 117–131.

Appendix A1
ICSEM SE Models Typology according to different countries

#	Country	SE Models according to ICSEM Working Papers	Source
1	Australia	Meeting unmet consumer needs of excluded groups or locales; Advancing charitable or community purpose; Creating opportunities for community participation; Providing work integration opportunities for disadvantaged groups; Promoting ethical consumption through ethical production and supply; Strengthening the social economy; Social and environmental innovation	Barraket et al. (2016)
2	Austria	Foundations, Cooperatives, Social Enterprises and Social Entrepreneurs	Anastasiadis and Lang (2016)
3	Belgium	Entrepreneurial non-profits, Social cooperatives and Social ventures	Huybrechts et al. (2016)
4	Brazil	Service provision and community development; Support for productive activities of members; Work and primary income generation for members; Work and income complement for members; Work solidarity economy enterprises (EESs) with insufficient payment of members	Gaiger et al. (2015)
5	Cambodia	Trading non-profit organisations; Work integration social enterprises (WISEs); Non-profit cooperatives; Non-profit/for-profit partnerships; Community development enterprises	Lyne et al. (2015)
6	Canada (national)	Cooperative; Non-profit organisation; Community development/interest organisation; First Nation businesses; Business with a social mission	McMurtry et al. (2015)
7	Canada (Quebec)	Institutionalised social economy; Social economy periphery or inclusive social economy movement; Social purpose enterprises	Bouchard et al. (2015)
8	Chile	Traditional cooperatives; Non-profits (corporations, foundations, some NGOs); B Corps; Community enterprises	Giovannini and Nachar (2017)
9	Croatia	Social enterprises driven by employment ('people-driven' SEs); Social enterprises driven by financial sustainability ('income-driven' SEs); Social enterprises driven by innovative solutions ('innovation-driven' SEs)	Vidović and Baturina (2016)

(Continued)

#	Country	SE Models according to ICSEM Working Papers	Source
10	Czech Republic	Model of social enterprise from the civic sector: Association, Public benefit organisation, Institute, Foundation, Church legal person; Model of social enterprise from the cooperative sector: The cooperative; Model of social enterprise from the business sector: The limited liability company, The public company, The self-employed individual from disadvantaged social groups; Work integration social enterprise	Dohnalová et al. (2015)
11	Equador	Cooperatives; Community-based organisations; Organisations embedded in social movements; New popular economy ventures	Ruiz Rivera and Lemaître (2017)
12	Finland	Identification of social enterprise models: Institutionalised social enterprises – Work integration social enterprises; Non-institutionalised social enterprises: New cooperatives, Other organisations providing work integration, Social and welfare service organisations (owned by associations and foundations), Soci(et)al impact-oriented small businesses ('smart-ups'); New typology of Finnish social enterprises: Social enterprises providing public (welfare) services; Emerging alternative economic initiatives; Impact businesses and 'smart-ups'; Social impact redistributors	Kostilainen et al. (2016)
13	France	General interest and multiple stakeholder organisations; Entrepreneurial associations; Commercial businesses with a social purpose and social entrepreneurs	Fraisse et al. (2016)
14	Germany	Older social economy movements: The cooperative model; The welfare model; The model of foundations; The model of traditional associations Younger social economy movements: Integration enterprises; Volunteer agencies; Self-managed enterprises of alternative-, women- and eco-movements; Self-help initiatives; Socio-cultural centres; German work integration enterprises; local exchange and trading systems; Neighbourhood and community enterprises; SE; mutual insurance systems	Birkhölzer (2015)
15	Hungary	Public service provision social enterprises; Enterprising civil society organisations (CSOs); Work integration CSOs; Local development community enterprises; Social start-up enterprises; Solidarity economy initiatives	Fekete et al. (2017)
16	Indonesia	Entrepreneurial non-profit organisation (NPO); Social cooperative (SC) model; Community development enterprise (CDE) model; Social business (SB) model	Pratono et al. (2016)
17	Ireland	WISE operational model	O'Hara and O'Shaughnessy (2017)
18	Israel	Social businesses; NPOs; Cooperatives	Gidron et al. (2015)

#	Country	SE Models according to ICSEM Working Papers	Source
19	Italy	Social cooperatives; Social enterprises under the form of associations; Social enterprises under the form of foundations and religious institutions; Limited company social enterprises	Borzaga et al. (2017)
20	Japan	Health co-op model; Koseiren model	Kurimoto (2015)
		Earned-income non-profits approach; Non-profit/ cooperative approach; Social business approach	Nakagawa and Laratta (2015)
21	Mexico	Rural organisms; Organisations of workers; Cooperatives; Exclusive or majority companies of workers; Workers' savings associations; Credit unions; Community financial societies (SOFINCOs); Unregulated multiple object financial societies (SOFOMs); Social groups	Conde (2015)
22	New Zealand	Trading not-for-profits and community economic development; Social innovation through youth and technology; Māori social enterprises	Grant (2015)
23	Poland	Cooperatives; Entrepreneurial non-profit organisations; Work and social integration social enterprises	Ciepielewska-Kowalik et al. (2015)
24	Rwanda	NGOs; Cooperatives; Informal associations; Social entrepreneurs; Public/private partnerships; Companies carrying out social activities	Rwamigabo (2017)
25	South Africa	Not-for-profit models: Voluntary associations; Trusts; Non-profit companies (NPC); For-profit models: Private companies ([Pty] Ltd); Personal liability companies (Inc.) and public companies (Ltd); Close corporations (CC); Cooperatives; Sole proprietorship; Hybrid structures	Claeyé (2016)
26	South Korea	The 'self-sufficiency' metamodel; The 'SEPA' (Social Enterprise Promotion Act) metamodel; The 'social economy' metamodel	Bidet and Eum (2015)
		Work integration social enterprises; Social services provision social enterprises; Regional regeneration social enterprises; Alter-economy social enterprises	Hwang et al. (2016)
27	Spain	The traditional model mainly corresponding to WISEs; The intermediate model; The emerging model in specific areas such as culture, fair trade and sustainable development	Díaz-Foncea et al. (2017)
28	Sweden	WISEs; Non-profit social enterprises; Social purpose businesses; Societal entrepreneurship	Gawell (2015)
29	Switzerland	Actors originally described as social enterprises: WISE; Hybrid, economic social service actor; Actors referring to a specific conception of the economy: Social enterprises as SSE organisations; Social enterprises and the economy for the common good; The SE actors; Cooperatives: Consumer cooperatives; Worker cooperatives; Agricultural and producers' cooperatives; Actors at the periphery: Third sector actors with no business activity; Third sector actors with separate business activity; Small and medium enterprises with strong (family) values and local anchorage	Gonin and Gachet (2015)

(Continued)

104 Giorgi Jamburia and Jean-Marie Courrent

#	Country	SE Models according to ICSEM Working Papers	Source
30	Taiwan	Work integration or affirmative enterprises; Local community-based social enterprises; Social enterprises trading/providing social services and products; Venture capital business created for the benefits of NPO; Social cooperatives	Kuan and Wang (2015)
31	The Philipines	Social cooperatives (social coops); Social mission-driven microfinance institutions (SMD-MFIs); Fair trade organisations (FTOs); Trading development organisations (TRADOs); New generation social enterprises (New-Gen SEs)	Dacanay (2017)
32	United Arab Emirates	Publicly owned social enterprises; Privately owned social enterprises: Self-contained social enterprises; Social enterprises incubated by a company's corporate social responsibility (CSR) department; Social enterprises which are part of an international non-profit organisation but are independently licenced in the UAE	Johnsen (2016)
34	The UK	Co-operatives; Charity social enterprises; For-profit social enterprises; Community interest companies (CICs)	Spear et al. (2017)
35	Ukraine	The entrepreneur support model; The employment (work integration) model; The service subsidisation model; The fee-for-service model; The organisational support model	Bibikova (2015)
36	The USA	WISEs, Low-profit limited liability company (L3C); Benefit corporations	Cooney (2015)
37	Vietnam	Cooperatives; Social enterprises established and driven by social entrepreneurs; Social enterprises incubated by professional intermediaries; Social enterprises transformed from local NGOs	Pham et al. (2016)

Source: Author's own table.

Appendix References

Anastasiadis, M. and Lang, R. (2016) *Social Enterprise in Austria: A Contextual Approach to Understand an Ambiguous Concept*, ICSEM Working Papers, No. 26. www.iap-socent.be/sites/default/files/Austria%20-%20Anastasiadis%20%26%20Lang.pdf (Accessed 6 August 2017)

Barraket, J., Douglas, H., Eversole, R., Mason, C., McNeill, J. and Morgan, B. (2016) *Social Enterprise in Australia: Concepts and Classifications*, ICSEM Working Papers, No. 30. www.iap-socent.be/sites/default/files/Australia%20-%20Barraket%20et%20al.pdf (Accessed 6 August 2017)

Bibikova, V. (2015) *Social Enterprise in Ukraine*, ICSEM Working Papers, No. 12. www.iap-socent.be/sites/default/files/Ukraine%20-%20Bibikova.pdf (Accessed 6 August 2017)

Bidet, E. and Eum, H. (2015) *Social Enterprise in South Korea: General Presentation of the Phenomenon*, ICSEM Working Papers, No. 06. www.iap-socent.be/sites/default/files/South%20Korea%20-%20Bidet%20%26%20Eum.pdf (Accessed 6 August 2017)

Birkhölzer, K. (2015) *Social Enterprise in Germany: A Typology of Models*, ICSEM Working Papers, No. 15. www.iap-socent.be/sites/default/files/Germany%20%28part%20B%29%20-%20Birkh%C3%B6lzer.pdf (Accessed 6 August 2017)

Research on social entrepreneurship 105

Borzaga, C., Poledrini, S. and Galera, G. (2017) *Social Enterprise in Italy: Typology, Diffusion and Characteristics*, ICSEM Working Papers, No. 44. www.iap-socent.be/sites/default/files/Italy%20-%20Borzaga%20et%20al.pdf (Accessed 6 August 2017)

Bouchard, M.J., Cruz Filho, P. and Zerdani, T. (2015) *Social Enterprise in Québec: The Social Economy and the Social Enterprise Concepts*, ICSEM Working Papers, No. 23. www.iap-socent.be/sites/default/files/Canada%20%28Quebec%29%20-%20Bouchard%20et%20al.pdf (Accessed 6 August 2017)

Ciepielewska-Kowalik, A., Pieliński, B., Starnawska, M. and Szymańska, A. (2015) *Social Enterprise in Poland: Institutional and Historical Context*, ICSEM Working Papers, No. 11. www.iap-socent.be/sites/default/files/Poland%20-%20Ciepielewska-Kowalik%20et%20al.pdf (Accessed 6 August 2017)

Claeyé, F. (2016) *Social Enterprise in South Africa: A Tentative Typology*, ICSEM Working Papers, No. 38. www.iap-socent.be/sites/default/files/South%20Africa%20-%20Claeye%CC%81.pdf (Accessed 6 August 2017)

Conde, C. (2015) *Social Enterprise in Mexico: Concepts in Use in the Social Economy*, ICSEM Working Papers, No. 22. www.iap-socent.be/sites/default/files/Mexico%20-%20Conde_0.pdf (Accessed 6 August 2017)

Cooney, K. (2015) *Social Enterprise in the United States: WISEs and Other Worker-Focused Models*, ICSEM Working Papers, No. 09. www.iap-socent.be/sites/default/files/USA%20-%20Cooney.pdf (Accessed 6 August 2017)

Dacanay, M.L. (2017) *Social Enterprise in the Philippines: Social Enterprises with the Poor as Primary Stakeholders*, ICSEM Working Papers, No. 49. www.iap-socent.be/sites/default/files/The%20Philippines%20-%20Dacanay.pdf (Accessed 17 March 2018)

Díaz-Foncea, M., Marcuello, C., Marcuello, C., Solorzano, M., Navío, J., Guzmán, C., de la O Barroso, M., Rodríguez, M.J., Santos, F.J., Fisac, R., Alguacil, P., Chaves, R., Savall, T. and Villajos, E. (2017) *Social Enterprise in Spain: A Diversity of Roots and a Proposal of Models*, ICSEM Working Papers, No. 29. www.iap-socent.be/sites/default/files/Spain%20-%20Di%CC%81az-Foncea%20et%20al.pdf (Accessed 17 March 2018)

Dohnalová, M., Guri, D., Hrabětová, J., Legnerová, K. and Šlechtová, V. (2015) *Social Enterprise in the Czech Republic*, ICSEM Working Papers, No. 24. www.iap-socent.be/sites/default/files/Czech%20Republic%20-%20Dohnalova%20et%20al_0.pdf (Accessed 6 August 2017)

Fekete, É.G., Hubai, L., Kiss, J. and Mihály, M. (2017) *Social Enterprise in Hungary*, ICSEM Working Papers, No. 47. www.iap-socent.be/sites/default/files/Hungary%20-%20Fekete%20et%20al.pdf (Accessed 6 August 2017)

Fraisse, L., Gardin, L., Laville, J.-L., Petrella, F. and Richez-Battesti, N. (2016) *Social Enterprise in France: At the Crossroads of the Social Economy, Solidarity Economy and Social Entrepreneurship?*, ICSEM Working Papers, No. 34. http://iap-socent.be/sites/default/files/France%20-%20Fraisse%20et%20al_0.pdf (Accessed 6 August 2017)

Gaiger, L.I., Ferrarini, A. and Veronese, M. (2015) *Social Enterprise in Brazil: An Overview of Solidarity Economy Enterprises*, ICSEM Working Papers, No. 10. www.iap-socent.be/sites/default/files/Brazil%20-%20Gaiger%20et%20al.pdf (Accessed 6 August 2017)

Gawell, M. (2015) *Social Enterprise in Sweden: Intertextual Consensus and Hidden Paradoxes*, ICSEM Working Papers, No. 08. www.iap-socent.be/sites/default/files/Sweden%20-%20Gawell.pdf (Accessed 6 August 2017)

Gidron, B., Abbou, I., Buber-Ben David, N., Navon, A. and Greenberg, Y. (2015) *Social Enterprise in Israel: The Swinging Pendulum between Collectivism and Individualism*, ICSEM Working Papers, No. 20. www.iap-socent.be/sites/default/files/Israel%20-%20Gidron%20et%20al.pdf (Accessed 6 August 2017)

106 *Giorgi Jamburia and Jean-Marie Courrent*

Giovannini, M. and Nachar, P. (2017) *Social Enterprise in Chile: Concepts, Historical Tra-jectories, Trends and Characteristics*, ICSEM Working Papers, No. 45. www.iap-socent. be/sites/default/files/Chile%20-%20Giovannini%20%26%20Nachar.pdf (Accessed 17 March 2018)

Gonin, M. and Gachet, N. (2015) *Social Enterprise in Switzerland: An Overview of Existing Streams, Practices and Institutional Structures*, ICSEM Working Papers, No. 03. www. iap-socent.be/sites/default/files/Switzerland%20-%20Gonin%20%26%20Gachet_0.pdf (Accessed 6 August 2017)

Grant, S. (2015) *Social Enterprise in New Zealand: An Overview*, ICSEM Working Papers, No. 01. www.iap-socent.be/sites/default/files/New%20Zealand%20-%20Grant_0.pdf

Huybrechts, B., Defourny, J., Nyssens, M., Bauwens, T., Brolis, O., De Cuyper, P., Degavre, F., Hudon, M., Périlleux, A., Pongo, T., Rijpens, J. and Thys, S. (2016) *Social Enterprise in Belgium: A Diversity of Roots, Models and Fields*, ICSEM Working Papers, No. 27. www.iap-socent.be/sites/default/files/Belgium%20-%20Huybrechts%20 et%20al.pdf (Accessed 6 August 2017)

Hwang, D.S., Jang, W., Park, J.-S. and Kim, S. (2016) *Social Enterprise in South Korea*, ICSEM Working Papers, No. 35. www.iap-socent.be/sites/default/files/Belgium%20 -%20Huybrechts%20et%20al.pdf (Accessed 6 August 2017)

Johnsen, S. (2016) *Social Enterprise in the United Arab Emirates: A Concept in Context and a Typology of Emerging Models*, ICSEM Working Papers, No. 42. www.iap-socent. be/sites/default/files/UAE%20-%20Johnsen.pdf (Accessed 6 August 2017)

Kostilainen, H., Houtbeckers, E. and Pättiniemi, P. (2016) *Social Enterprise in Finland*, ICSEM Working Papers, No. 37. www.iap-socent.be/sites/default/files/Finland%20 -%20Kostilainen%20et%20al.pdf (Accessed 6 August 2017)

Kuan, Y.-Y. and Wang, S.-T. (2015) *Social Enterprise in Taiwan*, ICSEM Working Papers, No. 13. www.iap-socent.be/sites/default/files/Taiwan%20-%20Kuan%20and%20 Wang.pdf (Accessed 6 August 2017)

Kurimoto, A. (2015) *Social Enterprise in Japan: The Field of Health and Social Services*, ICSEM Working Papers, No. 07. www.iap-socent.be/sites/default/files/Japan%20 -%20Kurimoto.pdf (Accessed 6 August 2017)

Lyne, I., Khieng, S. and Ngin, C. (2015) *Social Enterprise in Cambodia: An Over-view*, ICSEM Working Papers, No. 05. www.iap-socent.be/sites/default/files/ Cambodia%20-%20Lyne%20et%20al.pdf (Accessed 6 August 2017)

McMurtry, J.J., Brouard, F., Elson, P., Hall, P., Lionais, D. and Vieta, M. (2015) *So-cial Enterprise in Canada: Context, Models and Institutions*, ICSEM Working Papers, No. 04. www.iap-socent.be/sites/default/files/Canada%20%28national%29%20 McMurtry%20et%20al.pdf (Accessed 6 August 2017)

Nakagawa, S. and Laratta, R. (2015) *Social Enterprise in Japan: Notions, Typologies, and Institutionalization Processes through Work Integration Studies*, ICSEM Working Papers, No. 17. www.iap-socent.be/sites/default/files/Japan%20-%20Nakagawa%20 %26%20Laratta.pdf (Accessed 6 August 2017)

O'Hara, P. and O'Shaughnessy, M. (2017) *Social Enterprise in Ireland: WISE, the Domi-nant Model of Irish Social Enterprise*, ICSEM Working Papers, No. 41. www.iap-socent. be/sites/default/files/Ireland%20-%20O%27Hara%20%26%20O%27Shaughnessy.pdf (Accessed 6 August 2017)

Pham, T.V., Nguyen, H.T.H. and Nguyen, L. (2016) *Social Enterprise in Vietnam*, ICSEM Working Papers, No. 31. www.iap-socent.be/sites/default/files/Vietnam%20 -%20Pham%20et%20al.pdf (Accessed 6 August 2017)

Research on social entrepreneurship   107

Pratono, A.H., Pramudija, P. and Sutanti, A. (2016) *Social Enterprise in Indonesia*: Emerging Models under Transition Government, ICSEM Working Papers, No. 36. www.iap-socent.be/sites/default/files/Indonesia%20-%20Pratono%20et%20al.pdf (Accessed 6 August 2017)

Ruiz Rivera, M.J. and Lemaître, A. (2017) *Social Enterprise in Ecuador: Institutionalization and Types of Popular and Solidarity Organizations in the Light of Political Embeddedness*, ICSEM Working Papers, No. 39. www.iap-socent.be/sites/default/files/Ecuador%20-%20Ruiz%20Rivera%20%26%20Lemai%CC%82tre.pdf (Accessed 6 August 2017)

Rwamigabo, E.R. (2017) *Social Enterprise in Rwanda: An Overview*, ICSEM Working Papers, No. 46. www.iap-socent.be/sites/default/files/Rwanda%20-%20Rwamigabo.pdf

Spear, R., Teasdale, S., Lyon, F., Hazenberg, R., Aiken, M., Bull, M. and Kopec, A. (2017) *Social Enterprise in the UK: Models and Trajectories*, ICSEM Working Papers, No. 40. www.iap-socent.be/sites/default/files/UK%20-%20Spear%20et%20al.pdf (Accessed 6 August 2017)

Vidović, D. and Baturina, D. (2016) *Social Enterprise in Croatia: Charting New Territories*, ICSEM Working Papers, No. 32. www.iap-socent.be/sites/default/files/Croatia%20-%20Vidovic%20%26%20Baturina_0.pdf (Accessed 6 August 2017)

5 Eco-entrepreneurship as a promising drive for financial performance

A literature review

Chandrika Hemanthi Wijayasinghe, Dilrukshi Krishanthi Yapa Abeywardhana, and Chandralal Thilakerathne

Introduction

There is a growing tendency for scholarly investigations related to green aspects; thus, a vital need has emerged to gather knowledge in this segment. The purpose of this paper is to present a comprehensive literature review to identify the existing gaps in the literature, theory and practice on the association of green practices and financial performance. This paper reviews literature on the green practices adopted by small and medium-sized enterprises (SMEs). Accordingly, this article has been divided into three broad segments. The first section discusses the theoretical and empirical backgrounds for evolving the green practices to the enterprise sector. Under this section, the evolution of the environmental entrepreneurship, definitions, theories, different views of the impact of green practices on financial performance, impact changes against the socio-cultural context and ways of sustainability reporting have been discussed. The second section consists of an assessment of citation and thematic analyses. This section elaborates the findings of the thematic and citation analyses carried out by the authors considering 155 research papers. The thematic analysis helps to get a better overview of different themes and categories which have been previously researched. The citation analysis facilitates to identify the most cited papers within those selected categories. The third section provides a discussion on emerging interest towards green practices and a way forward with implications of environmental entrepreneurship for future research.

The evolution of the theoretical and empirical background

The first course in entrepreneurship was offered by Harvard Business School in 1947. Peter Drucker started a course in entrepreneurship and innovation in 1953 at New York University. Early courses primarily dealt with small business management. The domain of 'Eco-entrepreneurship' had started in the early stages of 1970 by way of publishing the first article (Quinn, 1971) related to eco-entrepreneurship, released by the *Harvard Business Review*. This article emphasised that 'the ecology movement could provide profitable new markets for business expansion rather than simply being a drain on economic activity' (Quinn,

Eco-entrepreneurship: a literature review   109

1971). The 'Ecopreneurship' emerged for making money being an environmentally friendly manner (Schuyler, 1998). Ecopreneurs are entrepreneurs who create sustainable ventures. They make good money by developing eco-friendly businesses through sustainable ideas. Thus, different phrases are used to illustrate this new phenomenon. Sometimes, the terminology in this field referred to as 'green entrepreneurship' (Bennett, 1991; Berle, 1991), 'environmental entrepreneurship' (Keogh & Polonsky, 1998), 'ecopreneurship' (Schaper, 2002) and 'ethical entrepreneurship' (Taylor & Walley, 2003). The term ecopreneurship began to be widely used in the twenty-first century. Till now, a number of scholars (Schuyler, 1998; Schaper, 2002; Taylor & Walley, 2003; Kirkwood & Walkton, 2010) have provided several definitions for ecopreneurs (Table 5.1). Out of which, the most referred definition for ecopreneurs is proposed by Kirkwood and Walkton (2010).

There is no nationally accepted definition for ecopreneurs in Sri Lanka. However, there are several definitions for 'entrepreneurs' adapted by various institutions such as Department of Census and Statistics, Industrials Development Board, Department of Small Industries, Sri Lanka Export Development Board, Central Bank of Sri Lanka and lots more. Out of which, the most referred definition was proposed by the Department of Census and Statistics,

Table 5.1 Definitions of 'Ecopreneurs'

#	Author	Definitions of 'Ecopreneurs'
01	Murphy, Poist, and Braunschweig, (1995)	'Entrepreneurs who respond to environmental issues in a socially responsible manner'.
02	Anderson (1998)	'Entrepreneurs who using business tools to preserve open space, develop wildlife habitat, save endangered species and generally improve environmental quality'.
03	Schuyler (1998)	'Entrepreneurs whose business efforts are not only driven by profit, but also by a concern for the environment'.
04	Pastakia (1998)	'Individuals or institutions that attempt to popularize eco-friendly ideas and innovations either through the market or non-market routes may be referred to as ecopreneurs'.
05	Taylor and Walley (2003)	'Ecopreneurs are considered as change drivers'.
06	Cohen and Winn (2007)	'Ecopreneurs are effectively decisive change agents, enabling the world to change its path, are highly motivated in making a difference and displacing unsustainable means an important transitional role in sustainability'.
07	Kirkwood and Walkton (2010)	'Ecopreneurs are those entrepreneurs who start for-profit businesses with strong underlying green values and who sell green products or services'.
08	Schaltegger and Wagner (2011)	'Ecopreneurs are visionaries, with the ability to foresee a demand for fundamental innovations in traditional markets'.
09	Issak (2016)	'A person who seeks to transform a sector of the economy towards sustainability by starting up a business in that sector with a green design, with green processes and with a life-long commitment to sustainability'.
10	Ecopreneur. BusinessDictionary. com (2018)	'Entrepreneur who creates and sells environmentally friendly products and services including organic food, recycling efforts, or green construction'.

Source: Author's own table.

110   *Chandrika Hemanthi Wijayasinghe et al.*

The 'ecopreneur' is a subcategory of entrepreneurs and considered as a vital tool to mitigate the harmful practices to the environment. According to the literature, exploratory researches on the theme of eco-entrepreneurship have started since the beginning of the twenty-first century. Accordingly, the number of studies on green adaptation of the entrepreneurs has increased (Shaper, 2016). The consumers are willing to pay a premium amount when purchasing eco-friendly products. Accordingly, the consumer demand and purchase of environmentally friendly products have gone up; similarly, a trend for value-driven environmentalism has emerged (Bansal & Roth, 2000). The environmental entrepreneurs make money while creating the world a better place; they have a desire to improve the environment by changing the world. Similarly, several theories and models have been developed by the scholars (Huber, 2000; Murphy & Gouldson, 2000; Witt, 2002; York & Rosa, 2003; Lee, 2009) to prove the relationships among various environmental practices and economic success. According to Huber (2000), 'the environmental problems facing the world today, act as a driving force for future industrial activity and economic development'. Huber's Ecological Modernisation Theory duly provides a theoretical rationale for environmental entrepreneurship. It highlights that the entrepreneurs are the central agents to find solutions to protect the environment. Similarly, the theory illustrates that the higher concern towards environment would be a path to promote the economic benefits of a business (Murphy & Gouldson, 2000). Roberts and Colwell (2011) explain the way of 'economizing ecology' and highlight that 'ecological modernization is possible to integrate the goals of economic development, social welfare, and the environmental protection'.

The original Russian version of the Economic Development Theory was first published in 1911 under the name 'Theorie der wirtschaftlichen Entwicklung' and the first English edition was published in 1934. According to this theory, entrepreneurship is an engine for economic development which can eventually act as a driving force of 'destructive innovation' (Witt, 2002). This theory also highlights that environmental innovation could expand the monetary value of a business. Although both these theories have contributed towards increasing the theoretical strength of this area, they are not providing adequate provisions to justify whether the green practices could enhance the financial performance of a business entity. The link between green practices and financial performance has been widely debated in the literature during the first decade of the 21st century. One view is that green practices mainly causes extra costs and thus negatively affect financial performance (Gilley, Worrell, Davidson, & El–Jelly, 2000; Wagner, Van Phu, Azomahou, & Wehrmeyer, 2002). The opposite view is that green practices may improve the financial performance of a business (Melnyk, Sroufe, & Calantone, 2003; Zhu & Sarkis, 2004). Both views have not been concluded so far. It has revealed that several quantitative and qualitative studies (Gilley et al., 2000; Melnyk et al., 2003) have tested the relationship between green practices and financial performance. Annex A1 shows the different empirical studies with diverse green management practices and different financial/statistical analysis methods practiced by different scholars. The results are varied, according to the profession of the respondents and the researched context (King & Lenox, 2001; Wagner, 2005; Manaktola & Jauhari, 2007). In most of the environment-related

Eco-entrepreneurship: a literature review 111

studies, the corporate social responsibility (CSR) has been identified as a common feature (Babiak & Trendafilova, 2011; Orlitzky, Siegel, & Waldman, 2011). Traditionally, business performances were measured through 'profit' or 'loss' and the cost of the societal and environmental impact was not considered as a compulsory requirement (Kennerley & Neely, 2003). In other words, the CSR has not been considered for their cost–benefit analyses. According to Taylor and Walley (2003), there are two categories of environmental entrepreneurs, namely 'profit-/economic-oriented' entrepreneurs and 'sustainability-oriented' entrepreneurs. However, starting an entrepreneurial business is primarily dependant on business skills and technical know-how of the starter. Therefore, lack of expertise can be adversely affected to start up a business (Gartner, Carter, & Reynolds, (2010). The opportunities can be converted into sustainable entrepreneurship through strategic thinking and strategic management (Mazzarol, 2004). However, according to Gartner (2004), the entrepreneurial background can be influenced by the nature of the business. Schaltegger (2005) emphasises that an entrepreneur must make a substantial contribution to the environment. He states that a real contribution could be given only if the manufacturing process, products and services are delivered according to an environmentally friendly manner. An 'ecopreneur' is an individual who does not harm the environment. Thus, ecopreneur tries to offer eco-friendly products and services while adopting environment-friendly practices.

Ecopreneurs try to achieve business success only through environmental solutions. Schaltegger (2005), in his business continuum, specifies the relationship between the environmental-oriented business goals and market effect. The combination of these two dimensions helps to distinguish ecopreneurship from other forms of corporate environmental activities. The authors identify the related literature and the applications of the Global Reporting Initiative (GRI) Standards towards green practices. The GRI Standards (36 Nos.) were released in October 2016, for the organisations to report about their impacts on the economy, environment and society (Global Reporting Initiative Standards, 2016). The environmental dimension of GRI Standards covers the organisation's impacts on land, air, water and ecosystems (Annex A2). As more companies are now adopting GRI standards, those companies eventually lead to the Sustainable Development Goals (SDGs). The information gathered by the environmentally responsible firms on GRI standards will benefit those companies when making management decisions towards SGDs. In general, Sri Lankans are not favourable towards entrepreneurship as an occupation since the education system of the country does not encourage self-employment; thus, limited provisions are allotted for entrepreneurship (Lussier, Bandara, & Marom, 2016). Financing is the major obstacle for Sri Lankan entrepreneurs to create a new venture (Lussier et al., 2016). Entrepreneurs in Sri Lanka are triggered by self-employed capitalists. Global Entrepreneurship Monitor (2015–2016), a special report on entrepreneurial finance, highlighted that '95% of the worldwide entrepreneurs have financed their own start-ups'. Larger firms always receive multi-stakeholder pressure to become more ethical. Although the SMEs are relatively small, their accumulated impact can be very high. In most of the developed and middle-income countries, SMEs represent more than 90% of the total firms.

112 *Chandrika Hemanthi Wijayasinghe et al.*

In Sri Lanka, the entrepreneurial businesses contribute 65% of the total workforce (Hirimuthugodage, Madurawala, Senaratne, Wijesinha, & Edirisinghe, 2014) and 80% to the total firms (Lussier et al., 2016). In addition, the SME sector in Sri Lanka accounts for over 50% of the GDP; thus, considered as the backbone of the Sri Lankan economy (Fairoz, Hirobumi, & Tanaka, 2010). By understanding the importance of this domain, the Sri Lankan government has provided concessions for green initiatives and promoted enterprises to go with green (Central Environmental Authority, 2017). Having discussed this evolution and theoretical background of eco-entrepreneurship, the next section reviews citation and thematic aspects of the study.

Citation analysis and thematic analysis

In the in-depth literature review, citation analysis is important because it gives an implication to the researches to use as a guide for the continuation of the research in the same field or associated areas. Research in green practices has considerably expanded during the past decade. In order to analyse the most recent literature on green practices, the authors have performed a systematic search of the literature. Only referred journal articles have been considered for this review since they are considered as authenticated knowledge. First, the authors identified the most important areas in this field. In order to make better perspective of the applications of the green practices, this study considered scholarly contributions made from Jan 2000 to Oct 2018 containing the keywords related to 'eco-entrepreneurship' and 'green/environmental practices'. Accordingly, a total of 155 papers addressing different aspects of green practices have been analysed. All 155 abstracts were read to ensure that the paper really addresses the scope of the study. In order to assess the most recent literature, the authors performed thematic and citation analyses.

A *thematic analysis* was carried out to explore the main categories, and the subcategories fall in line with the selected theme. The top-ranked most cited papers were then identified from the selected journal articles for the *citation analysis*. Both these analyses helped identify the main variables and new associations that correlated with financial performance. During the citation analysis, 40 papers were identified as the most influential papers that go with the theme. Initially, 155 research papers that directly address the main research theme were identified. After that, they were separated into main categories and subcategories that fall in line with the selected theme through skimming. Out of which, 40 papers that truly associate with different greening and economic aspects have been selected. The selected papers were further divided according to the variables tested against financial performance. It was found that different thoughts were being empirically developed on green practices and financial performance. Having discussed the methodology, the next section elaborates the results of the thematic and citation analyses.

Thematic analysis

A total of 155 research papers published between Jan 2000 and Oct 2018 have been considered for the thematic analysis. As the authors considered only the

Eco-entrepreneurship: a literature review   113

journal articles published during the past eighteen years for these analyses, most outdated researches had not come into the count. Then, the selected papers were classified into 10 main categories and further divided in to 20 subcategories through attentive reading according to the consistency in the content (Table 5.2). If the paper was based on two or more subcategories, the most relevant theme was chosen for the review. Table 5.3 shows the distribution of selected research papers by year.

Table 5.2 Distribution of papers by subcategory

Main Themes	Main Category	Subcategories	Total Papers
Green practices (total reviewed papers – 32)	EPC – 9 Papers	Dimensions of EPC	2
		Monitoring initiatives	3
		Prevention initiatives	2
		Impact of EPC on financial performance	2
	PS – 14 Papers	Utilisation of recyclable materials for manufacturing	3
		Green packaging	3
		Green initiatives and consumer behaviour	8
	URE – 9 Papers	Renewable energy	5
		Impact of renewable energy on sustainable development	4
Financial measures of green practices (total reviewed papers – 8)	ROA – 4 Papers	Positive impact of green practices on ROA	3
		Negative impact of green practices on ROA	1
	ROE – 4 Papers	Positive impact of green practices on ROE	1
		Negative impact of Green practices on ROE	3
Moderate variables (total reviewed papers – 12)	Financial Leverage – 3 Papers	Effect of financial leverage on financial performance	3
	Sales Growth rate – 4 Papers		
	Firm Size – 5 Papers	Effect of sales growth on financial performance	4
		Effect of firm size on financial performance	5
General topics related to the review (total reviewed papers – 103)	Link between green practices and financial performance values performance (literature) – 30 Papers	Impact of green practices on economic success	30
	Theoretical insights – 14 Papers	Theories, environmental-related variables, models and frameworks	14
	Previously validated questionnaires – 4 Papers	Data collecting equipment	4
	Entrepreneurship and related topics – 55 Papers	Entrepreneurial practices, definitions, sustainability and entrepreneurial profiles	55
TOTAL			155

Source: Author's survey, 2018.

Table 5.3 Distribution of research papers by year (2000–2018)

Category (variable)	2000	2001	2002	2003	2004	2005	2006	2007	2008	2009	2010	2011	2012	2013	2014	2015	2016	2017	2018	TOTAL
Environmental pollution	2	2			2						1		1	1						09
PS			2			1	1			1		2	2	2	2			1		14
URE	1	1				1	1		1	1			1			1	1			09
ROA		1			1								2							04
ROE			1			1			2											04
Financial leverage	1														1			1		03
Sales growth						1		1										1	1	04
Firm size		1				1			1	1								1		05
Green practices and financial performance	3	1	3	1	6	2	3	3	2	2						2	1	1		30
Theoretical insights	1	1	1	1				2	2	4						1		1		14
Previously validated questionnaires	1		1							1						1				04
Entrepreneurship and related topics	1	5	2	4	4	2	1	4	3	7	4		2	3	3	3	7			55
Total	10	11	08	14	09	06	11	09	17	05	03	08	08	09	06	08	04	01		155

Source: Author's own table.

Citation analysis

The citation analysis has been done considering the journal ranking system of the Association of Business Schools' (ABS) Academic Journal Guide 2015. Accordingly, 155 journal articles have further examined and the most influential research papers were selected from each category. The citation analysis procedure eventually helps to identify the most influential papers that define the main categories of the selected research field. Accordingly, ten main categories were identified under twenty different themes. All these selected articles had published in reputed journals, which fell under the ABS Academic Journal Guide 2015 ranking number 4 to 1, as listed in Table 5.4, which presents the classification of top-ranked, most cited research papers published during the years Jan 2000–Oct 2018.

When comparing the total citations of the entrepreneurial group categories, environmental pollution control (EPC) got the highest score of 4,068. The product stewardship (PS) and utilisation of renewable energy (URE) marked the total score of 1,086 and 1,760, respectively. Figure 5.1 showcases the graphical presentation of the citation analysis.

Having discussed the thematic and citation aspects of the review, main variables related to green practices have been derived, and accordingly the next section will showcase the link between the derived variables and the GRI Standards.

The GRI Standards, released in October 2016, are designed to be used by organisations to report about their impacts on the economy, society and the environment (Global Reporting Initiative, 2016). A total of 36 GRI Standards have been released to cover the sustainability reporting. The environmental dimension of GRI Standards covers the organisation's impacts on land, air, water and eco systems (Global Reporting Initiative, 2016). According to the findings of the thematic and citation analyses and by considering the GRI standards, three main variables, namely EPC, PS and URE have been identified as the most influential variable associated with the financial performance of the SMEs (Table 5.5).

Way forward and future implication

According to scholars, eco-entrepreneurship has grown rapidly, which helps to make the world a better place (Schaper, 2002; Taylor & Walley, 2003). Today, industrialists face growing pressure by society to become environmentally responsible. Therefore, there is an emerging requirement to investigate the real impact of green practices on economic success (Melnyk et al., 2003; Zhu & Sarkis, 2004; Wagner, 2005). Scholars have done several studies (Wagner, 2005; Manaktola & Jauhari, 2007) under different socio-cultural context. Some scholars (Cohen & Winn, 2007; Kirkwood & Walkton, 2010) have emphasised that this field of ecopreneurship is still in its infancy. Therefore, the empirical studies on green practices are inadequate and the research works on eco-entrepreneurship is comparatively limited. Green practices demonstrate

Table 5.4 Classification of top ranked, most cited research papers (2000–2018)

Variable	Group Category	Paper #	Author and Year	Journal	ABS Rank 2015	Cites	Total Cites
Green practices (total reviewed papers – 15)	EPC	01	Christmann (2000)	*AMJ*	4	1,750	4,068
		02	Rao and Holt (2005)	*IJOPM*	4	1,582	
		03	Filbeck and Goman (2004)	*E&RE*	3	210	
		04	Jasch (2000)	*JCP*	4	375	
		05	Yakhou and Dorweiler (2004)	*BS&E*	2	151	
	PS	06	Lewis (2005)	*ES&P*	3	53	1,086
		07	Masilamani et al. (2017)	*JCP*	4	3	
		08	Pujari (2006)	*Technovation*	3	465	
		09	Lee and Kim (2011)	*BS&E*	2	119	
		10	Pujari, Wright, and Peattie, (2003)	*JBR*	3	446	
	URE	11	Wüstenhagen and Menichetti (2012)	*EP*	2	253	1,760
		12	Yue, Liu, and Liou, (2001).	*EP*	2	73	
		13	Tsoutsos and Stamboulis (2005)	*Technovation*	3	187	
		14	Shen, Lin, Li, & Yuan, (2010)	*EP*	2	89	
		15	Stefan and Paul (2008)	*AMP*	3	1,158	
Green practices and financial performance (total reviewed papers – 8)	ROA	16	Ameer and Othman (2012)	*JBE*	3	263	2,766
		17	Lo, Yeung, and Cheng, (2012)	*IJPE*	3	116	
		18	King and Lenox (2001)	*JIE*	2	996	
		19	González-Benito and González-Benito (2006)	*IJPR*	3	237	
	ROE	20	Wagner et al. (2002)	*CSR and EM*	1	332	
		21	Wagner (2005)	*JEM*	3	280	
		22	Nakao, Amano, Matsumura, Genba, and Nakano. (2007)	*BS&E*	3	233	
		23	Aragon-Correa and Rubio-Lopez (2007)	*LRP*	3	309	

Moderating variables (total reviewed papers – 9)	Financial leverage	24	Delmar, McKelvie, and Wennberg, (2013)	*Technovation*	3	87	2,141
		25	Miroshnychenko, Barontini, and Testa, (2017)	*JCP*	4	15	
	Sales growth	26	Montabon, Sroufe, and Narasimhan, (2007)	*JOM*	4	527	
		27	Menguc and Ozanne (2005)	*JBR*	3	361	
		28	Zeng et al. (2011)	*JCP*	4	74	
	Firm size	29	Jermias (2008)	*BER*	3	106	
		30	Sarkis and Cordeiro (2001)	*EJOR*	4	264	
		31	Ramaswami, Srivastava, and Bhargava,(2009)	*AMSR*	2	236	
		32	Yang, Hong, and Modi, (2011)	*IJPE*	3	471	
General topics related to literature (total reviewed papers – 8)	Link between green practices and financial performance	33	Molina-Azorín, Claver-Cortés, López-Gamero, Tarí, (2009)	*MD*	2	317	3,151
		34	Schaltegger and Synnestvedt (2002)	*JEM*	3	546	
	Related theories	35	Witt (2002)	*I&I*	2	156	
		36	York and Rosa (2003)	*O&E*	2	47	
		37	Geng, Mansouri, and Aktas, (2017)	*IJPE*	3	23	
		38	Liñán and Fayolle (2015)	*IE&MJ*	1	181	
	Previously validated questionnaires	39	Melnyk et al. (2003)	*JOM*	4	1,064	
		40	Turker (2009)	*JBE*	3	817	

Source: Author's survey, 2018.

ABS RANK 4 journals – *IJOP&M – International Journal of Operations and Production Management, JCP – Journal of Cleaner Production, AMJ – Academy of Management Journal, JOM – Journal of Operations Management, EJOR – European Journal of Operational Research.*

ABS RANK 3 journals – *JBR – Journal of Business Research, IJPR – International Journal of Production Research, IJPE – International Journal of Production Economics, JBE – Journal of Business Ethics, LRP – Long Range Planning, E&RE – Environmental and Resource Economics, AMP – Academy of Management Perspectives, JEM – Journal of Environmental Management, BS&E – Business Strategy and the Environment, BER – The British Accounting Review, ES&P – Environmental Science and Policy, Technovation.*

ABS RANK 2 journals – *O&E – Organization and Environment, BS&E – Business Strategy and the Environment, MD – Management Decision, JIE – Journal of Industrial Ecology, AMSR – Academy of Marketing Science Review, EP – Energy Policy, I&I – Industry and Innovation.*

ABS RANK 1 journals – *CSR&EM – Corporate Social Responsibility and Environmental Management, IE&MJ – International Entrepreneurship and Management Journal.*

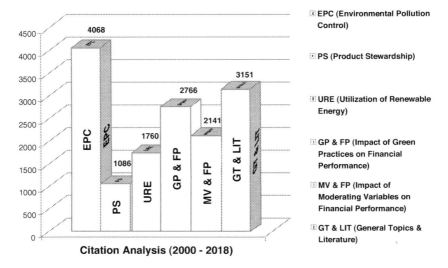

Figure 5.1 Graphical presentation of total citations.
Source: Author's own figure.

Table 5.5 The link between green variables and GRI standards

Dimension		Authors
Green Variables	*GRI Standards*	
EPC	GRI 306 (Effluents and Waste)	Christmann (2000), Jasch (2000), Filbeck and Goman (2004), Yakhou and Dorweiler (2004), Rao and Holt (2005)
PS	GRI 301 (Materials)	Jasch (2000), Pujari et al. (2003), Lewis (2005), Pujari (2006), Lee (2009), Lee and Kim (2011), Marques et al. (2014), Masilamani et al. (2017)
URE	GRI 302 (Energy)	Yue et al. (2001), Tsoutsos and Stamboulis (2005), Stefan and Paul (2008), Shen et al. (2010), Wüstenhagen and Menichetti (2012)

Source: Author's survey, 2018.

the diverse effect on financial performance in developing countries (Ali, Khan, Ahmed, & Shahzad, 2011; Suki, 2013). The interest towards green practices has increased in the past decade and more environmental practices are now being discussed under this domain. Thus, people across the world have increased awareness of green products and services. Accordingly, more and more consumers are willingly turning to eco-friendly alternatives; thus, the demand for those products has significantly increased (Forbes, Cohen, Cullen, Wratten, & Fountain 2009; Kang, Stein, Heo, & Lee, 2012; Atkinson & Kim, 2015). According to Schaper (2016), 'ecopreneurship' is a relatively under-researched field. However, in today's context, there is an emerging recognition for green entrepreneurs. Therefore, this study contributes to the further expansion of the green aspects. In addition, this paper will offer a better view of the subfields in relation to environmental practices. The scholarly findings may help the new entrepreneurs to understand the importance of the green practices and to promote newcomers to go with green. In addition, those findings would influence future researchers to conduct their studies on eco-entrepreneurship. New researches can focus on how to promote the entrepreneurs to go with green. The scholars can identify what important factors that they have to be considered when selecting ecopreneurship as a livelihood method. While understanding the importance of this theme, the Sri Lankan government now promotes new ventures to go with green (Samarasinghe, 2012).

Conclusion

The main contribution of this paper lies in the classification of the considerable amount of papers published between Jan 2000 and Oct 2018. According to the findings of the thematic and citation analyses, three main variables, namely EPC, PS and URE, have been identified as the most influential variables associated with the green aspects. The outcome of this review revealed that return on assets (ROA) and return on equity (ROE) are commonly used as a measure to ascertain the impact of the green practices on financial performance (Table 5.4 and Annex A1). On top of that, those researchers had duly applied moderate variables (firm size, sales growth and financial leverage) as proxy variables, which impact the financial performance of a firm (Table 5.4). Having identified the importance of this theme, the authors address research gaps for future consideration. Accordingly, the review addresses the gaps like survival rate of eco-entrepreneurs, barriers to eco-entrepreneurship, driving forces behind the sustainability of eco-entrepreneurial activities and so on, which may need further attention. This situation implies that further research is necessary to get the real picture of the relationships affiliated with green practices and financial performance. Hence, the findings of this paper would inspire new entrepreneurs to get the real picture of the relationships between green practices and the financial performance of an entrepreneurial business.

Annex 1

Table A1 Summary of methodologies

Author	Sample	Environmental variables	Performance variables	Main analysis	Major findings
Ameer and Othman (2012)	Top 100 sustainable global companies	Community index Diversity index Environmental index Ethical index	Sales growth, ROA, profit before taxation and cash flows	*Mann–Whitney U test*	Companies which place emphasis on sustainability practices have higher financial performance
Lo et al. (2012)	61 ISO 14000 certified fashion- and textiles-related firms	Environmental management system (EMS)	ROA, ROS	Sensitivity analysis	Environmental performance could improve firms' profitability through improving cost efficiency and sales performance
Nakao et al. (2007)	Environmentally friendly corporations in Japan	Environmental performance	ROA and ROE proxy variables: Tobins 'q – I' and earnings per share	Multiple linear regression analysis with pooled cross-section and time series	Firm's environmental performance has a positive impact on its financial performance
Aragon-Correa and Rubio-Lopez (2007)	Multinational companies and a sample of 140 food factories in France and the UK	Proactive environmental strategies	Total organic carbon/ sales Total organic carbon/ employees	Time series cross-sectional data analysis techniques Regression analysis Case analyses Simultaneous equation framework Event study methodology	Lack of relationship between total organic carbon certification and superior environmental performance

Author (Year)	Sample	Variables		Method	Findings
Gonzalez-Benito and Gonzalez-Benito (2006)	Four hundred and twenty-eight companies, 156 of which were in the chemical sector, 211 in the electronic and electric equipment sector and 61 in the furniture sector	The environmental pressure of the stakeholders and the managerial environmental awareness	Supply Purchasing Transportation Warehousing and distribution Reverse logistics and waste management	Regression analysis	The effect of the management's values influenced by the perception of environmental pressure of the stakeholders
Wagner (2005)	Firms from four European countries (Germany, Italy, the Netherlands and the UK) in the pulp and paper manufacturing center	Corporate environmental strategies – The SO_2 emissions, NOX emissions, COD emissions, total energy input and total water input	ROS, ROCE, ROE, debt-to-equity ratio, asset Turnover ratio	Regression analysis	The firms with pollution prevention-oriented corporate environmental strategies and the relationship between environmental and economic performance are more positive
Watson, Klingenberg, Polito, & Geurts, (2004)	Ten pairs of firms which represent EMS adopter	EMS	Price to earnings ratio (P/E ratio), market to book ratio (M/B ratio), return on invested capital (ROIC), ROA, profit margin, operating margin and beta	Wilcoxon signed-rank test	Implementation of an environmental management strategy does not negatively impacton firm's financial performance
King and Lenox (2001)	Six hundred and fifty-two US manufacturing firms	Total emissions (relative emissions and industry emissions)	Tobin's q (calculate Tobin's q by dividing the sum of firm equity value, book value of long-term debt and net current liabilities by the book value of total assets)	Least squares regression analysis	Total emissions are associated with superior financial performance

Source: Researcher's construction, 2018.

Annex 2

Table A2 Reporting Principles and GRI Standards

Universal GRI Standards	*Topic-Specific GRI Standards*		
	GRI 200 Economic	*GRI 300 Environmental*	*GRI 400 Social*
GRI 101 Foundation	GRI 201 Economic Performance	**GRI 301 Materials**	GRI 401 Employment
GRI 102 General Disclosures	GRI 202 Market Presence	**GRI 302 Energy**	GRI 402 Labour/ Management Relations
GRI 103 Management Approach	GRI 203 Indirect Economic Impacts	GRI 303 Water	GRI 403 Occupational Health and Safety
	GRI 204 Procurement Practices	GRI 304 Biodiversity	GRI 404 Training and Education
	GRI 205 Anti-Corruption	GRI 305 Emissions	GRI 405 Diversity and Equal Opportunity
	GRI 206 Anti-Competitive behaviour	**GRI 306 Effluents and Waste**	GRI 406 Non-Discrimination GRI 400
		GRI 307 Environmental Compliance	GRI 407 Freedom of Association and Collective Bargaining
		GRI 308 Supplier Environmental Assessment	GRI 408 Child Labour
			GRI 409 Forced or Compulsory Labour
			GRI 410 Security Practices
			GRI 411 Rights of Indigenous People
			GRI 412 Human Rights Assessment
			GRI 413 Local Communities
			GRI 414 Supplier Social Assessment
			GRI 415 Public Policy
			GRI 416 Customer Health Safety
			GRI 417 Marketing and Labelling
			GRI 418 Customer Privacy
			GRI 419 Socio-Economic Compliance

Source: Global Reporting Initiative Standards, 2016.

References

Ali, A., Khan, A. A., Ahmed, I., & Shahzad, W. (2011). Determinants of Pakistani consumers' green purchase behavior: Some insights from a developing country. *International Journal of Business and Social Science, 2*(3), 217–226.

Ameer, R., & Othman, R. (2012). Sustainability practices and corporate financial performance: A study based on the top global corporations. *Journal of Business Ethics, 108*(1), 61–79. doi: 10.1007/s10551-011-1063-y

Anderson, A. R. (1998). Cultivating the garden of Eden: Environmental entrepreneuring. *Journal of Organizational Change Management, 11*(2), 135–144.

Aragon-Correa, J. A., & Rubio-Lopez, E. A. (2007). Proactive corporate environmental strategies: Myths and misunderstandings. *Long Range Planning, 40*, 357–381. doi: 10.1016/j.lrp.2007.02.008

Atkinson, L., & Kim, Y. (2015). "I drink it anyway and I know I shouldn't": Understanding green consumers' positive evaluations of norm-violating non-green products and misleading green advertising. *Environmental Communication, 9*(1), 37–57. doi: 10.1080/17524032.2014.932817

Babiak, K., & Trendafilova, S. (2011). CSR and environmental responsibility: Motives and pressures to adopt green management practices. *Corporate Social Responsibility and Environmental Management, 18*(1), 11–24. doi: 10.5465/1556363

Bansal, P., & Roth, K. (2000). Why companies go green: A model of ecological responsiveness. *Academy of Management Journal, 43*(4), 717–736.

Bennett, S. J. (1991). *Ecopreneuring: 'The Complete Guide to Small Business Opportunities From the Environmental Revolution'*, Wiley, New York.

Berle, G. (1991). *The Green Entrepreneur: Business Opportunities that Can Save the Earth and Make You Money*, Liberty Hall Press, Blue Ridge Summit, PA.

Central Environmental Authority (CEA); Official website, (2017, May 3), Retrieved from www.cea.lk

Christmann, P. (2000). Effects of "best practices" of environmental management on cost advantage: The role of complementary assets. *Academy of Management Journal, 43*(4), 663–680.

Cohen, B., & Winn, M. I. (2007). Market imperfections, opportunity and sustainable entrepreneurship. *Journal of Business Venturing, 22*, 29–49. doi: 10.1016/j.jbusvent.2004.12.001

Delmar, F., McKelvie, A., & Wennberg, K. (2013). Untangling the relationships among growth, profitability and survival in new firms. *Technovation, 33*(8–9), 276–291. doi: org/10.1016/j.technovation.2013.02.003

Ecopreneur. BusinessDictionary.com. (2018). Retrieved July 26 from www.business dictionary.com/definition/ecopreneur.html

Fairoz, F. M., Hirobumi, T., & Tanaka, Y. (2010). Entrepreneurial orientation and business performance of small and medium scale enterprises of Hambantota District Sri Lanka. *Asian Social Science, 6*(3), 34.

Filbeck, G., & Gorman, R. F. (2004). The relationship between the environmental and financial performance of public utilities. *Environmental and Resource Economics, 29*(2), 137–157.

Forbes, S. L., Cohen, D. A., Cullen, R., Wratten, S. D., & Fountain, J. (2009). Consumer attitudes regarding environmentally sustainable wine: An exploratory study of the New Zealand marketplace. *Journal of Cleaner Production, 17*(13), 1195–1199.

124 *Chandrika Hemanthi Wijayasinghe et al.*

Gartner, W. B. (2004). Achieving 'Critical Mess' in entrepreneurship scholarship'. In: Katz, J. A. and Shepherd D. (eds.) *Advances in Entrepreneurship, Firm Emergence, and Growth* (pp. 199–216), JAI Press, Greenwich, CT. doi: 10.1016/S1074-7540(04)07008-4

Gartner, W. B., Carter, N. M., & Reynolds, P. D. (2010). Entrepreneurial behaviour: Firm organizing processes. In Z. J. Acs and D. B. Audretsch (eds) *Handbook of Entrepreneurship Research* (pp. 99–127), Springer, New York. doi:10.1007/978-1-4419-1191-9

Geng, R., Mansouri, S. A., & Aktas, E. (2017). The relationship between green supply chain management and performance: A meta-analysis of empirical evidences in Asian emerging economies. *International Journal of Production Economics, 183*, 245–258. doi: 10.1016/j.ijpe.2016.10.008

Gilley, K. M., Worrell, D. L., Davidson III, W. N., & El-Jelly, A. (2000). Corporate environmental initiatives and anticipated firm performance: The differential effects of process-driven versus product-driven greening initiatives. *Journal of Management, 26*(6), 1199–1216.

Global Entrepreneurship Monitor. (2015–2016) (p.05), Retrieved May 3, 2017 from www.babson.edu/Academics/centers/blank-center/global-research/gem/Documents/GEM%202015-2016%20Finance%20Report.pdf

Global Reporting Initiative (GRI). (2016). G4 Sustainability Reporting Guidelines: Reporting Principles and Standard Disclosures, Global Reporting Initiative, Amsterdam, (October 22, 2017). Retrieved from www.globalreporting.org/standards/gri-standards-download-center/

Gonza'lez-Benito, J., & Gonza'lez-Benito, O. (2006). Environmental proactivity and business performance: An empirical analysis. *Omega, 33*(1), 1–15.

Hirimuthugodage, D., Madurawala, S., Senaratne, A., Wijesinha, A., & Edirisinghe, C. (2014). *Female Entrepreneurship and the Role of Business Development Services in Promoting Small and Medium Women Entrepreneurship in Sri Lanka*, Institute of Policy Studies of Sri Lanka and Oxfam International, Sri Lanka.

Huber, J. (2000). Towards industrial ecology: Sustainable development as a concept of ecological modernization. *Journal of Environmental Policy and Planning, 2*(4), 269–285.

Isaak, R. (2016). The making of the ecopreneur. In Schaper, M. (ed) *Making Ecopreneurs* (pp. 63–78). Routledge, London.

Jasch, C. (2000). Environmental performance evaluation and indicators. *Journal of Cleaner Production, 8*(1), 79–88. PII: S0959-6526(99)00235-8

Jermias, J. (2008). The relative influence of competitive intensity and business strategy on the relationship between financial leverage and performance. *The British Accounting Review, 40*(1), 71–86. doi: 10.1016/j.bar.2007.11.001

Kang, K. H., Stein, L., Heo, C. Y., & Lee, S. (2012). Consumers' willingness to pay for green initiatives of the hotel industry. *International Journal of Hospitality Management, 31*(2), 564–572. doi: 10.1016/j.ijhm.2011.08.001

Kennerley, M., & Neely, A. (2003). Measuring performance in a changing environment. *International Journal of Operations & Production Management, 23*(2), 213–229. doi: 10.1108/01443570310458465

Keogh, P. D., & Polonsky, M. J. (1998). Environmental commitment: A basis for environmental entrepreneurship? *Journal of Organizational Change Management, 11*(1), 38–49.

King, A. A., & Lenox, M. J. (2001). Does it really pay to be green? An empirical study of firm environmental and financial performance. *Journal of Industrial Ecology, 5*(1), 105–116.

Eco-entrepreneurship: a literature review   125

Kirkwood, J., & Walton, S. (2010). What motivates ecopreneurs to start businesses? *International Journal of Entrepreneurial Behavior & Research, 16*(3), 204–228. doi: 10.1108/13552551011042799

Lee, K. H. (2009). Why and how to adopt green management into business organizations? The case study of Korean SMEs in manufacturing industry. *Management Decision, 47*(7), 1101–1121. doi: 10.1108/00251740910978322

Lee, K. H., & Kim, J. W. (2011). Integrating suppliers into green product innovation development: An empirical case study in the semiconductor industry. *Business Strategy and the Environment, 20*(8), 527–538. doi: 10.1002/bse.714

Lewis, H. (2005). Defining product stewardship and sustainability in the Australian packaging industry. *Environmental Science & Policy, 8*(1), 45–55. doi: 10.1016/j.envsci.2004.09.002

Liñán, F., & Fayolle, A. (2015). A systematic literature review on entrepreneurial intentions: Citation, thematic analyses, and research agenda. *International Entrepreneurship and Management Journal, 11*(4), 907–933.

Lo, C. K., Yeung, A. C., & Cheng, T. C. E. (2012). The impact of environmental management systems on financial performance in fashion and textiles industries. *International Journal of Production Economics, 135*(2), 561–567. doi: 10.1016/j.ijpe.2011.05.010

Lussier, R. N., Bandara, C., & Marom, S. (2016). Entrepreneurship success factors: An empirical investigation in Sri Lanka. *World Journal of Entrepreneurship, Management and Sustainable Development, 12*(2), 102–112. doi: 10.1108/WJEMSD-10-2015-0047

Manaktola, K., & Jauhari, V. (2007). Exploring consumer attitude and behaviour towards green practices in the lodging industry in India. *International Journal of Contemporary Hospitality Management, 19*(5), 364–377. doi: 10.1108/09596110710757534

Marques, R. C., da Cruz, N. F., Simões, P., Ferreira, S. F., Pereira, M. C., & De Jaeger, S. (2014). Economic viability of packaging waste recycling systems: A comparison between Belgium and Portugal. *Resources, Conservation and Recycling, 85*, 22–33. doi: 10.1016/j.resconrec.2013.12.015

Masilamani, D., Srinivasan, V., Ramachandran, R. K., Gopinath, A., Madhan, B., & Saravanan, P. (2017). Sustainable packaging materials from tannery trimming solid waste: A new paradigm in wealth from waste approaches. *Journal of Cleaner Production, 164*, 885–891. doi: 110.1016/j.jclepro.2017.06.200

Mazzarol, T. (2004). Strategic management of small firm: A proposed framework for entrepreneurial venture. 17th Annual SEAANZ Conference, 26–29 September 2004, Brisbane Queensland, Australia.

Melnyk, S. A., Sroufe, R. P., & Calantone, R. (2003). Assessing the impact of environmental management systems on corporate and environmental performance. *Journal of Operations Management, 21*(3), 329–351. PII: S0272-6963(02)00109-2

Menguc, B., & Ozanne, L. K. (2005). Challenges of the "green imperative": A natural resource-based approach to the environmental orientation–business performance relationship. *Journal of Business Research, 58*(4), 430–438. doi: 10.1016/j.jbusres.2003.09.002

Miroshnychenko, I., Barontini, R., & Testa, F. (2017). Green practices and financial performance: A global outlook. *Journal of Cleaner Production, 147*, 340–351. doi: 10.1016/j.jclepro.2017.01.058

Molina-Azorín, J. F., Claver-Cortés, E., López-Gamero, M. D., & Tarí, J. J. (2009). Green management and financial performance: A literature review. *Management Decision, 47*(7), 1080–1100. doi: 10.1108/00251740910978313

126 Chandrika Hemanthi Wijayasinghe et al.

Montabon, F., Sroufe, R., & Narasimhan, R. (2007). An examination of corporate reporting, environmental management practices and firm performance. *Journal of Operations Management, 25*(5), 998–1014. doi: 10.1016/j.jom.2006.10.003

Murphy, J., & Gouldson, A. (2000). Environmental policy and industrial innovation: Integrating environment and economy through ecological modernisation. *Geoforum, 31*(1), 33–44. PII: S 0 0 1 6-7 1 8 5 (9 9) 0 0 042-

Murphy, P. R., Poist, R. F., & Braunschweig, C. D. (1995). Role and relevance of logistics to corporate environmentalism: An empirical assessment. *International Journal of Physical Distribution & Logistics Management, 25*(2), 5–19. doi: 10.1108/096000 39510083916

Nakao, Y., Amano, A., Matsumura, K., Genba, K., & Nakano, M. (2007). Relationship between environmental performance and financial performance: An empirical analysis of Japanese corporations. *Business Strategy and the Environment, 16*(2), 106–118. doi: 10.1002/bse.476

Orlitzky, M., Siegel, D. S., & Waldman, D. A. (2011). Strategic corporate social responsibility and environmental sustainability. *Business & Society, 50*(1), 6–27.

Pastakia, A. (1998). Grassroots ecopreneurs: Change agents for a sustainable society. *Journal of Organizational Change Management, 11*(2), 157–173. doi: 10.1108/ 09534819810212142

Pujari, D. (2006). Eco-innovation and new product development: Understanding the influences on market performance. *Technovation, 26*(1), 76–85. doi: 10.1016/j. technovation.2004.07.00

Pujari, D., Wright, G., & Peattie, K. (2003). Green and competitive: Influences on environmental new product development performance. *Journal of Business Research, 56*(8), 657–671. doi: 10.1016/S0148-2963(01)00310-1

Quinn, J. (1971). Next big industry: Environmental improvement. *Harvard Business Review, 49*(5), September–October, 120–131.

Ramaswami, S. N., Srivastava, R. K., & Bhargava, M. (2009). Market-based capabilities and financial performance of firms: Insights into marketing's contribution to firm value. *Journal of the Academy of Marketing Science, 37*(2), 97. doi: 10.1007/ s11747-008-0120-2

Rao, P., & Holt, D. (2005). Do green supply chains lead to competitiveness and economic performance? *International Journal of Operations & Production Management, 25*(9), 898–916. doi: 10.1108/01443570510613956

Roberts, P., & Colwell, A. (2001). Moving the environment to centre stage: A new approach to planning and development at European and regional levels. *Local Environment, 6*(4), 421–437. doi: 10.1080/13549830120091716

Samarasinghe, R. (2012). The influence of cultural values and environmental attitudes on green consumer behaviour. *International Journal of Behavioral Science (IJBS), 7*(1). ISSN: 1906-4675

Sarkis, J., & Cordeiro, J. J. (2001). An empirical evaluation of environmental efficiencies and firm performance: Pollution prevention versus end-of-pipe practice. *European Journal of Operational Research, 135*(1), 102–113. PII: S0377-2217(00)00306-4

Schaltegger, S. (2005). A framework and typology of ecopreneurship: Leading bioneers and environmental managers to ecopreneurship. *Making Ecopreneurs: Developing Sustainable Entrepreneurship*, 43–60.

Schaltegger, S., & Synnestvedt, T. (2002). The link between 'green' and economic success: Environmental management as the crucial trigger between environmental and economic performance. *Journal of Environmental Management, 65*(4), 339–346. doi: 10.1006/jema 2002.0555

Eco-entrepreneurship: a literature review 127

Schaltegger, S., & Wagner, M. (2011). Sustainable entrepreneurship and sustainability innovation: Categories and interactions. *Business Strategy and the Environment, 20*(4), 222–237. doi: 10.1002/bse.68

Schaper, M. (2002). The essence of ecopreneurship. *Greener Management International, 38*, Summer, 26–30.

Schaper, M. (Ed.). (2016). *Making Ecopreneurs: Developing Sustainable Entrepreneurship* (2nd ed., p. 342). eBook, CRC Press, Routledge, London. doi: 10.4324/9781315593302

Schuyler, G. (1998). Merging Economic and Environmental Concerns through Ecopreneurship. Digest Number 98-8.

Shen, Y. C., Lin, G. T., Li, K. P., & Yuan, B. J. (2010). An assessment of exploiting renewable energy sources with concerns of policy and technology. *Energy Policy, 38*(8), 4604–4616. doi: 10.1016/j.enpol.2010.04.016

Stefan, A., & Paul, L. (2008). Does it pay to be green? A systematic overview. *The Academy of Management Perspectives, 22*(4), 45–62.

Suki, N. M. (2013). Green Awareness effects on consumers purchasing decision: Some insights from Malaysia. (Penerbit USM), *International Journal of Asia-Pacific Studies, 9*(2), 49–62.

Taylor, D. W., & Walley, E. E. (2003). The green entrepreneur: Visionary, maverick or opportunist? Retrieved from http://e-space.mmu.ac.uk/1465/

Tsoutsos, T. D., & Stamboulis, Y. A. (2005). The sustainable diffusion of renewable energy technologies as an example of an innovation-focused policy. *Technovation, 25*(7), 753–761. doi: 10.1016/j.technovation.2003.12.003

Turker, D. (2009). Measuring corporate social responsibility: A scale development study. *Journal of Business Ethics, 85*(4), 411–427. doi: 10.1007/s10551-008-9780-6

Wagner, M. (2005). How to reconcile environmental and economic performance to improve corporate sustainability: Corporate environmental strategies in the European paper industry. *Journal of Environmental Management, 76*(2), 105–118. doi: 10.1016/j.jenvman.2004.11.021

Wagner, M., Van Phu, N., Azomahou, T., & Wehrmeyer, W. (2002). The relationship between the environmental and economic performance of firms: An empirical analysis of the European paper industry. *Corporate Social Responsibility and Environmental Management, 9*(3), 133–146. doi: 10.1002/csr.22

Watson, K., Klingenberg, B., Polito, T., & Geurts, T. (2004). Impact of environmental management system implementation on financial performance. *Management of Environmental Quality, 15*(6), 622–628. doi: 10.1108/14777830410560700

Witt, U. (2002). How evolutionary is Schumpeter's theory of economic development? *Industry and Innovation, 9*(1–2), 7–22. doi: 10.1080/13662710220123590

Wüstenhagen, R., & Menichetti, E. (2012). Strategic choices for renewable energy investment: Conceptual framework and opportunities for further research. *Energy Policy, 40*, 1–10. doi: 10.1016/j.enpol.2011.06.050

Yakhou, M., & Dorweiler, V. P. (2004). Environmental accounting: An essential component of business strategy. *Business Strategy and the Environment, 13*(2), 65–77. doi: 10.1002/bse.395

Yang, M. G. M., Hong, P., & Modi, S. B. (2011). Impact of lean manufacturing and environmental management on business performance: An empirical study of manufacturing firms. *International Journal of Production Economics, 129*(2), 251–261. doi: 10.1016/j.ijpe.2010.10.017

York, R., & Rosa, E. A. (2003). Key challenges to ecological modernization theory: Institutional efficacy, case study evidence, units of analysis, and the pace of eco-efficiency. *Organization & Environment, 16*(3), 273–288. doi: 10.1177/1086026603256299

128 Chandrika Hemanthi Wijayasinghe et al.

Yue, C. D., Liu, C. M., & Liou, E. M. (2001). A transition toward a sustainable energy future: Feasibility assessment and development strategies of wind power in Taiwan. *Energy Policy, 29*(12), 951–963. PII: S0 301-4 215(0 1)00025-8

Zeng, S., Meng, R., Zeng, R. C., Tam, C. M., Tam, V. W. Y., & Jin, T. (2011). How environmental management driving forces affect environmental and economic performance of SMEs: A study in the Northern China district. *Journal of Cleaner Production, 19*(13), 1426–1437. doi: 10.1016/j.jclepro.2011.05.002

Zhu, Q., & Sarkis, J. (2004). Relationships between operational practices and performance among early adopters of green supply chain management practices in Chinese manufacturing enterprises. *Journal of Operations Management, 22*(3), 265–289. doi: 10.1016/j.jom.2004.01.00

6 Female empowerment through social entrepreneurship in Indonesia

A conceptual framework

Prameshwara Anggahegari, Gatot Yudoko, Bambang Rudito and Melia Famiola

Introduction

According to Danone Ecosysteme, around 70% of the poor people in the world are female. This number also aligns with the number acquired from Indonesia's statistics bureau. Of around 250 million people that are listed as Indonesian citizens, around 6% of the 125 million of productive age in the labour force are listed as unemployed, and almost 12% are listed as people who live in poverty. However, in the lowest income bracket are households headed by female. These female have become household heads due to several reasons: death of their spouses; divorce; polygamous husbands; migrated husbands; permanently ill husbands; and unemployed husbands, among others. According to the Community-Based Welfare Monitoring System Survey (*Sistem Pemantauan Kesejahteraan Berbasis Komunitas* [SPKBK]), there are more than 50% families in the lowest welfare level headed by female.

Moreover, according to the data taken from the National Economics Census Data (SUSENAS) in 2007, the number of female household heads in Indonesia is steadily increasing. It shows that female between eighteen and eighteen years old head one in every four households; they have one to six dependents per family (www.pekka.or.id/index.php/id/, 2017). This problem is one of the topics that most researchers will raise along with poverty alleviation, as these female are seen as trying to break the social stereotyping and limitations that burden them. In addition to the economic problems, and before the waves of the feminist movement were introduced, female live in conditions where they are oppressed by male dominance. They have limited rights – neither voice nor prospect.

These phenomena are happening in other patriarchal countries, where female are subjugated. Marriage Law No. 1/1974, for example, explicitly mentions husbands or men as the recognised heads of households, and this is reflected in the entire social, economic and political systems. These huge numbers, taken from the Statistics Bureau, are using the household unit as their variable in counting, for example, counting governments aids such as those receiving Conditional Cash Transfers (*Program Keluarga Harapan*). Therefore, there is a possibility

130 *Prameshwara Anggahegari et al.*

that the number of these female household heads is actually higher, since female are still seen as the 'hidden number'. As a consequence, female are not recognised as household heads, leading to discrimination in their social and political lives. As a result, these circumstances have led to appalling issues, as female become enlightened by the fact that they have the skills, knowledge and the motivation to earn an income. Moreover, economic hardship is one of the many problems they need to face every day; for female to earn a decent income by working outside their homes in standard working hours is still considered difficult. They are also constricted by conditions such as having several children or the need to take care of sick family members, as well as illiteracy, which hinders them from getting decent work in a factory or an office. Therefore, there are several proposals that we will discuss in this chapter, with data taken from observations and indepth interviews as well as from research of six female social enterprises owners.

Problem formulation

1 Stereotyping and dependency has taken root in every single aspect of our lives. It is also barred by cultural limitations where female are not encouraged to develop themselves.
2 Natural tendencies in female are in motivating and nurturing others; thus they are quite fit to perform social entrepreneurial activities. On one hand, it may help develop themselves and on the other, they may help empowering others.
3 Social entrepreneurship to create sustainability in a social platform has not been applied appropriately, as it should be to empower people, especially female. Thus, the management of social enterprise is facing a lot of difficulties in order to be scaled-up or even survive.

Research questions

Based on the previously mentioned conditions, we formulate several related research questions:

RQ 1: What kind of support and barriers did the female social entrepreneurs encounter?
RQ 2: Why are female considered fit in performing social entrepreneurship?
RQ 3: How is the organisation of their social enterprises?

Literature review

Gender pressure and patriarchy

There are many researches regarding gender and entrepreneurship focusing on the distinctive sex of the entrepreneurs such as their personality traits, demographic background, motivations, educational and occupational experiences

Empowerment through social entrepreneurship 131

(Brush, 1992; Fagenson, 1993; Buttner and Moore, 1997), business characteristics, strategies, problems, management styles and networking behaviours. However, gender differences in socialisation may result in female lacking the attitudes of risk taking and internal locus of control that are deemed important to the success of small businesses. The 'invisibility' of the female contributes towards and reinforces a dominant discourse of entrepreneurship, usually described as individualistic, gender-biased and discriminatory. These points have been seen as major drawbacks that the culture embeds in a patriarchal country such as Indonesia.

Entrepreneur: push or pull

There are two types of female entrepreneurs: the first is an entrepreneur by passion and the second an entrepreneur by conditions. Most businesspeople in the first category already have aspirations to become entrepreneurs, which may be influenced by demographic, role model, culture counterpart and economic characteristics that form individual preferences, whereas entrepreneurs by condition are businesspeople who have no background (family/social/cultural/educational/class) that led them on the entrepreneurial path; they are forced into entrepreneurship because they have no other options.

The conditions that forced them became reasons why they choose this path to perform in a company. Other reasons are that it may be difficult for them to work outside their homes due to reasons mentioned earlier (Goffee and Scase, 1985; Chaganti, 1986; Scott, 1986; Cromie and Hayes, 1988; Holmquist and Sundin, 1988; Kaplan, 1989; Brush, 1990; Parasuraman and Simmers, 2001; DeMartino and Barbato, 2003; Collins-Dodd et al., 2004; Hughes, 2006). Other studies demonstrate that family-related factors at the household level, such as motherhood and spousal self-employment as well as family-oriented initiatives at the state level such as childcare and maternity leave policies, impact the likelihood that female will pursue self-employment, already explored by notable researchers.

Buttner and Moore (1997) also supported these findings that differentiate between traditional and modern female entrepreneurs. A comparative study of sexes shows that usually it is a woman who becomes an entrepreneur after she has completed her family obligations (Sarri and Trihopoulou, 1997). These findings are also related with the 'push' and 'pull' factors that may be appropriate in explaining the motivation of female entrepreneurs (Hisrich and Brush, 1985; Buttner and Moore, 1997; Brush, 1999) in creating a business. The 'pull' factors refer to the need for independence, achievement, personal development, seeking challenge, self-fulfilment and social status, all of which may be quite important for business. In contrast, limited advancement opportunities, job frustration, boredom or avoiding undesirable working conditions (Hisrich and Brush, 1985) are considered 'push' factors. Based on those researches, many literatures agreed to a postulation that female are more 'pushed' rather than 'pulled' in becoming an entrepreneur.

132   *Prameshwara Anggahegari et al.*

Social entrepreneurship as one of the viable option

It has been more than thirty years since studies on female entrepreneurship transpired in many literatures (Schwartz, 1976; DeCarlo and Lyons, 1979; Hisrich and O'Brien, 1981; Sexton and Kent, 1981; Pellegrino and Reece, 1982). Entrepreneurship is one of the few options that most female choose in order to earn an income and also look after their families. The problems that female face have already grabbed the attention of scholars to contribute to the social and economic problems in our surroundings. One suggestion is how we may be able to help them be economically independent, since this is one of the surging problems today.

A resource-pulling on the talent and potential of female is quite vital in entrepreneurship since they can be expected to make changes. Female have certain characteristics, such as having a high need for achievement, willingness to take risks, tolerance for ambiguity, creative intuition, flexibility, high need for autonomy, self-confidence, internal locus of control, adaptability, dominance, low need for conformity, commitment, proactivity and sense of observation, even though in some literatures they are considered to be less risk-taking and avoid uncertainty. Besides, female entrepreneurs are considered to be more supportive, socially and emotionally, in nurturing relationships rather than advancing their careers compared with men.

Another research in small enterprises by GEM (2013) indicates that female are most likely to engage in social and environmental activity compared with men. Nevertheless, many female spend most of their time in developing other activities and involve their kin in their networks; they also tend to be more trusting, since it is crucial in maintaining networks. However, both men and female are motivated by equal economical needs, even though self-fulfilment, job satisfaction and achievement are primary reasons for becoming self-employed (Schwartz, 1976; Hisrich and O'Brien, 1981; Buttner and Moore, 1997).

In relation with female as the main originator of their acts of social entrepreneurship, they not only try to gain as many benefits as possible, they also try to captivate the local wisdom values and virtues of their surroundings in order to enrich themselves socially as well as generate profit for their well-being. So, their social enterprises are mostly based on social action problems. Therefore, female are 'fit' enough to be considered as change makers, even though there are only a small number of scholars who discuss how female are able to empower others (Kabeer, 2001; Malhotra and Schuler, 2005) in their acts of social entrepreneurship by the sharing process (Hutchings and Michailova, 2004).

Research by Eagly and Carli (2003) shows that a woman has the tendency to empower others and to be more collaborative. According to McKinsey's report in 2009, female leadership styles are people-based. They implement a more

Empowerment through social entrepreneurship 133

participative style, where their subordinates are also included in decision-making processes (Eagly and Johnson, 1990). They also provide intellectual stimulations for their employees, not only helping with their personal development in correlation with their career path, but also with the character building that correlates more with ethics. This can be done through mentoring, workshops or any other empowerment programmes.

Research method

This research used both deductive and inductive reasoning by using the mixed-method data collection. On the one hand, this research uses deductive reasoning since it is also based on critical literature review in order to find the gaps and propose some other framework to fill in those gaps, and on the other, due to the recent phenomenon of social entrepreneurship, it is considered as grounded research since it focuses on interactions with the community where we blended in, thus creating a bottom-up perception. This type of research is needed, since qualitative approach is one of the perfect options to capture a glimpse regarding research on female.

However, it is also based on literatures in order to ground it based on formal theories and framework. Nevertheless, this research is using the mixed-method data based on interpretive paradigm, which is underpinned by observation and interpretation; thus, to observe is to collect information about events, while to interpret is to make meaning of that information by drawing inferences or by judging the match between information and abstract patterns. Thus, the methods that we used have taken us a few steps further. In order to capture the phenomenon and categorise it into a more fitting context-based story, we did literature studies and several in-depth interviews as well as observation on six social enterprise initiators. This is a theoretical sampling (Yin, 2015) based on the understanding that this research aims to indulge deeper perspectives based on theoretical ideas in order to answers questions raised from the analysis. These six female social entrepreneurs were chosen based on the various types of empowerment that they have already with a minimum of five years of empowerment. This observation and in-depth interviews are a part of the longitudinal study that we have embarked on since 2014. After conducting field observation as well as several in-depth interviews, we did some validating through several secondary data and triangulations. We also tried to create concepts based on unstructured interviews, observations and writing field notes or memos as well as gaining data from available documents (Wolcott, 1990; Alvermann et al., 1996) as part of the data formulation process.

After these data were gathered, we categorised and coded different types of actions based on it. Figure 6.1 shows the process in which these data were collected and coded. The second stages involved initial coding in which we tried comparing data based on the initial codes; there are 257 labelled codes,

43 tentative categories and 27 categories. There are merging and clarification of data in this process, since it is a rough data that should be formulated. The third stage is axial coding, wherein data are put together to connect categories during the analytical processes, which resulted in 85 generated concepts and 13 tentative categories. The next few procedures involved selective coding by using a set of core codes that was already determined beforehand and did theoretical sampling and theoretical codes to see the correlation of each theory. At this stage, researchers crosschecked the first gathered evidences, memos and documents.

By using a qualitative view, this research tried to generate a grounded research of social entrepreneurship by using several case studies and observations, since the knowledge regarding female's leadership as a part of basic humanity and instincts is already there. Therefore, the next step is to formulate the management of the social enterprises based on the gathered data. The result of this process has five dimensions: self-drives, contentment, learning process, unavoidable predictors, and continuity.

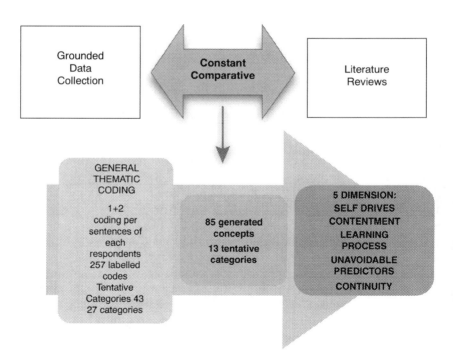

Figure 6.1 The process of data collection and dimensions of female social entrepreneur in Indonesia.
Source: Author's own figure.

Results and discussion

Based on the field observations and in-depth interviews as well as focus group discussions, there are several major points which emerged from the inductive process. There are some notable fragments from the in-depth interviews and focus group discussions that we will highlight in this part. Findings and discussion in the research questions can also be seen from the proposition.

RQ 1: What kind of support and barriers have these female social entrepreneurs encountered?

The following dimensions are being presented by each construct. The first dimension is self-drive, in which these female social entrepreneurs usually have their own motivation in doing the entrepreneurial activities, either external or internal motivations. The external motivations comprises of sets of problems or phenomenon that are daily encountered by them, which somehow triggers the awareness of the unfortunate conditions that most people combat every day, including poverty and social conditions.

> I live in a city near Bandung, and I always observe that every weekends there are small children and teenagers wearing punk outfit. I saw where they live, it's a slum area and they hitch into some pickup and went to the city. I think they will do mischievous things. So I kept thinking what can we contribute for them? How can we help them? We have obligation to help them.
>
> When I first met them, I feel that this (my acts) will be quite impactful. We are females, we are on the same age, and the place where they live is not very far from Bandung, which is a big city. But I compare options that I have with them. I can graduate and get job offers, my friends can continue pursue her master degree or open businesses. We have got plenty of options. Apparently options that they had, were that much.
>
> There are plenty former inmates that I have met. This is, for me, the main problem. Government and private company won't help and give them jobs. Who knows that they already learned from their mistakes and will not do the same criminality? Or, even, they were only trapped in those conditions but it is not their wrongdoings? But no one would give them second-chances. Not many cares.

These fragments are several motivations based on the external conditions; however, there are some other forces which urge these female to conduct social entrepreneurship. This is also related to the second research question, which shows the correlation between the self-drives with the reasons of context-based fit.

RQ 2: Why are female considered to be fit in performing social entrepreneurship?

In relation with the next research question, the following are the fragments that correlated with the internal motivation:

> If we help people, Allah will help us. By helping others, I believe that we will get both margin, in this world and in the afterlife.

136   *Prameshwara Anggahegari et al.*

In front of Allah, the one that will be respected is the pious. Good suggestion will lead to good acts, and I believe we will be awarded for it.

These fragments show that some values these female believed in had a direct impact towards their motivation and urges towards their acts. The first two lists of fragments show the basic ground on why they did these things. The following fragments show the unavoidable predictors that these female encounter in the process of the initiation of social enterprises:

I am a widow with 3 children, when I first came into this community, they are sceptical and pretentious. They are afraid of my motivation in helping them. I faced rejection, but I continue doing it, because I know that my intention is good.

We have had rejection from the parents of the children that we wanted to help. They said that they don't need it, but we give them understanding and encouragement. After several hard work, they finally came into their mind that it (education) is important.

They (the people and neighbours) said did not want my help. But I saw them being lazy and did not do a thing to help their own selves and their family. At first I pitied them and help them by provided them with their basic needs. But they kept coming asking for more money and nothing changes. I gave them loans because they said they wanted to open some business, but nothing happens. They did not pay back the loans and they have no business whatsoever. Apparently they used the money to paid the loan sharks, gambles, and drink alcohols. I was furious. But I will not stop; I know that people can change. I just need to find another way.

From these statements, we find the correlation of what these females are facing during the initiation of the social enterprises to help the empowerment processes. They are motivated by both internal and external motivation as self-drives in continuing their actions. The next fragments show that these female social entrepreneurs were content with their acts. This feeling, fortunately, is correlated deeply with the desires to help others as well:

There is in this hadith, if you have problems then go help the orphans. It's just that simple. I am grateful of doing this (empowerment)… Because I know that knowledge sharing will be rewarded by goodness.

When I saw that they (the empowered) feeling happy and able to get back on their own feet, I feel glad. I cannot describes this feeling, but seeing smiles on their faces makes me wanted to do more.

In relation with the last research questions, the next two lists of fragments show the tendency of female social entrepreneurs to self-develop and develop others through the organisation of their social enterprises.

RQ 3: What is the organisation of social enterprises?

Empowerment through social entrepreneurship 137

Following are several fragments regarding their enterprises management and funding related with the social enterprises learning process that align with the needs to empower the employees and the volunteers as well:

> Maybe this is one of my weaknesses, but I don't want to ask for donations. We can still use our own resources, even though I did not close the opportunity for other people to do good by giving donations. But I want it to be more professional as well. This is also part of learning for my friends (the one that help to run the activities). Giving is better than receiving.
>
> So we don't have to necessarily accept everything, but we may be able to utilize things that we currently have. Based on that we can be more independent.
>
> At first, we got help from several institutions, not only in terms of money but also training and coaching. But in the end, we try to struggle and educate others to use the resources that we have. Thank God we survive and able to expand our business.

The last dimensions gathered from the grounded research are the continuity of social enterprises. These fragments show that the continuity of the social enterprises and the empowerment process relies heavily on the sustainability of the activities later on:

> We actually wanted to help them one time only. I mean, we did not want them to be dependent on us. So, we also give them the understanding that they also need to be able to stand on their own. It is hard, yes we know, but it is possible. We try to make them aware of the condition that they need to strive more, for their own sake.
>
> This business model were also replicated somewhere else, we did the same thing on some other areas. However, we observe and ask them first, what do they truly need. So we really hit the core of the problems.

Even though the number of entrepreneurs and social entrepreneurs is still considered less than expected, the growth is prospective and relatively high. With the support from all the stakeholders, the number of entrepreneurs is hoped to be increasing in the near future. There are many proposed activities that the government will articulate, for example, the revision for microcredit financing, online registration to update the number of businesses in Indonesia and the strengthening of the laws for business are among the top list of their plan, not to mention non-governmental and not-for-profit organisations that also have the same proposals in luring new entrepreneurs. These plans, too, are one of the strategies to lure new entrepreneurs in general and female entrepreneurs in particular. However, there are better options to empower them through social entrepreneurship.

Based on these findings, we may see that these dimensions were found relevant with the conditions of female social entrepreneurs today. Most of the entrepreneurs that we met during the data collection were not fully aware that they are classified as social entrepreneurs, even though during the past five years some have already understood the concept. According to several in-depth interviews and observations, there are several things that become the main starting points on why a female initiator creates social enterprises.

Some are moved due to the social and economical problems around them and some by their own conditions, which then led them to the need to empower others. This also aligned with the literatures of the push and pull factors. However, some are able to capture the social and economic phenomenon around them and create an enterprise as a catalyst for changes. Based on the coding result, following is the model from which the female social entrepreneurship may be comprehended (Figure 6.2).

Based on this concept, female social entrepreneurs were facing both support and barriers in initiating their social enterprises. This can be seen from the result from the finding that shows the transcripts of the in-depth interviews and observations. However, both these factors apparently give these female social entrepreneurs higher motivations in developing themselves as well as empowering others. Meanwhile, they are also content by conducting these acts in which shows that by feeling content, they are willing to spend more time and energy in not only developing themselves, but also others' as well. The contentment and the learning process matters a great deal in shaping the female social entrepreneurs.

Therefore, it is important that they feel content since it directly influences the learning process and the entire system in which they become leaders. However, this paper also provides the novelty and recommendation of three types of social entrepreneurs that are emerging from the inductive process. The first is continuity that motivates female woman in doing more for her surroundings. However, this type of empowerment is still on the first phase of impact; thus, their characteristics are still dependent on the social entrepreneur. The second shows that the empowered are already self-reliant. They are not fully

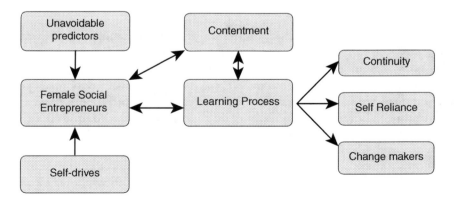

Figure 6.2 Conceptual framework on female empowerment through social entrepreneurship.
Source: Author's own figure.

Empowerment through social entrepreneurship   139

dependent and have already created innovations, at the very least in helping themselves.

However, the third types are those who are change makers. They are doing some learning process in which they may feel content as well as the need to continue their activities, as it has become one of the enablers on the needs to become social entrepreneurs based on the needs to develop themselves and to capture problems within their surroundings as well as from the urges that come from their beliefs. By using the feminine management style, which tends to be more assertive, these female initiators decided to create a business which is not only profit-oriented, but also based on social investments. They are already considered to be self-reliant and also grow with the sense of empowerment towards others, either by replicating the business model of their patron or even develop and tailor their own business model.

Based on this conceptual framework explanation, there are several propositions that are related with the empowerment processes.

Proposition 1: The barriers and support that are felt the female social entrepreneurs are coming from both the internal motivations as well as from their surroundings

Proposition 2: Female are driven by their emotional closeness with those who are being empowered as part of the contentment

Proposition 3: Female social entrepreneurs tend to use the knowledge sharing process as one of the initial learning process for their organisations and cadres.

Based on these findings and conceptual framework, it can be seen that there are more types of empowerment that emerge from the fields. The first one remains on the continuity of the activities, the second one is the self-reliance activities and the third one is when these female become one of the change makers.

Research contribution and further directions

Based on this research, the problems within social economics surely can be handled by tapping resources from female empowerment. One of the main aims is to create the awareness to shift the paradigm that they need to be always given help or assistance. The first proposal is quite aligned with the second proposal, since after they initiate their own enterprise, they can also help empowering other female; based on the findings, they have the motivation to help other people due to the nature as a woman.

Further research is required in order to help female to self-actualise by empowering themselves in building their own economy by being independent as well as finding contentment from both self-development and empowering others. This area should be larger in order to capture this phenomenon into a more generalised setting. More studies should be directed towards the micro, messo, and macro level of analysis in which we might be able to give a deeper analysis

140   *Prameshwara Anggahegari et al.*

towards the female social entrepreneurship as a movement. The practical implications of this research are the suggestion to create a social replication platform, in which female social entrepreneurs will be actively engaged in creating a sustainable reproduction of their concept of social entrepreneurship thoroughly. However, this is part of a larger setting that will involve every related stakeholder, for example, the government, civil society organisations, educational institutions and lots more. By creating a great ecosystem, we believe that these movements will also help the encouragement of social entrepreneurial movement in a larger basis.

Nevertheless, the limitations of this study are on the scope of research boundaries and time limitations. Therefore, we encourage further research that can capture broader scope in the area of observation and probably can be deepened into a more quantitative study to give insights on how many social enterprises are initiated by female and what kind of contribution and scope of impacts that they have covered.

References

Alvermann, D. E., O'Brien, D. G., & Dillon, D. R. (1996). Conversations on writing qualitative.

Brush, C. G. (1992). Research on women business owners: Past trends, a new perspective and future directions. *Small Business: Critical Perspectives on Business and Management,* 1038–1070.

Brush, C. G. (2002). A gendered perspective on organizational creation. *Entrepreneurship Theory and Practice,* 16, 5–30.

Buttner, E. H., & Moore, D. P. (1997). Women's organizational exodus to entrepreneurship: Self-reported motivations and correlates with success. *Journal of Small Business Management,* 35(1), 34.

Chaganti, R. (1986). Management in women-owned enterprises. *Journal of Small Business Management,* 24, 18.

Collins-Dodd, C., Gordon, I. M., & Smart, C. (2004). Further evidence on the role of gender in financial performance. *Journal of Small Business Management,* 42(4), 395–417.

Cromie, S., & Hayes, J. (1988). Towards a typology of female entrepreneurs. *The Sociological Review,* 36(1), 87–113.

DeCarlo, J. F., & Lyons, P. R. (August 1979). A comparison of selected personal characteristics of minority and non-minority female entrepreneurs. In *Academy of Management Proceedings* (Vol. 1979, No. 1, pp. 369–373). Academy of Management.

DeMartino, R., & Barbato, R. (2003). Differences between women and men MBA entrepreneurs: Exploring family flexibility and wealth creation as career motivators. *Journal of Business Venturing,* 18(6), 815–832.

Eagly, A. H., & Carli, L. L. (2003). The female leadership advantage: An evaluation of the evidence. *The leadership quarterly,* 14(6), 807–834.

Eagly, A. H., & Johnson, B. T. (1990). Gender and leadership style: A meta-analysis. *Psychological Bulletin,* 108(2), 233.

Fagenson, E. A. (1993). Personal value systems of men and women entrepreneurs versus managers. *Journal of Business Venturing,* 8(5), 409–430.

Empowerment through social entrepreneurship 141

Goffee, R., & Scase, R. (1985). *Women in charge: The experiences of female entrepreneurs.* Allen & Unwin.

Hisrich, R. D., & Brush, C. G. (1985). Women and minority entrepreneurs. In *Frontiers of Entrepreneurship Research* (pp. 566–587), Eds. J. A. Hornaday, B. A. Kirchhoff, O. J. Krashner & KH Vesper Babson College, Wellesley, Maine.

Hisrich, R. D., & O'Brien, M. (1981). The woman entrepreneur from a business and sociological perspective. *Frontiers of Entrepreneurship Research, 21,* 19–23.

Holmquist, C., & Sundin, E. (1988). *Women as entrepreneurs in Sweden: Conclusions from a survey, frontiers of entrepreneurship research.* Wellesley: Babson College.

Hughes, K. D. (2006). Exploring motivation and success among Canadian women entrepreneurs. *Journal of Small Business & Entrepreneurship, 19*(2), 107–120.

Hutchings, K., & Michailova, S. (2004). Facilitating knowledge sharing in Russian and Chinese subsidiaries: The role of personal networks and group membership. *Journal of Knowledge Management, 8*(2), 84–94.

Kaplan, S. (1989). The effects of management buyouts on operating performance and value. *Journal of Financial Economics, 24*(2), 217–254.

Parasuraman, S., & Simmers, C. A. (2001). Type of employment, work–family conflict and well-being: A comparative study. *Journal of Organizational Behavior, 22*(5), 551–568.

Pellegrino, E. T., & Reece, B. L. (1982). Perceived formative and operational problems encountered by female entrepreneurs in retail and service firms. *Journal of Small Business Management, 20*(2), 15–24.

Sarri, K., & Trihopoulou, A. (2005). Female entrepreneurs' personal characteristics and motivation: A review of the Greek situation. *Women in Management Review, 20*(1), 24–36.

Schwartz, E. B. (1976). Entrepreneurship: A new female frontier. *Journal of Contemporary Business, 5*(1), 47–76.

Scott, C. (1986). Why more women are becoming entrepreneurs. *Journal of Small Business Management, 24*(4), 37–44.

Sexton, D. L., & Kent, C. A. (1981). Female executives and entrepreneurs: A preliminary comparison. *Frontiers of Entrepreneurship Research,* 40–55.

Wolcott, H. F. (1990). Making a study "more ethnographic". *Journal of Contemporary Ethnography, 19*(1), 44–72.

Yin, R. K. (2015). *Qualitative research from start to finish.* Guilford Publications.

7 Competences in social business

An analysis of the narratives about the experiences of a group of social entrepreneurs in the State of Alagoas

Ibsen Mateus Bittencourt

Introduction

This study takes place in the context of strengthening the discussion about the entrepreneurial culture in Brazil and in the world. However, the focus of interest lies in a particular type of entrepreneurship, the social one, which has also been gaining strength and focus in recent years (Oliveira, 2004; Bose, 2013; Bittencourt et al., 2016) as a business setting that seeks innovative solutions to social and environmental problems while pursuing profitable goals. The development of competencies of the entrepreneurs to work in organisations with this characteristic is the driving theme of the present investigation.

The concern to promote a discussion about social entrepreneurship under the lens of competency studies is justified for a few reasons. First, when defining goals and purposes that are not part of the *core business* of the corporate world, these companies require a different set of business as well as incorporating qualitative indicators that act beyond the mathematical-financial result (Parrish, 2010), which demands new skills from its leaders. And this is not a concern about knowing if it is important to develop another set of skills besides the traditional ones, but how we can develop better competencies (Ruth, 2006) in a context of social and environmental challenges in which the corporate world is being called upon to produce answers.

But, above all, not only is the subject still lacking studies and researches yet, but there also is a predominance of a rather rationalist view in the works already published, which, despite all its contribution to the field, leaves open subjective aspects of the competence process that need to be seized and analysed. This is because of how little is known about social business skills that have been developed by social entrepreneurs and what nature of meanings and actions has been unleashed by those who run these businesses. The interpretative look for competences, whose basis is phenomenological, places attention on the human experience, lived, felt, perceived, signified, created and continually recreated at work (Sandberg, 2000). Therefore, it is understood that competence attributes – knowledge, skills and attitudes – are mobilised by the subjects in the experience in accordance with their conceptions about what the work means for them. And especially, it is concerned

Competences in social business 143

with understanding the process of how people become 'comes to be' competent, as they experience and put meaning into their work.

Thus, it was understood that analysing the development of competence, the 'coming to be', from the trajectories of entrepreneurs who have been achieving publicly recognised results would contribute to a better understanding of this phenomenon. Then, the main question of the research is formulated: *Considering the experiences of a group of social entrepreneurs, what can be learned about the process of developing their competencies that allowed the achievement of social impact and financial sustainability?*

The objective was to describe and analyse the trajectory of a group of social entrepreneurs in the State of Alagoas, in order to understand through the narratives of the partners-owners the elements underlying the process of becoming social entrepreneurs. The intention was to discuss the development of skills for social business of a group of social entrepreneurs living in the State of Alagoas, which has 20.5% of its population, approximately 700,000 people, living with an income of R\$ 70.00 per capita per month. This represents less than R\$ 2.50 per day.

Although Brazil has been presenting positive numbers in recent years, Alagoas has one of the worst life expectancies rates in addition to having a low education level expectancy. It presents the highest rate of illiterate and functional illiterates, with a ratio of approximately 63% of the population aged fifteen years or older. It has the highest infant mortality rate and the lowest HDI in the country. However, many social businesses have emerged in recent years, with the goal of solving social problems not fully addressed by governments. This movement has been presenting results at the national and international level of companies that have received awards and professional and financial recognition. Therefore, we analysed the experiences of a group of social entrepreneurs in the State of Alagoas, whose companies are recognised for their work in the areas in which they operate.

Social business in the world: a look at international literature

Faced with a new type of business model, there is a need to conceptualise and understand the model better, given the diversity of nomenclatures defined by social businesses. With this goal, the different theoretical perspectives for social business in the literature are approached. According to Comini and colleagues (2012), three different perspectives define social business: European, North American and emerging countries. According to Young (2009), the initial motivation for creating social enterprises in Europe was to offer services that belonged to the public sector but at a much lower cost, thereby generating employment opportunities for the unemployed and marginalised population. With this scenario, social enterprises have their business activities well defined, but also engage in social issues. Thus, the European perspective arises from the tradition of social economy, with associations and cooperatives, emphasising the role of civil society organisations with public functions.

144 *Ibsen Mateus Bittencourt*

Social business in the North American perspective emerged with actions that involved income generation in civil society organisations from several different parties such as corporations, NGOs, governments, consumers and investors (Young, 2009). This movement caused the NGOs to begin expanding their commercial activities, thus resulting in social enterprise. Kerlin (2006) defines social enterprises as dual-purpose companies that fit profit targets with social (hybrid) objectives or non-profit organisations committed to developing commercial activities that support the execution of their mission (organisations with social ends).

From the perspective of the developing countries, the concept of social business is seen under two different views: the Latin American one, which uses the term inclusive businesses, and the Asian view of Yunus (2010), which uses the term social business. Fischer and Comini (2012) and Teodosio and Comini (2012) emphasise that social businesses are market initiatives aimed at reducing poverty, transforming the social conditions of marginalised or excluded individuals.

For Yunus (2010), there are two types of social business: type 1, composed of companies whose focus is on creating social benefits and not maximising profits for their owners, and type 2, social businesses, whose objective is to maximise profits for their owners in a state of poverty, which means associative forms and cooperatives of companies that contribute to their members getting together to leave this condition.

In Brazil, the most commonly used term is 'social business'; however, some organisations and academics still use the term 'inclusive business' or 'business that generates social impact'.

Both Teodosio and Comini (2012) cut and differentiate the two terms, considering inclusive businesses as a subcategory of social business, because inclusive businesses are only concerned with including people and giving access to products and services that enable improvement in quality of life, while social businesses develop models that enable people to emerge from extreme poverty, developing all the capacities of people or communities to create new businesses that generate social impact.

For this study, we use the social business perspective of emerging countries by Fischer and Comini (2012) and Teodosio and Comini (2012) in the Latin American perspective, with the business principle of emphasising market initiatives aimed at reducing poverty, transforming the social conditions of marginalised or excluded individuals.

Competences in the interpretative view: coming to be competence

In this research, the interpretative paradigm is used, supported by the model of Sandberg (1991). The concept of competence discussed in the interpretative perspective takes into account the experience, context and meaning attributed to the work rather than considering competencies only as a set of generic attributes such as knowledge, skills and attitudes.

Competences in social business 145

The interpretative paradigm uses the principle in which social reality does not exist in concrete terms, but as a product of people's intersubjective experiences. This means that people are the ones who construct and symbolically define reality.

From this perspective, the subject's experience and understanding of his work environment is more important to his competence than his personal attributes (Sandberg, 2000). Thus, it is emphasised that for competency studies, it is necessary to mainly understand the subjects' understanding and describe the meaning that people attribute to their work. If competence is the result of the meaning we build with our work, its development must be understood based on organisational practices, analysis of experiences and intersubjective experiences. More specifically, the development of skills involves the refinement or change in the structure and meaning of work practices (Sandberg and Dall'Alba, 2006). Thus, in this research, the competences of social entrepreneurs are associated with their understanding or the way they see and experience social business and refine and/or break old thinking and acting patterns.

The discussion of social business skills in literature

The literature on social business skills does not address directly and explicitly the relation between competencies in social business, only referring to the term competencies and/or social business alone. Therefore, it has performed a systematic review in the literature to identify possible theoretical gaps using the two constructs and their synonyms.

Part of the identified social skills competency studies, more than anything else, deal with the subject from the perspective of developing competencies in higher education. In what concerns now, the studies of competences in social businesses identified in the literature that do not focus on the universe of education try specifically to present models and point some tendencies in social business.

Pless and Maak (2008) discuss the concept of business in society competence. They address the qualities that leaders must present in order to act responsibly and effectively. In the same direction, Nga and Shamuganathan (2010) take into account that personality traits such as affability, frankness, understanding, generosity and awareness generally have a positive influence on the actions of social entrepreneurs.

As for Orhei and colleagues (2012), they list the skills that a social entrepreneur needs to develop. They treat competence as a set of social attributes.

Moreau and Mertens (2013) developed a model based on seven competences for the context of social enterprises in Europe based on knowledge, know-how and attitudes. Knowledge is understood as the ability to manage a social business, being the result of the assimilation of information through learning; know-how as the skills to apply the knowledge and be able to complete the activities; and attitudes, the ability to behave appropriately in the organisation and interpersonal relationships.

Methodological procedures

This study is delineated under the interpretative paradigm, assuming, forcibly, a qualitative and descriptive character. For Gephart (1999), the interpretive paradigm presupposes that reality is intersubjective and socially constructed, and the researcher has the task of searching for patterns of meanings, describing and analysing them. Its purpose is to understand the subject's worldview, examining how reality is produced, reproduced and modified. It is about understanding the interactions of individuals with each other and with the environment in which they live (Merriam, 2002). What is under analysis is the social experience of the subject and how it was constructed from the sense that individuals give to the world, how subjects attribute meaning to a given phenomenon and which experiences were lived (Merriam, 2002).

Coherent with the interpretative look at competences that seek senses and meanings that lead to competent action in the process of becoming entrepreneurial, the strategy of narrative studies is chosen as a research proposal. Narrative interviews were the main strategy of data construction, followed by documentary analysis. In order to analyse the collected data, we chose the thematic analysis of narrative proposed by Riessman (2008), because the intention was to preserve the sequential and structural characteristics of the narratives.

It was defined as the object of study of this research the experience of 13 founding partners of four social businesses in the State of Alagoas: MeuTutor, Hand Talk, Osório Cardoso Clinic and Association of Friends and Parents of Special People (AAPPE):.

i   These are not initiatives of corporative social responsibility;
ii   the main goal of the company must be of socio-environmental nature and its main activity must seek this goal;
iii businesses with a purely environmental goal will not be eligible;
iv   it must have at least one year of formal operation;
v   people of low income or in situations of social vulnerability must be part of the value chain or be client of it;
vi   at least 50% of the company's revenue must come from the sale of producer/ services;
vii must have the prospect of operating indeterminately without the need for donations.

Description and analysis of narratives

Four stories are told from the narrative of the partners and founders. Two of them refer to technology-based companies and the other two to companies that provide medical services. The construction of the competences of these companies will be described and analysed separately, because the nature of the enterprises (IT and Health) and their trajectories explain the success of the initiatives in a different way. There are five central elements that are revealed in

Competences in social business 147

the narratives built by the owners, telling the story of the construction of their enterprise and how they developed skills that led them to recognition.

Analysis of the narratives of technologically based companies

In Figure 7.1, we have the flow of the central elements of analysis that follows a sequence using the experiences of the entrepreneurs as its basis.

We comprehend here the competence not from management logic, but from a pragmatic, measurable and quantifiable management model that will play a role of evaluation, monitoring and decision-making in the context of people management. The competence being analysed here is the capacity of coming to be, the process of becoming competent by giving meaning to the work and triggering actions in this direction.

Direct contact with the problems of social reality

The idea of the company and its materialisation in social entrepreneurial action begins with the direct contact of the entrepreneurs with the problematic social reality. Here is revealed the importance of direct and meaningful living with the social problems. The problems emerge as an annoyance and lead them to think about how they could improve their social reality.

For the entrepreneurs of MeuTutor, some of the annoyances started during the training process. Ig Ibert and Seiji Isotani failed to conform when they came across the biggest IT event in education in the world, and the two were the only Brazilians at the event. In this context, they wondered how this could be possible, since Brazil presents numerous education problems and there was not

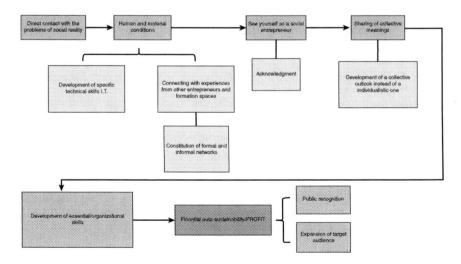

Figure 7.1 Flow of the central elements of analysis: MeuTutor and Hand Talk.
Source: Developed by the author.

148   *Ibsen Mateus Bittencourt*

another Brazilian researcher in the space to discuss with the international community of the area. They began to think and align ideas of what they could do to improve and impact Brazilian education together with their students, who developed an educational platform. During the validation process, they encountered and witnessed the real problems of Brazilian education *in locu*. This contact with reality reinforced the action of the entrepreneurs.

The same situation happened with the entrepreneurs of Hand Talk when they wanted to change the way society communicated with the Deaf people of Brazil. The entrepreneurs in contact with the problem found that more than 70% of Deaf people in Brazil do not understand Portuguese and cannot communicate.

Faced with this reality, the problems identified by entrepreneurs are being attacked using top level IT. With new technologies and increased exchanges between markets as well as frustration with government actions and state organisations in addressing social issues, they expand the creation of new business formats in search of creative and innovative solutions.

The experience of Professor Alan Pedro in having direct contact with the social reality and with the problems faced by many students in the interior of the State of Alagoas made him think that he could and should do something. 'It begins to foster the idea of making a big impact for people who really wanted to study and grow and did not have the opportunity'.

The contact with social problems and social reality that MeuTutor and Hand Talk entrepreneurs have been able to experience has changed the way they understand their work environment. This was more important for the development of their skills than having only one set of attributes. It was necessary for the entrepreneurs to have the material and human conditions and experience the problem in order to be able to build the meaning that the work had for them and transform it into a self-sustaining business.

Development of specific IT technical skills

The two companies had similar trajectories for the consolidation of their products and services in the market. For MeuTutor entrepreneurs, the material and human conditions for advanced research and technological development at the university were aligned with the desire to expand the knowledge generated in the graduate program beyond the walls of the university. As for Hand Talk, it also emerged as a project within the university. This is the university environment, regardless of influence in creating the conditions for the emergence of successful businesses.

However, MeuTutor entrepreneurs had to make decisions to be able to design the company for the development of new technologies. The same happened with the entrepreneurs of Hand Talk, as they decided to use applications for mobile devices when there was no type of application for Deaf people in the world, and little was said about this type of solution.

For the entrepreneurs, the process began with formatting the idea into a product concept and later a business project. These were the basis for obtaining the financial resources that made it possible to enter the market. Daily life has led

Competences in social business 149

entrepreneurs to develop fundamental skills for solving technical problems such as web development, artificial intelligence, semantic web, ontology and software engineering and intelligent tutoring systems, among others.

It should be noted that some of the technical skills developed are similar for both companies, because they are technology based; however, some are more specific to one or the other because the type of business, specificity of its application and end users differs.

During the process of undertaking the collective learning process as fundamental, as described by Tadeu Luz, one of the entrepreneurs of Hand Talk: 'It is inevitable, you end up learning a lot during the process, and you have to learn very fast'.

Connecting with experiences of other social entrepreneurs and training spaces

For the entrepreneurs, a very important moment in their formation was when they had contact with Endeavor and Artemisia, two social business accelerators.

The contact of the entrepreneurs with the institutions that disseminate the social business culture in Brazil and provides mentoring and subsidies for the business was fundamental for the development of the market view of social entrepreneurs.

The differential for the two companies during the acceleration programmes were the mentors involved in the process. This was crucial in the initial phase. According to Ribeiro and colleagues (2015), the body of intensively active mentors is a trait that differentiates accelerators from other incubation and business development programs. Certainly, the support of the accelerators was significant, so that the entrepreneurs had more chances of success in the market.

See yourself as a social entrepreneur: consciousness' awareness

The act of becoming and seeing themselves as social entrepreneurs occurred in the process of building the company and not a priori. The realisation of them being social entrepreneurs emerged in the process of building and consolidating the company.

During the process, these entrepreneurs' experience in accelerators was critical to developing a critical awareness of their own business.

These entrepreneurs had no practical experience when they started the company. As they had no experience, this was not the starting point for wanting to undertake a new venture.

For the entrepreneurs of MeuTutor, they wanted only to appropriate the research developed at the university and put into practice. For Hand Talk, they report that:

> We fell from the skies with parachutes without knowing what a social business was. I knew I was creating something that was going to impact people's lives, and it had the potential to be profitable, but we did not have that much in mind.

150   *Ibsen Mateus Bittencourt*

The fact that they wanted to test solutions was not the point that led them to realise what they were actually doing, but experiences during the process of undertaking and recognising the business as being social. Ronaldo Tenório from Hand Talk thought during the process: 'Hey, I have a social business and I'm making a social impact. We realized where we were'.

The fact that they did not have previous experiences was reported by all the entrepreneurs. They consider that the experience of entrepreneur was fundamental to learn the importance of the business and how much they were making a difference. For entrepreneur Ig Ibert: 'Undertaking socially is trying to change social indices. It means not being comfortable with the state of our society'.

The narratives present elements of how entrepreneurs see themselves inside the society, somehow perceiving in some fashion that the contact with the target public and social problems promotes professional learning, which leads them to see themselves as social entrepreneurs and as agents of change.

Sharing collective meanings

The shared meaning in both cases is, above all, the passage from an eminently individualistic and technical view to a collective/social one. Professional technical experts broaden and deepen their vision of what their work means from more superficial conceptions (solving technical/technological problems) to deeper ones (what is the ultimate goal and purpose of my work, for the society, community and collective).

The process of becoming entrepreneurs occurred during the trajectory of changing from an individualistic and technical view to a more collective and macro view. During the trajectory of the company, the entrepreneurs were transforming themselves and realising the personal change in the work and the behaviour before the society. For Wilkson Eldon of MeuTutor, 'I did not deal with people, I dealt more with the online part, now it's very different and very nice dealing with people', and for Thyago Tenório, 'at first I did not think much about people's problems. Today, when I see a problem, I feel obligated to solve'.

There is a significant change in their point of view – from a technician one to a more collective one. And that also appears in Tadeu Luz's narrative of Hand Talk: 'IT WAS NOT ONLY A TECHNICAL CHALLENGE ANYMORE, BUT ALSO A SOCIAL CHALLENGE, and I was realizing the importance of what I was doing as something much more social'.

During the process, naturally, entrepreneurs realised that the solutions developed were actually helping people.

The competence developed occurs through the changes provoked in the organisational environment by the people, and especially by the entrepreneur himself to reach his social objectives. What greatly reflected in the development of some skills and knowledge was the change of perception and meaning that led them to important conducts for the success of the business.

Development of essential/organisational skills

The construction of an identity as a social entrepreneur and the definition of the mission, vision and values of the business as such are fundamental elements for a company, but none of the entrepreneurs had this very clear in their minds.

In Drucker's view (1994), a company is composed of three parts: (i) premises of the organisation's environment; (ii) the company's mission and (iii) the core competencies – those that must be developed to fulfil the mission of the organisation.

According to Prahalad and Hamel (1990), the essential competences are the collective learning process in the organisation, especially how to coordinate several skills and integrate multiple streams of technology. Consider the ability of MeuTutor to provide a customised and tailored learning to the students, in which the skills are appropriate to the development of the platform and interrelate between them and the others (Figure 7.2).

The essential competence is related to the harmonisation of technology chains and is also associated with the organisation of work and the delivery of value; this occurring both in MeuTutor and Hand Talk which has as a product, a platform for automatic translation of texts, picture, sound and video for sign language (Figure 7.3).

Essential competence, according to Prahalad and Hamel (1990), is communication, involvement and a deep commitment to work beyond organisational boundaries. In this case, it involves the entire organisation engaged and committed to achieving the mission and objectives. The companies, after having developed the necessary skills to fix their products/services in the market, focused towards the financial sustainability of the business.

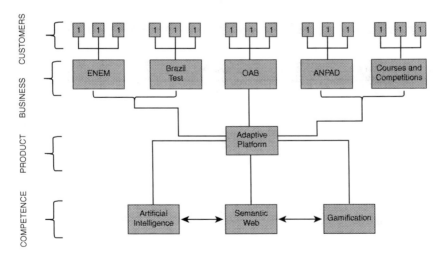

Figure 7.2 Essential skills versus final MeuTutor products.
Source: Developed by the author.

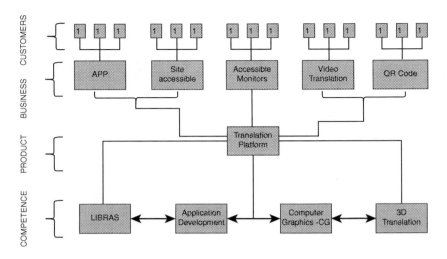

Figure 7.3 Essential skills versus end products – Hand Talk.
Source: Developed by the author.

Medical service companies

Even if the narrated stories point to an almost heroic and romanticised view of the social concern that triggered the business – and this altruistic desire only partly explains the birth of the enterprise – there are elements of the narrative that allow us to observe central aspects of becoming competent and that can contribute to infer the processes that led to the success of the business. Figure 7.4 shows the flow of the central elements of analysis.

Direct contact with the problems of social reality

The direct contact of entrepreneurs with social reality since childhood and the early involvement in social causes was the trigger for them to start fostering the idea of changing the situation they faced. In the narratives, the direct and significant experience of entrepreneurs with social problems is revealed, like Maria José being taken by her mother to show the reality that there are people who have many needs, without a home to live or simply do not have a plate of food on the table to eat, or Iraê Cardoso reporting her own suffering and significative experience, but that was vital for her to trace the course of her life.

The problems that generated the origin of the social concern led the entrepreneurs to think about how they could contribute to improve the social reality that they experienced. Maria José, with a medical background, started a medical referral centre in the countryside of the State of Alagoas to meet the people of her hometown and surrounding communities. Iraê Cardoso, with the experience of a brother with hearing impairment, had the idea of providing a reference centre

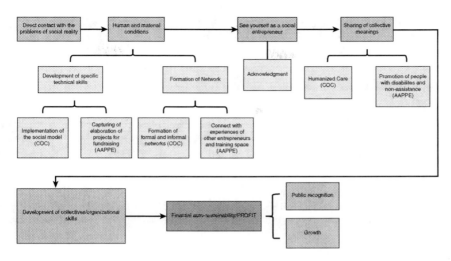

Figure 7.4 Flow of the central elements of analysis: Osório Cardoso and AAPPE.
Source: Developed by the author.

with a bilingual approach (Portuguese and sign languages) based on the needs of the Deaf capable of supplying the entire state.

For entrepreneurs to idealise the business they wanted to build, they needed to understand and analyse adequately the social problems and the target audience they wanted to impact. The analysis of social problems requires efforts to find solutions in the intervention of social reality. It takes more than knowing how to 'work really hard'. The entrepreneur needs to be a resource articulator, a deep knower of the industry, someone who uses creativity, the ability to identify opportunities, seek and manage resources and to take risks.

For De Mello et al. (2008), the recognition of business opportunities can be divided into three competencies: identification, evaluation and search for market opportunities. Such competencies suggest that an entrepreneur must be able to identify the scenarios favourable to the social objectives and to act on the potential business chances through their evaluation, in order to transform them into positive situations.

Material and human conditions

Creating the material and human conditions for the idealisation of reference centres for medical services in the State of Alagoas was the desire of the entrepreneurs. For Dr. Maria José, the project was almost completed after the end of her medical residency in Rio de Janeiro, when she decided to return to her hometown and not to work in a major centre in Southeastern Brazil. As for Iraê Cardoso, who already had a life experience with a Deaf brother, the trigger was the trip to a house in a neighbourhood of the city of Maceió and found a Deaf

154 *Ibsen Mateus Bittencourt*

child dying, which recalled her trajectory with the brother, and from that moment on she decided to put into practice what she had already thought of.

The two entrepreneurs had similar life trajectories to consolidate their businesses in the market. They left cities in the interior, had to go initially to large centres to study and capacitate themselves, and then return to Alagoas. They still had to abdicate and sacrifice many things in relation to their personal lives, according to their own accounts.

Development of specific technical skills

The process of undertaking for Maria José started when she returned to her city and began to provide medical care for the community and surrounding cities.

For Iraê Cardoso, it started when she decided to take over the direction of the AAPPE and redirect the focus of action in the care of the hearing impaired.

For the entrepreneurs to put into practice what they were planning, they needed to have the necessary conditions to idealise their business. At that moment, the entrepreneurs had two different paths to follow.

The focus of action to consolidate the business of the Osório Cardoso Clinic was in the implementation of a social assessment model of the patient's profile to know if the patient had financial conditions or not to pay a consult and/or procedure. For the AAPPE, it was directed at the elaboration of projects to attract funds from various sectors of the economy, including public and private institutions, as well as important work to consolidate the disability rights law in Alagoas.

The two companies developed specific customer service techniques. Dr. Maria José with her peculiar technique in the diagnosis of her patients, listening and understanding the suffering before taking some invasive procedure and intervention in the most serious cases. Iraê Cardoso, with her ability to write projects, has been able to improve the care of the hearing impaired.

It should be noted that not only did they develop individual skills, but also group skills. The entrepreneurs had to develop new knowledge and techniques for the collective development to consolidate the business.

Dr. Maria José with her techniques managed to make the patients look for the clinic, even with it being located in the countryside, becoming a reference in their area despite the long wait for medical care. As for Iraê Cardoso, with her ability to write and manage complex projects and reading contexts, has been able to capture the resources needed to build nine rehabilitation centres for the hearing impaired and multiple physical disabilities.

The entrepreneurs could consolidate their businesses as health centres of excellence and work to make their projects become actions that promote the development of their communities and their target audience.

Networking and training spaces

Although their narratives are being analysed together, here is an exception due to the specificity of each entrepreneur. Dr. Maria José managed to establish a network of contacts around her business and Iraê Cardoso besides forming a network, also connected directly with other social entrepreneurs and training spaces for entrepreneurs.

Networking is important to exchange information, experiences and actions in the market. According to Dr. Maria José, the network of contacts is important to put their actions in practice from the clinic attendance until its action in the founded NGOs. Its professional contact involved from doctors in this area and other specialties to the judiciary, businessmen, educational institutions and organised civil society.

Iraê Cardoso formed a network constituted by people of the organised civil society and of the judiciary powers, executive and legislative. Her objective has always been the capture of resources directed solely and exclusively for the attendance of its public. However, the contact with other social entrepreneurs and the involvement with the actions of the accelerator Artemisia enabled the entrepreneur to expand the network of contacts in the business scope. The relation was built with social entrepreneurs and entrepreneurs from several areas of the economy. With the support of the network of contacts and the experiences with other entrepreneurs, the security in the performance increased and also improved the meaning that the work has for them; this led them to increase the service to its public.

Seeing yourself as a social entrepreneur: awareness

The process of becoming social entrepreneurs and developing skills in social business did not happen before, but after and during the experiences of undertaking.

The two learned during the process of building their business that the focus of the entrepreneurs was only to be able to provide a decent and quality service to people in need; however, for lack of experience, they could not reach the public and neither expand the business.

Dr. Maria José has been professionalising in management over the years, implanting step by step a specific sector to carry out a diagnosis of the social profile of the patient, who did not have or declared themselves unable to pay for consultation and/or procedure.

Iraê Cardoso, when having contact with other social entrepreneurs, realised that she had a social business and that it should focus specifically on her public rather than working a policy of assistance.

The entrepreneurs start then to develop a critical capacity and reflection regarding the acquired knowledge and begin a process of awareness. This process leads them to rethink the business. This phase happened when Dr. Maria José implemented the sector of analysis of social profile and Iraê Cardoso ended the practice of welfare. The truth is that awareness brings entrepreneurs closer to their target audience. If they were used to be concerned only with caring for people, today they are concerned about who, how and why you are caring for the person.

Sharing of collective meanings

Differently from the two IT companies analysed that transitioned from an eminently individualistic vision to a collective one, the medical companies have, at the front of their management, entrepreneurs who always had a collective oriented look.

156   *Ibsen Mateus Bittencourt*

Dr. Maria Jose was always looking to help other people, dedicating to multiplying this service to others. Iraê Cardoso, with the enterprising inclination, always looked for something to market, but it was with the social work that can give free expression to its entrepreneurial potential.

The fact that the entrepreneurs were always concerned about the collective did not mean that they were generating a significant social impact. To do this, it was necessary to make the organisational environment converge with the ideas of the entrepreneurs, and that employees and collaborators could understand that the role of each one was fundamental to directly impact socially vulnerable people.

Osório Cardoso Clinic has approximately 20 staff members. However, the number of professionals working indirectly is even greater, because Dr. Maria José performs more complex procedures in public and private hospitals. The employees and partners are many and range from professionals to doctors.

Iraê Cardoso could consolidate a structure with nine referral centres focused on the treatment of people with multiple disabilities distributed geographically and strategically to serve a large part of the population in Alagoas. It has approximately 300 people, from general service people to trainees and volunteers.

According to Miller et al. (2012), some skills need to be developed so that the business has possibilities of success in the market. It is emphasised that it is necessary to build effective teams capable of realising the objectives of the business. However, it is not enough just to form the teams, you have to be able to lead and develop the people in the organisation. The two entrepreneurs with interpersonal communication skills were able to train and develop professionals so that they could create a significant social impact.

Development of collective/organisational skills

In the beginning, the two entrepreneurs had only a functional view of their work. For Dr. Maria José, it was already very professionally fulfiling, and Iraê Cardoso felt very good about working on the capture of special projects. However, when they realised that they could improve the quality of life of the public who attended their services and understand the impact that this could cause in the lives of these people, they began to mobilise the knowledge and develop new skills necessary for this to happen.

They transited then from a technical and individual vision of their work to a more managerial one. The change of vision allowed the two entrepreneurs to see beyond what they were doing, consolidating themselves as centres of reference. For this, the need to learn how to capture and allocate material and human resources, deal with suppliers, measure results, analyse some decision-making within the scope of action and knowing how to guide the support team and the professionals involved were fundamental for the growth of business.

For Dr. Maria José, with the planning, it was possible to perceive the impediments of the business and to implant a flow of processes that could in fact identify the people who had a socio-economic profile.

As for Iraê Cardoso, the accomplishment of a business plan aligned to the strategic planning provided the implantation of eight AAPPE units distributed geographically in the State of Alagoas.

The planning was necessary so that the two entrepreneurs could structure the business, in which the relationship between the organisation and the internal and external environment was defined as well as the social objectives defining the necessary strategies to achieve the established goals.

The Osório Cardoso Clinic, in addition to structuring the flow of processes, has also changed its operational model – from the network of contacts of Dr. Maria José. The Clinic has a structure divided by sectors that has the function of giving information more fluidity.

The AAPPE has a stronger administrative structure compared to the Osório Cardoso Clinic. The structure is divided by departments and then by specific sectors, with the goal of achieving efficiency and improve interdepartmental and inter-sector relations.

Both Dr. Maria José from Osório Cardoso Clinic and Iraê Cardoso from AAPPE were only able to consolidate their business, grow and have public recognition because they changed the conception of work, moving from a more paternalistic practice to a non-paternalistic one, and a more technical performance to a more professional one, mobilising all the theoretical and practical resources and developed the skills necessary for business success.

Conclusion

This research did not discuss competencies as a phenomenon of people management or even had as its purpose to present a set of attributes that added or modified those already known in the literature as relevant to the ability of social entrepreneurs to carry out their projects. The proposal was to understand the competence built in the trajectory of a group of social entrepreneurs in the State of Alagoas, in order to analyse the experiences lived in the course, from the constitution of the business to its consolidation; and finally, to bring to the fore the course and with it the elements of experience that help to explain the emerging character of competence and which can contribute to the consolidation of knowledge in this area, in an interpretative perspective, still little explored in the literature on skills and business social policies.

In order to do so, the use of narratives (Riessman, 2008) was chosen because they externalise through history and language the meaning given to the situations confronted, and thus the universe of beliefs that constitute action, that is, values, ideals, roles, in short, everything that mobilises subjects and helps to explain the phenomenon in research, decoding it and interpreting it. By organising their experiences in the narratives, the entrepreneurs reveal their doing, which, grouped in a set of stories, shows a course in which the central elements of competence are revealed.

In this effort to understand the process of development of competences of social entrepreneurs and favoured experiences, a systematic review of the literature

158 *Ibsen Mateus Bittencourt*

was carried out. This organises the knowledge, above all, from a set of attributes that in part reproduces the expected capabilities of any traditional enterprise: capacity to manage teams, make decisions, seize opportunities not yet explored and so on (Timmons, 1978, Hornaday, 1982, Meredith et al., 1982, Filion, 2000). But it also incorporates new elements, such as emotional skills, skills to identify and solve social problems and desire and ability to create a significant social impact (Pless and Maak, 2008, Nga and Shamuganathan, 2010, Miller et al., 2012, Oorhei, Bibu and Vinke, 2012, Moreau and Mertens, 2013).

Considering this literature, it is possible to identify, through the narratives analysed, the presence of many of the competencies. It is noted that many of the competencies of the social entrepreneurs that were subjects of this study are like all four businesses analysed; however, some are specific to one type of business and not another. It is highlighted, for example, the capacity to measure results, create/assess the feasibility and implementation of a business plan, identification, evaluation and exploitation of opportunities and the ability to develop the organisation for its perpetuation and/or expansion. All these competences were developed by MyTutor, Hand Talk, AAPPE and the Osório Cardoso Clinic. However, it is worth mentioning that the Osório Cardoso Clinic is the only company that has no prospect of expansion and growth over the years, especially the maintenance of care.

However, in spite of the relevance of these specific competences, the entrepreneurs' experiences pointed to the flow with which these constituent aspects of competence were mobilises in the context and re-signified actions in a process towards social entrepreneurship (Sandberg and Dall'Alba, 2006). Five central elements were revealed in the narratives built by the members, telling the story of the construction and consolidation of the business, and how they developed competencies that led them to public recognition and financial self-sustainability.

The first element refers to the **direct contact of the partners-owners with the problems of the social reality**. For IT companies, the contact with this problematic reality emerged as an issue that led them to think how they could improve the social reality found. For the medical companies, this contact happened since the beginning of the project, serving as a trigger for the entrepreneurs to begin to foster the idea of changing the situation they lived and witnessed.

The second element is **the material and human conditions** that led to the creation of the business. Entrepreneurs have developed their competences and technical skills specific to each business in connection with other entrepreneurs and training spaces as well as networking. Technical and specific skills aligned with a good network of contacts and training spaces were one of the factors that enabled entrepreneurs to leverage their ideas and projects in the beginning of the business until they became a reference in the area in which they were working.

The third emerging element, in turn, was the fact that partners-owners **see themselves as social entrepreneurs** during the process of building the company and not a priori. The awareness that what they did could be classified as social entrepreneurship emerged in the process of building and consolidating business.

Competences in social business 159

The fourth element, however, elucidates the **sharing of meanings**. There was a shift from an eminently individualistic and technical vision to a collective/social one in the case of the entrepreneurs of MyTutor and Hand Talk. For the women entrepreneurs in the medical area, what they socialised was the logic from a welfare practice to a non-paternalistic one and an unprofessional management for a professional one, generating more and better impact for the public they attended.

The fifth and final element was the **development of skills.** Here, it is revealed that the materialisation of the competences developed and assimilated by any organisation constituted from the products of MyTutor, with the creation of an adaptive educational platform that helps students with the contents for ENEM and the Provinha Brazil programme, and Hand Talk with the development of a mobile solution that enables Deaf people and the community in general to communicate. For healthcare companies, this is the offer of specialised services in ocular problems, with a focus on humanisation of the patient, ranging from the initial care with the receptionist until the patient returns for a consultation and/or procedure, and for the AAPPE, it is a centre of reference in the care of people with hearing loss and multiple disabilities.

Thus, from the point of view of theoretical implications, what these constitutive elements of the narratives have shown is that although technology- and healthcare-based companies are very different, they have revealed *a very similar flow in the process of becoming competent social entrepreneurs.* The way these entrepreneurs told their stories and explained the development of individual and collective competence and the underlying elements of their success brought attention to a path that allowed us to point out the following reflections:

1   The need to pay attention to triggers and preconditions that trigger and support the emergence of competence flow. In this case, the nuisance and proximity to the social reality that is the focus of action as well as the way of creating the material and human conditions to execute the enterprise.
2   The creation and strengthening of an identity of social entrepreneurs, which makes social objectives take precedence in discourse and in entrepreneurial action.
3   The attention directed to the connections in networks of entrepreneurs or professionals and spaces of formation that amplify the social action.
4   The consolidation and sharing of the meaning of social business collectively.
5   The materialisation of business competence in reference products and services.

Notably, there is a combination of aspects of personal history with others of a structural and material nature that allow the execution of ideas in business. But above all, it is the development of an identity of social entrepreneurs that has been shared and strengthened in this process. When this becomes a collective understanding, it is understood as something natural, adequate, implicit, *taken for granted* (Sandberg and Targama, 2007). And as a consequence, it made that

160   *Ibsen Mateus Bittencourt*

competence visible. The creation of meaning of social, non-paternalistic and professional focused in solving problems of social nature was intensive and shared collectively. Above all, a social business identity was created and communicated, which emerges in discourse as an existential crisis: we must do something for education, for health, for the handicapped and for those who cannot afford it, but also something that becomes feasible to materialise as a profitable business.

From the point of view of practical implications, the flow identified with the central elements can serve as a benchmark for new and developing companies to self-analyse their own trajectory, identifying the advances in the construction of a social business identity collectively that strengthens the business competence. In the same way, it can also serve as a reference for the training processes of new social entrepreneurs in universities, either in business incubators or in the classrooms of business schools.

Regarding the methodology, the use of narrative research as a methodological option stands out. In the systematic review of the literature of the last ten years, no national and/or international empirical study written in English, Portuguese or Spanish addressed the development of competences in social affairs and the use of narratives. This option proved to be rich and interesting to understand qualitatively the phenomenon of the development of competence in social business.

For all of this, it is expected that this research should contribute and bring more elements to the literature on social business skills, mapping the dynamics of social entrepreneurs and bringing to light the mechanisms inherent in the process of becoming entrepreneurial social.

References

Bittencourt, Ibsen et al. Systematic review of the literature social entrepreneurship and skills development: An analysis of past 10 years. *International Journal of Innovation*, v. 4, n. 1, p. 33–45, 2016.

Bose, Monica. *Empreendedorismo social e promoção do desenvolvimento local*. 2013. Tese de Doutorado. Universidade de São Paulo.

Comini, G.; Barki, Edgard; Aguiar, Luciana Trindade de. A three-pronged approach to social business: A Brazilian multi-case analysis. *Revista de Administração (São Paulo)*, v. 47, n. 3, p. 385–397, 2012.

De Mello, Sérgio C. Benício; Fonsêca, Francisco Ricardo Bezerra; De Paiva Júnior, Fernando Gomes. Competências empreendedoras do dirigente de empresa de base tecnológica: um caso empresarial de sucesso. *Revista de Administração Mackenzie*, v. 8, n. 3, 2008.

Drucker, Peter F. The theory of the business. *Harvard Business Review*, v. 72, n. 5, p. 95–104, 1994.

Filion, Louis. Empreendedorismo e gerenciamento: processos distintos, porém complementares. *Rev. adm. empres.*, São Paulo, v. 40, n. 3, set. 2000.

Fischer, Rosa Maria; Comini, Graziella. Sustainable development: From responsibility to entrepreneurship. *Revista de Administração (São Paulo)*, São Paulo, v. 47, n. 3, set. 2012.

Competences in social business 161

Gephart, R. *Paradigmas and Research Methods*. (1999). Disponível em: http://division.aomonline.org/rm/1999_RMD_Forum_Paradigms_and_Research_Methods.htm. Acesso em 10 abr. 2013.

Hornaday, John. *Research About Living Entrepreneurs*. In. Encyclopedia of Entrepreneurship, Kent/Sexton/Vesper eds., copyright, 1982. Englewood Cliffs, NJ: Prentice Hall, Inc., p. 25–27.

Kerlin, J. Social enterprise in the United States and Europe: Understanding and learning from the differences. *Voluntas: International Journal of Voluntary and Nonprofit Organizations*, v. 17, n. 3, p. 246–262, 2006.

Meredith, Geoffrey; Nelson, Robert; Neck, Philip. *The Practice of Entrepreneurship*. 1982. Geneva: International Labour Office.

Merriam, S. B. *Qualitative Research in Practice. Examples for Discussion and Analysis*. 2002. San Francisco: Jossey-Bass.

Miller, Toyah; Wesley, Curtis; Williams, Denise. Educating the minds of caring hearts: Comparing the views of practitioners and educators on the importance of social entrepreneurship competencies. *Academy of Management Learning & Education*, v. 11, n. 3, p. 349–370, 2012.

Moreau, Charlotte; Mertens, Sybille. Managers' competences in social enterprises: Which specificities? *Social Enterprise Journal*, v. 9, n. 2, p. 164–183, 2013.

NGA, Joyce; Shamuganathan, Gomathi. The influence of personality traits and demographic factors on social entrepreneurship start up intentions. *Journal of Business Ethics*, v. 95, n. 2, p. 259–282, 2010.

Oliveira, Edson. *Empreendedorismo social no Brasil: atual configuração, perspectivas e desafios – notas introdutórias*. Revista FAE, v.7 n. 2, p. 9–18, jul./dez. 2004.

Orhei, Loredana; BIBU, Nicolae; VINKE, Joop. The competence of social entrepreneurship in Romania. A profile from experts in the field. *Managerial Challenges of the Contemporary Society*, v. 4, p. 73–79, 2012.

Parrish, Bradley. Sustainability-driven entrepreneurship: Principles of organization design. *Journal of Business Venturing*, v. 25, n. 5, p. 510–523, 2010.

Pless, N. M.; Maak, Thomas. Business-in-society competence for leading responsibly in a global environment. *INSEAD Faculty & Research Working Paper*. 2008.

Prahalad, Coimbatore; HAMEL, Gary. The core competence of the corporation. *Harvard Business Review*, v. 68, n. 3, p. 79–93, 1990.

Ribeiro, Artur; PLONSKI, Guilherme; ORTEGA, Luciane. Um fim, dois meios: aceleradoras e incubadoras no Brasil. *Altec*, 2015.

Riessmann, Gerhard. *Narrative Methods for the Human Sciences*. 2008. Thousand Oaks: Sage Publications.

Ruth, Damian. Frameworks of managerial competence: limits, problems and suggestions. *Journal of European Industrial*, v. 30, n. 3, p. 206–226, 2006.

Sandberg, Jörgen. *Competence as International Achievement: A Phenomenographic Study*. Occasional Paper 91.4. Melbourne: ERADU, 1991.

———. Understanding human competence at work: An interpretative approach. *Academy of Management Journal*, v. 43, n. 1, p. 9–25, 2000.

———; DALL'ALBA, G. Reframing competence development at work. In: Castleton, G., Gerber, R.; Pillay, H. (Orgs.) *Improving workplace learning*. Nova: New York, 2006.

Sandberg, Jörgen; Targama, Axel. Share understanding: The basis for collective competences and its development. *Management understanding in organizations*. SAGE: London, 2007, p. 89–108.

162 *Ibsen Mateus Bittencourt*

Teodosio, Armindo; Comini, Graziella. Inclusive business and poverty: Prospects in the Brazilian context. *Revista de Administração (São Paulo)*, São Paulo, v. 47, n. 3, set. 2012.

Timmons, Jeffry A. Characteristics and role demands of entrepreneurship. *American Journal of Small Business*, v. 3, n. 1, p. 5–17, 1978.

Young, Dennis. Alternative perspectives on social enterprise. In: CORDES, Joseph; STEUERLE, Eugene. (Ed.). *Nonprofits and business*. Washington: The Urban Institute Press, p. 21–46, 2009.

Yunus, Muhammad. *Creating a world without poverty: Social business and the future of capitalism*. Public Affairs, 2010.

8 Communities, diversity and entrepreneurship

Future trends

Vanessa Ratten

Introduction

The role of diversity and communities in entrepreneurship is undervalued, which has impeded the advancement of the literature. The reason for this comes from the majority of entrepreneurship research still focusing on single entrepreneurs rather than communities. This has meant that the role of communities in entrepreneurship has been underplayed despite the increasing number of communities involved in entrepreneurship and their role in encouraging diversity. Nevertheless, the role played by communities has become a growing subject due to the realisation social nuances are important in understanding entrepreneurial behaviour (Etemad, 2015). Community entrepreneurship is a specific research domain but lags behind more well-known areas of entrepreneurship such as social and sustainability. Community-specific studies can help inform entrepreneurship practices by understanding barriers and challenges within them.

Community-based enterprises are defined as 'a community acting corporately as both entrepreneur and enterprise in pursuit of the common good' (Peredo and Chrisman, 2006:309). Traditionally, most communities were viewed as social parts of society that were largely engaged in non-profit activities. This has changed with governments and councils relying more on user pays funding models. This chapter will evaluate and analyse community enterprises in order to clarify their position in society and role in diversity management. Communities are defined as having a 'shared geographical location, generally accompanied by collective culture and/or ethnicity and potentially other shared relational characteristics' (Peredo and Chrisman, 2006:315). Communities have an entrepreneurial orientation due to their need to strategically manage their resources. The key dimensions of entrepreneurial orientation are innovativeness, proactiveness and risk taking, which are important in ensuring diversity within community practices (Anggadwita et al., 2017). An entrepreneur is an individual who provides management to a firm by assuming risk (Kilby, 1977). This broad definition of an entrepreneur fits most studies that integrate a community aspect into their research (Hayton, 1996). Thereby, most entities that are part of the entrepreneurial ecosystem in a community can be considered entrepreneurs (Ferreira, Fernandes and Ratten, 2017).

164   *Vanessa Ratten*

To date, little research has focused on communities, diversity and entrepreneurial activity. The purpose of this chapter is to examine how diversity in entrepreneurship affects communities and how important communities are for societal advancement. Culture and social norms play a role in the development of a community and the inclusion of underrepresented segments of society. This chapter lays the groundwork for future studies examining diversity and entrepreneurship in communities. To improve the success rate of entrepreneurship, communities need to provide training to encourage local businesses to be entrepreneurial. Educating businesses about management and networking skills can provide support to other entrepreneurs. This is important as there is a scarcity of scholarly literature on diversity, communities and entrepreneurship.

Entrepreneurship

There are three main schools of thought about entrepreneurship in economics theory: German, new classical and Austrian (Gu, Qian and Lu, 2017). The German school incorporates the writings of Baumol and Schumpeter, who are well known for proposing that entrepreneurs are focused on innovation as a way of responding to market needs. The new classical school, whilst also well known but to a lesser extent than the German school, highlights the role of risk in recognising opportunities that have uncertain outcomes. The Austrian school is famous for the work of Kirzner, who analysed how opportunities are recognised, then evaluated by entrepreneurs. These different schools of thought are useful in community entrepreneurship as a way of understanding the link between citizens, governments and entrepreneurs (Ferreira, Ratten and Dana, 2017).

Gu, Qian and Lu (2017) considered entrepreneurship through innovation, business and risk taking. Innovation entrepreneurship deals mostly with management and technology processes. Thus, changing production costs and methods of manufacturing are important. As customer needs continually change based on environmental pressures, innovation entrepreneurship provides a way of keeping abreast of new technology development (Tsujimoto et al., 2018). Being at the front end of technology change is crucial for entrepreneurs wanting to keep or progress their position in the market. Competitiveness is a way for entrepreneurs to open up to new possibilities and expand their businesses; these are often done through innovation focusing on social issues (Ratten, 2014). Social innovations are defined as 'innovative activities and services that are motivated by the goal of meeting a social need' (Mulgan, 2006:146). These social needs often include incorporating more diverse members of society, which is often referred to as social entrepreneurship. Lortie and Cox (2018:1) state that 'the sub-field of social entrepreneurship also shares many commonalities with various sub-fields of larger fields of research such as corporate social responsibility, base of pyramid, non-profit management, social innovation and impact investing'.

In the field of entrepreneurship, the community concept is gaining traction as a way of understanding changes in the ecosystem (Ratten and Welpe, 2011).

Communities, diversity and entrepreneurship   165

This book poses three basic questions about diversity and entrepreneurship in communities. First, what is the meaning of communities in an entrepreneurship context? Second, what are the main issues facing communities when engaging in diversity through entrepreneurship? Third, what does the future hold for communities in terms of diversity in entrepreneurship? In order to clarify these questions, a number of different perspectives are included in this book. This enables an overview of the topics about diversity and community entrepreneurship to be discussed.

Community influence mechanism for diversity

There are three main ways communities influence diversity in entrepreneurship. First, by providing capital support to help finance new business activity; but depending on the type and size of a business it can be hard to obtain financing. Communities can use traditional funding mechanisms such as grants to encourage business activity, but can also introduce novel funding mechanisms such as crowdfunding and online competitions (Ratten, 2017). In emerging industries, communities can strengthen the appeal of their regions by focusing on strategic growth areas (Kalafatoglu and Mendoza, 2017). This helps to reduce uncertainties but can also encourage production in high-value areas. Communities need to realize that they need to support businesses in their region and help them particularly in stressful times (Lortie and Cox, 2018).

Second, communities need to provide education and training for entrepreneurs. This helps build management know-how and business acumen (Mulgan, 2006). Often, new entrepreneurs need to learn basic skills such as accounting and bookkeeping that take time to master (Gu, Qian and Lu, 2017). Thus, communities can provide a platform for individuals to share knowledge (Peredo and Chrisman, 2006). This would enable better social relations and help foster collaboration amongst entrepreneurs. By actively participating in training, entrepreneurs can expect to obtain new knowledge. Communities can also provide planning support that enables objectives to be met. Effective financial management is important for entrepreneurs, particularly in terms of managing cash flow (Ratten, 2006).

Third, communities need to build an entrepreneurial ecosystem in order to make their region a nice place to do business (Kilby, 1977). Entrepreneurial ecosystems can be geographically based or digital ones depending on the industry. Anyway, knowledge-intensive business services are increasing due to the importance of the digital innovation. Thus, a futuristic approach combining both geographical and online ecosystems is needed by communities. To create a good business atmosphere, there needs to be an emphasis on start-ups. This can be facilitated by business plan competitions that encourage people to become entrepreneurs (Somerville, 2007). However, communities need to balance social and financial goals of entrepreneurs in terms of quality of life for their citizens (Somerville and McElwee, 2011).

166 Vanessa Ratten

Implications for community and diversity managers

This book attempts to clarify diversity and the community concept in terms of its contribution to entrepreneurship research. Communities are essentially a social tool for individuals to cooperate and feel a sense of belonging. The community concept comes from the sociological research field, but is increasingly used in entrepreneurship studies. Communities by definition are an evolving topic that changes in meaning depending on societal trends. There are some similarities with communities and other concepts such as ecosystems that are currently a hot topic in the literature. Communities operate the same way as ecosystems but are considered as more static entities. This is seen as communities usually tending to focus on more social issues rather than digital changes evident in the ecosystems. However, the terms community and ecosystem can be used in a similar way depending on the circumstances. The main difference between the concepts is in digital ecosystems acknowledging the internet and information technology paradigm.

There tends to be a positive perception about the nature of communities in society. With the digital revolution, we have seen a trend towards going back to communities as a way to increase social cohesion in an area. However, communities compete with each other not only for the attention of citizens, but also for resources. Overall, this book uncovers some factors connecting entrepreneurship and communities. Each chapter developed theoretical reflections about the way diversity in entrepreneurship and communities are changing in society.

From this book, several implications for community managers emerge about the role of entrepreneurship. First, the impact of entrepreneurship as part of a community's development needs to be prioritised by managers. At the moment, managers are taking a retroactive instead of proactive approach to managing diversity in entrepreneurship. Instead of relying on the community to act entrepreneurial, managers need to spread the word about the impact of entrepreneurship. The characteristics of individual communities need to be considered when enhancing the visibility of entrepreneurship programmes.

Future research directions

There are areas yet to be discovered surrounding the role of diversity in entrepreneurship in communities. This book represents a holistic overview of research, but more practical examples are needed. As communities are an ongoing and evolving phenomena, they require constant study. By reflecting on the changes in communities, it can help new practices emerge. There are new configurations of communities emerging that take into account online and digital platforms. Whilst most of the research in this book focuses on diversity in physical communities characterised by geographical boundaries, there needs to be more investment on research about digital communities. Online portals are enabling groups of people to come together and discuss issues in an electronic format. This has changed the way debates are managed in communities and provide an

Communities, diversity and entrepreneurship   167

added dimension to the role of diversity in entrepreneurship and communities. In addition, entrepreneurship in this book has been considered as more physical activities such as manufacturing, but can also include virtual or electronic forms of entrepreneurship. Thus, future research needs to test our theoretical conceptualisation of communities to take into account changes in society. This would help reveal insightful considerations about the process of entrepreneurship in communities.

Further research is recommended on entrepreneurship and communities to establish a deeper understanding of the phenomenon. This will enable important questions still unanswered to be analysed as a way of predicting future trends. There are still issues about what diversity in entrepreneurship and communities really means and how are communities dependent on entrepreneurship yet to be answered in the literature. Additionally, it is beneficial to know more about entrepreneurial ecosystems in communities and how to target better performance outcomes. There is a great deal of opportunities available for researchers interested in diversity, entrepreneurship and communities.

In this book, we have seen how research on diversity in entrepreneurship and communities is bringing new perspectives. There are many promising research directions to pursue in terms of building new theories about diversity in entrepreneurship and communities. In sum, the chapters in this book present multiple themes worthy of further research. Fruitful avenues for further scholarly inquiry include questions about community responses to entrepreneurship, market access in communities, community management capacity and ethical business practices.

I believe that the chapters in this book provide for some interesting future research issues. The following is a list of main topics identified in this book as being potentially lucrative research areas:

1   Corporations and community responsibility
    How do corporations view the actions of communities practicing entrepreneurship?
    Does social value creation mean the same in corporations and communities?
    Are communities more effective at social entrepreneurship?
    What contexts help communities to act like corporate entrepreneurs?
    Is social innovation an effective marketing strategy for communities?
2   Developing and developed community economies and partnerships
    How do economic conditions affect community development?
    What kinds of partnerships provide the best source of entrepreneurship in communities?
    What strategies can communities use to design diverse entrepreneurial ecosystems?
    What can we learn from cooperation and competition in communities?
    What different kinds of diverse partnerships help govern the ideation process?
    How does trust evolve amongst entities in communities?

Conclusion

This book celebrates the role of entrepreneurship in communities and calls for more research into community/entrepreneurship relations. It also provides a fertile ground for studying diversity, entrepreneurship and communities and its influence on regional development. With a few notable studies, most of the literature on diversity in entrepreneurship has focused on social interactions and shied away from broader conceptualisations. The chapters in this book present excellent efforts in understanding diversity entrepreneurship. This conclusion chapter notes the contextualisation of entrepreneurship/community relations and plants the seeds for further research. Naturally, it is hoped the chapters in this book will be further used in more studies. This book complements and extends existing research on diversity in entrepreneurship. Each of the chapters in this book are discussed and organised by using a diversity and community perspective. Based on this approach, promising and important areas for future research are stated.

References

Anggadwita, G., Luturlean, B. S., Ramadani, V. and Ratten, V. (2017) 'Socio-cultural environments and emerging economy entrepreneurship: Women entrepreneurs in Indonesia', *Journal of Entrepreneurship in Emerging Economies*, 9(1): 85–96.

Etemad, H. (2015) 'Entrepreneurial orientation-performance in the international context', *Journal of International Entrepreneurship*, 13: 1–16.

Ferreira, J. J., Fernandes, C. I. and Ratten, V. (2017) 'Entrepreneurship, innovation and competitiveness: what is the connection?', *International Journal of Business and Globalisation*, 18(1): 73–95.

Ferreira, J. J., Ratten, V. and Dana, L. P. (2017) 'Knowledge spillover-based strategic entrepreneurship', *International Entrepreneurship and Management Journal*, 13(1): 161–167.

Gu, W., Qian, X. and Lu, J. (2017) 'Venture capital and entrepreneurship: A conceptual model and research suggestions', *International Entrepreneurship and Management Journal*, In Press.

Hayton, K. (1996) 'A critical examination of the role of community business in urban regeneration', *Town Planning Review*, 67(1): 1–20.

Kalafatoglu, T. and Mendoza, X. (2017) 'The impact of gender and culture on networking and value creation: An exploratory study in Turkey and MENA regions', *Cross Cultural & Strategic Management*, 24(2): 332–349.

Kilby, P. (1977) *Entrepreneurship and economic development*, New York, Free.

Lortie, J. and Cox, K. C. (2018) 'On the boundaries of social entrepreneurship: A review of relationships with related research domains', *International Entrepreneurship and Management Journal*, 14(3): 639–648.

Mulgan, G. (2006) 'The process of social innovation', *Innovations: Technology, Governance, Globalization*, 1: 145–162.

Peredo, A. and Chrisman, J. (2006) 'Toward a theory of community-based enterprise', *Academy of Management Review*, 31(2): 309–328.

Ratten, V. (2006) 'Policy drivers of international entrepreneurship in Europe', *Euromed Journal of Business*, 1(2): 15–28.Ratten, V. (2014) 'Future research directions for collective entrepreneurship in developing countries: A small and medium-sized enterprise perspective', *International Journal of Entrepreneurship and Small Business*, 22(2): 266–274.

Ratten, V. (2017) 'Entrepreneurial universities: The role of communities, people and places', *Journal of Enterprising Communities: People and Places in the Global Economy*, 11(3): 310–315.

Ratten, V. and Welpe, I. (2011) 'Community-based, social and societal entrepreneurship', *Entrepreneurship & Regional Development*, 23(5–6): 283–286.

Somerville, P. (2007) 'Cooperative identity', *Journal of Co-operative Studies*, 40(1): 5–17.

Somerville, P. and McElwee, G. (2011) 'Situating community enterprise: A theoretical exploration', *Entrepreneurship & Regional Development*, 23(5–6): 317–330.

Tsujimoto, M., Kajikawa, Y., Tomita, J. and Matsumoto, Y. (2018) 'A review of the ecosystem concept – Towards coherent ecosystem design', *Technological Forecasting & Social Change*, 136: 49–58.

Index

Alagoas 142, 143, 146, 148, 152–7

biology 2
block mobility theory 5

collaborative learning 5
creative environment 1
cultural attitudes 7
cultural capital 9

disadvantaged 5, 6, 9, 10, 15, 84, 90, 101, 102
diaspora-based networks 10
disadvantage theory 11, 40, 45
diversity management 1, 2, 5, 163

eco-entrepreneurship 108, 110, 112, 115
entrepreneurial development 5, 32, 35
entrepreneurial style 4
ethnic minority 2, 10, 12, 13, 14, 24, 26, 29, 33, 45, 46, 47, 48, 51, 52
ethnic product 4, 13
ethnic traits 2

female empowerment 129, 138, 139

Greek 4, 9

human capital 1, 5, 40, 74

Indonesia 102, 129, 131, 134, 137

knowledge community 5

languages 3–5, 14–16, 51, 151, 153, 157
linguistic ability 10

migration 5, 26, 28, 29, 40, 43, 45, 48, 50, 51
minority entrepreneurship 2, 4, 5, 6, 9, 10, 12–19, 24, 29, 33, 45, 46, 48, 52
migration traditions 5
mixed embeddedness 4, 12, 32, 35–9, 46, 47

opportunity structure theory 11

partnerships 6, 101, 103, 167
prejudices 2, 15
profitability 5, 120

racial discrimination 5
refugee entrepreneurship 23–54
regulations 4
religion 2, 4, 11, 19

sexuality 1, 16, 17
sexual preference 2
social business 76, 77, 83, 89, 102, 103, 142–6, 149, 150, 155, 159, 160
social capital 7, 17, 31, 32, 35, 63, 74, 78
social entrepreneurship 30, 31, 33, 63, 64, 65, 73, 77, 80, 81, 91, 129, 130, 132–6, 138, 140 158, 164, 167
social networks 5, 12, 14, 16, 17, 30, 52, 73, 74
social network theory 5, 34
sociology 1, 10, 23
spatial differences 4

United Kingdom 4

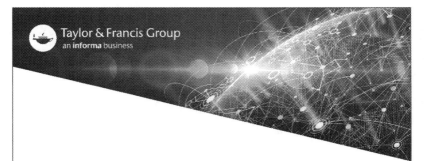

Printed in the United States
by Baker & Taylor Publisher Services